Casserole Cook Book

By the Editors of

Better Homes and Gardens

Around-the-world favorites

Souffles and omelets

Casseroles, like Classic Chicken Divan, are the stars of this complete roundup of delicious main dishes. "Supporting cast" is shown in border.

Speedy skillet meals

Chafing-dish classics

Contents

Cooking gear. *Pointers on use, care* . . .4

Casseroles. *Prize winners from hamburger, sausage; hearty "meat 'n potato" bakes; wonderful ways with chicken, sea food, and fish; sunny cheese and egg casseroles; garden-row bakes; perky casserole trims; main-dish freezing helps; casseroles and a shopping guide for 24* . . . 6

Skillet meals. *Popular quick suppers with hamburger and sausage; man-style beef, veal combos; sea-food sauces; egg and cheese specials* . . . 54

Traveler's choice. *Favorites from the Old World —England and Scandinavia, Turkey, Hungary and France; specialties of sunny coast countries— Mexico, Brazil, and Spain; Italian pasta, pizza, and casseroles; flavor adventures from the exotic Orient; zesty curries of India, Pakistan* . . . 68

Souffles and omelets. *Airy golden souffles; delicious French omelets; fancy supper scrambled eggs; light-as-air fluffy omelets* . . . 90

Chafing-dish classics. *Cook-at-the-table meats; superb sea-food sauces; elegant chicken a la King; cheese fondue and saucy rabbits; pretty shells* . . 100

Chowders, soups, and stews. *Meal-in-a-bowl soups and hearty chowders; savory stews and speedy toppers with a package start* . . . 116

Speedy suppers. *Fast fix-ups with meat; sleight-of-hand main dishes with chicken and sea food—all on yellow-bordered pages for quick reference* . . . 130

Encore—luscious leftovers. *Twice-good beef and pork; tag-ends of chicken and turkey* . . . 144

Whole-meal sandwiches. *Hearties by the yard; stuffed rolls, stacked sandwiches* . . . 152

Index . . . 158

Supper sandwiches

Stews, hearty soups

All recipes in this book are Test-Kitchen *endorsed.* Each has been tested over and over till it rates tops in practicality, family appeal, and downright goodness!

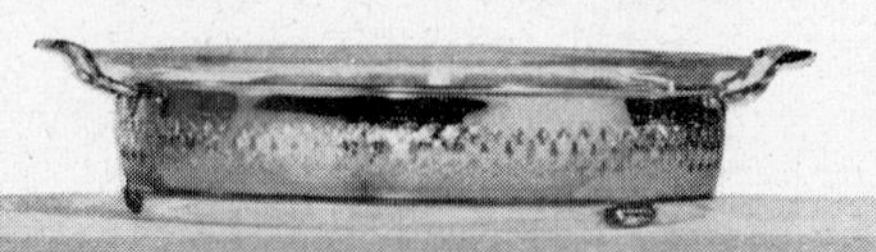

Covered baking dish is basic to a casserole wardrobe. It's often round, but may be oblong, oval, or square. Common sizes are 1-, 1½-, and 2-quart. Handles may be "ear" or hollow saucepan style.

Shallow rectangular baker is basic, too. Common sizes: 10x6x1½ inches (1½-quart); 11½x7½x1½ inches (2-quart); 13x9x2 inches (3-quart). Some are oval, some divided for baking main dish *and* vegetable.

Shallow round open baking dish is double-purpose—it's casserole *and* cake dish. Shallow round individuals are designed for shirred eggs, au gratin bakes. Handy to have: Handsome trivets, warmers, or made-to-match holders.

Cooking gear to make the fixing easy, fast, fun—

Outfit yourself from this wonderful variety of helpers—some make main-dish cooking speedy and convenient, some are gay and glamorous.

Start with covered baking dishes and shallow rectangular bakers—in company and family sizes. Choose skillets designed for your favorite top-of-range recipes (or at-table cooking); a Dutch oven for stews, pot roasts.

Electric appliances eliminate guesswork, "watch the pot" for you, cook in dining room or outdoors. Nice to have—portable electric tray to keep main dish, vegetables warm on buffet.

Chafing dishes and individual bakers, an old-time beanpot, and buffet warmers are handy when you entertain. If egg dishes are your specialty, consider souffle dishes, omelet pans.

Electric saucepan minds soups, stews, and creamed dishes with a minimum of fuss, keeps them warm on table till serving time. On handle: Time-temperature guide.

China skillet takes to top-of-range cooking *or* to baking. Directions suggest you use an asbestos pad when cooking skillet-style, and avoid sudden heating or cooling. This skillet goes directly from range to table, matches ovenproof dinnerware.

Omelet pan can be any heavy skillet with sloping sides, or you may want a classic French omelet pan. For French omelets, a small 8-inch skillet is best. If you make omelets often, keep one skillet just for them and avoid scouring it.

Electric Dutch oven. Plug in for effortless soup, stew, or meat! Constant temperature means no pot-watching required!

Dutch oven, top of range—your choice for foods that are best when gently simmered at a lazy bubble.

Beanpot—just like Grandma used! Bake quick from-a-can beans, or make "from scratch."

Individual casseroles dress up the main dish. To find out capacity, measure water required to fill one. A recipe designed for a 1-quart casserole will fill four 1-cup individuals. (Bake till hot.)

Earthenware (terra cotta) casseroles have charm that's hard to beat. Earthenware "stockpots" are available for stewing and braising, too. Do avoid sudden contrasts of temperature or heating baker when empty.

Souffle dish is straight-sided, especially designed to help your souffle rise to puffy heights. For individual souffles, or eggs en casserole, choose ramekins.

Double boiler provides gentle heat for cheese sauces, scrambled eggs, avoids constant stirring. Always cook over *hot, but not boiling,* water.

Single-pan chafing dish cooks over direct heat only. Special *deep* ones hold hot oil for meat fondues. A chafing dish may be heated by alcohol, canned heat, or electricity.

Bain-marie chafing dish is two pans. You can cook directly over the heat in the blazer pan *or* double-boiler style over the water bath. It can serve as warmer, too.

Super-ceramic skillet can go directly from freezer to electric base which cooks or keeps food warm. Or use skillet on top of range or in the oven. Handle comes off with a flick of the wrist to turn skillet into a casserole! Versatile!

Cast-iron skillet is especially practical when dish cooks top of range, then bakes in the oven. Look for porcelain-enameled cast-iron skillets *and* casseroles—all make handsome servers, too.

Electric skillet lets you cook where you eat! Have all ingredients ready for Sukiyaki or some such, then cook at the table when folks are seated. Take skillet to patio, or to living room for piping-hot snacks. Or use as a chafing dish.

Buffet server keeps supper hot at table, without unit doubles as casserole.

Pressure saucepan, top of range. Soup to dessert, you short-cut cooking with a pressure pan. Tops for less-tender beef cuts.

Electric pressure pan cuts cooking time, holds pressure automatically. You are free to put together rest of the meal.

Glamorous and good—it's Creamy Chicken-Rice Casserole

Fast, flavorful! One-apiece Hamburger Pielets with onion-ring topknots.

Casseroles

It's no wonder that cooks love casseroles! They're fast to fix, make most of the meal. And your oven takes over the main dish while you put together a salad and dessert. Dinner's ready—call the clan! Your family and guests will rave about these casseroles. Wonderful food combinations coupled with superb seasoning—your meal becomes a certain success! Serving a crowd? Take a look at our recipes for 24. We give tips, too, for freezing main dishes for busy days. Casserole trims and toppers, meal plans aplenty—all this and more!

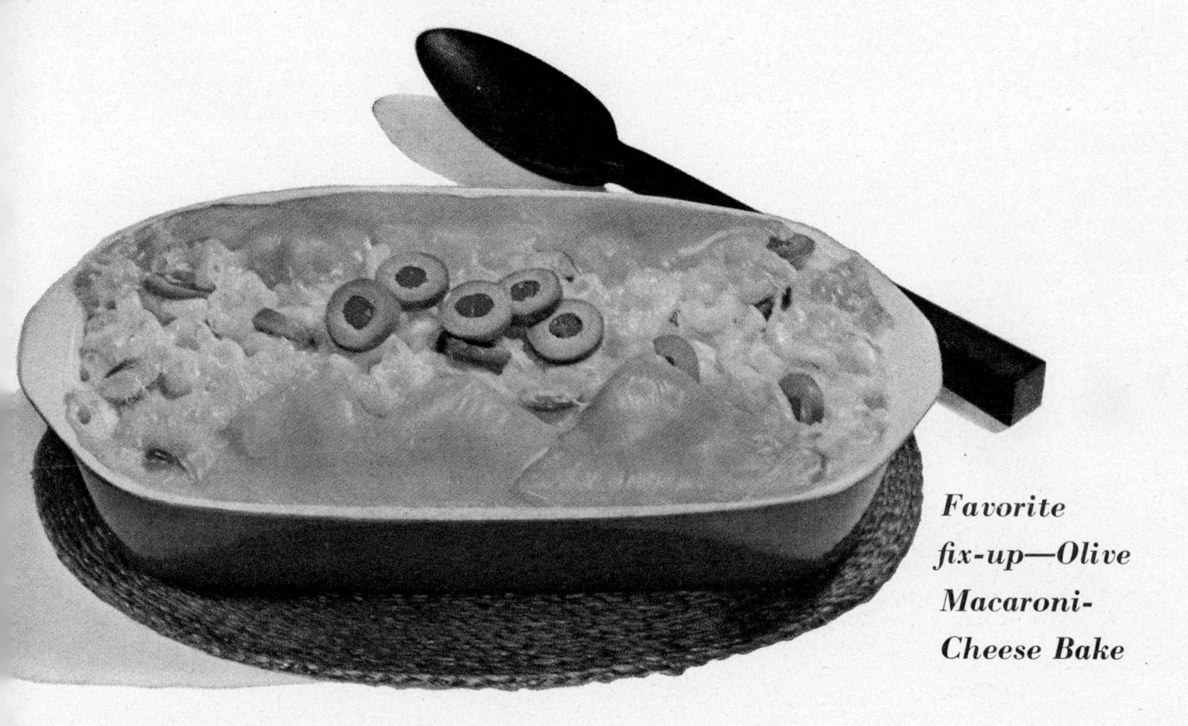

Favorite fix-up—Olive Macaroni-Cheese Bake

Handy hamburger, sausage

Prize winner from ground beef—Stuffed Manicotti, with cheese filling, rich meat sauce atop

Fill the hollows of jumbo macaroni, like *manicotti* or *tufoli*, with cottage-cheese or Ricotta stuffing. (Use a pastry tube or split the macaroni and fill.) Bake in a savory tomato meat sauce; top with Romano. Delicious!

You can use smaller pasta too, like *rigatoni*. Instead of filling, bake in layers of the cheese and sauce.

If your baking dish is an unusual size or shape, like this hand-crafted one, you can find out its size by measuring the amount of water needed to fill it. Mark volume on bottom with nail polish. Check casserole size and volume equivalents at right to know which recipes will fit in your baker.

Here begins a treasure chest of wonderful casseroles—easy, budget-minded, good!

You'll need a baking dish or two—perhaps a shallow rectangular baker and a deep round casserole. Common sizes in shallow bakers are 10x6x1½ (1½ quarts); 11½x7½x1½ (2 quarts); and 13x9x2 (3 quarts). Family-size deep casseroles measure 1, 1½, and 2 quarts. You can choose from other sizes, shapes, too, and a variety of materials. (Note care directions for earthenware, china.) Today's casseroles are pretty *and* practical, the main dishes served in them company-good! Starter below is the long-time favorite on cover—Hamburger Pie.

Hamburger Pie

1 medium onion, chopped
1 pound ground beef
¾ teaspoon salt
Dash pepper
1 1-pound can (2 cups) cut green beans, drained, *or* ½ pound green beans, cooked and drained
1 can condensed tomato soup
Potato Fluff Topper

Cook onion in small amount hot fat till tender but not brown. Add meat and seasonings; brown lightly. Add drained beans and soup; pour into greased 1½-quart casserole.

Drop Potato Fluff Topper in mounds over meat. If desired, sprinkle potatoes with ½ cup shredded process cheese. Bake at 350° for 25 to 30 minutes. Makes 6 servings.

Potato Fluff Topper

5 medium potatoes, cooked*
½ cup warm milk
1 beaten egg

Mash potatoes while hot; add milk and egg. Season. Drop in mounds over casserole.

*For speed, use packaged instant mashed or whipped potatoes. Prepare enough for 4 servings, according to package directions, but reserving half the milk. Add egg to potatoes; season. Add reserved milk slowly so you can omit a little, if necessary to make potatoes stiff enough to hold shape. Make Fluffs.

Hamburger Pielets

2 pounds ground beef
2 cups chopped onion
1½ cups bias-sliced celery
⅔ cup chopped green pepper
2 teaspoons chili powder
2 teaspoons salt
¼ teaspoon pepper
2 cans condensed tomato soup
2 cloves garlic, minced
Canned or frozen French-fried onions*

Combine ground beef, onion, celery, and green pepper in large skillet. Cook till meat is browned. Add remaining ingredients except onion rings; simmer 5 minutes.

Pour into 6 or 7 individual casseroles. Bake at 425° for 12 to 15 minutes. Last few minutes, arrange French-fried onions atop each pielet. Makes 6 or 7 servings.

*Or use a biscuit topper from page 46.

Hamburger-Biscuit Bake

1 tablespoon instant minced onion
⅔ cup milk
2 cups packaged biscuit mix
1 pound ground beef
1 tablespoon instant minced onion
1 cup shredded sharp process cheese
¼ cup mayonnaise
3 tablespoons snipped parsley
1 tablespoon butter, melted
1 teaspoon instant minced onion

• • •

Vegetable Sauce:
1 can condensed cream of vegetable soup
⅓ cup milk
¼ teaspoon monosodium glutamate

Soak 1 tablespoon instant minced onion in ⅔ cup milk. Prepare biscuit mix according to package directions for rolled biscuits, using milk-onion mixture for the liquid. Roll in two 8-inch circles, about ¼ inch thick. Press one circle into well-greased 8-inch shallow round baking dish.

Brown ground beef in skillet; spoon off excess fat. Stir in 1 tablespoon instant minced onion. Add cheese, mayonnaise, and parsley. Spread over biscuit in baking dish. Top with second biscuit. Flute edge.

Bake at 375° 15 to 20 minutes. Drizzle melted butter over top; sprinkle with 1 teaspoon instant minced onion. Bake 2 minutes or till onion is toasty. Cut in wedges. Pass Vegetable Sauce. Makes 5 or 6 servings.

Vegetable Sauce: Mix soup, ⅓ cup milk, and monosodium glutamate. Heat.

Slick way to grease a casserole—use a piece of bread!

When the recipe calls for a greased casserole, use a piece of bread to spread the butter, margarine, or salad oil. When you've finished, just cut up the bread and add it to the casserole mixture. (You can add it whole to some dishes.)

Stuffed Manicotti

Manicotti is such giant macaroni you can fill it! Dandy company casserole—

1 pound ground beef
¼ cup olive or salad oil

• • •

½ cup chopped onion
1 large clove garlic, minced
2 6-ounce cans (1⅓ cups) tomato paste
2 cups water
1½ teaspoons salt
Dash pepper
2 tablespoons chopped parsley
4 teaspoons basil
1 teaspoon aniseed (optional)

• • •

¾ pound fresh Ricotta cheese *or* 1½ cups cream-style cottage cheese
⅓ cup grated Romano or Parmesan cheese
1 beaten egg
2 tablespoons chopped parsley
¼ teaspoon salt
Dash pepper

• • •

8 ounces *manicotti*
Grated Romano or Parmesan cheese

Brown meat lightly in hot oil. Add next 9 ingredients. Simmer uncovered about 45 minutes, stirring occasionally. Meanwhile, combine next 6 ingredients.

Cook manicotti in boiling salted water till tender; drain; rinse in cold water. Use pastry tube to stuff manicotti with cheese mixture (or cut the macaroni lengthwise with scissors, open and fill).

Pour half the tomato-meat sauce into an 11x7x1½-inch baking dish. Arrange stuffed manicotti in a layer, overlapping slightly. Top with remaining sauce. Sprinkle with Romano cheese.

Bake in moderate oven (350°) 25 to 30 minutes. Makes 6 to 8 servings.

Salmagundi Bake

¾ cup uncooked long-grain rice
1½ teaspoons salt
Dash pepper
2 8-ounce cans seasoned tomato sauce
1 cup hot water
1 cup chopped onion
½ cup chopped green pepper
1 pound ground beef
1 teaspoon salt
½ teaspoon monosodium glutamate
1 12-ounce can (1½ cups) whole kernel corn, drained
2 to 3 teaspoons chili powder
4 slices bacon

In ungreased 2-quart casserole, place layer of uncooked rice. Sprinkle with 1½ teaspoons salt and dash pepper; pour over *1 can* of tomato sauce and the hot water. Add a layer of onion and green pepper, then a layer of ground beef. Sprinkle with 1 teaspoon salt and the monosodium glutamate. Top with a layer of corn. Add chili powder to remaining can of tomato sauce and pour over corn. Top with bacon slices.

Cover and bake in moderate oven (375°) 1 hour; uncover and bake 15 minutes longer or till rice is done. Garnish with tomato slices, topped with green-pepper rings and crisp bacon curls. Makes 5 or 6 servings.

Hamburger-Corn Casserole

1½ pounds ground beef
1 cup chopped onion
1 12-ounce can (1½ cups) whole kernel corn, drained
1 can condensed cream of chicken soup
1 can condensed cream of mushroom soup
1 cup dairy sour cream
¼ cup chopped pimiento
¾ teaspoon salt
½ teaspoon monosodium glutamate
¼ teaspoon pepper
3 cups medium noodles, cooked

• • •

1 cup soft bread crumbs
3 tablespoons butter, melted

Brown meat. Add onion; cook till tender but not brown. Add next 8 ingredients; mix well. Stir in noodles. Pour into 2-quart casserole.

Mix crumbs and butter; sprinkle over top. Bake in moderate oven (350°) 30 minutes or till heated through. Snip parsley over top. Makes 8 to 10 servings.

Burger-Noodle Bake

Noodles bake in rich, spicy meat sauce—

1 pound ground beef
½ pound ground pork
⅔ cup finely chopped onion
2 cans condensed tomato soup
1 3-ounce package cream cheese, diced
2 tablespoons sugar
2 to 3 teaspoons Worcestershire sauce
1½ teaspoons salt

• • •

8 ounces wide noodles

• • •

½ cup corn-flake crumbs
1 tablespoon butter or margarine, melted

Combine meats and brown lightly in 12-inch skillet; *drain off excess fat;* add onion and cook till tender but not brown. Add soup, cheese, sugar, and seasonings. Simmer uncovered 15 minutes, stirring occasionally.

Meanwhile, cook noodles in boiling salted water till tender; drain. Combine with sauce. Turn into an 11½x7½x1½-inch baking dish.

Mix corn-flake crumbs and butter; sprinkle over top. Bake in moderate oven (350°) about 20 minutes or till hot. Makes 8 servings.

Burger Chili and Chips

A quickie, with South-of-the-border flavor—

1 pound ground beef
½ cup chopped onion
¼ cup diced celery

• • •

1 teaspoon salt
¼ teaspoon pepper
1 1-pound can (2 cups) chili con carne with beans

• • •

1 cup corn chips
1 cup (½ pound) diced process American cheese

Brown meat. Add onion and celery and cook till tender but not brown. Season with salt and pepper. Add chili and mix.

Place layer of corn chips in greased 1½-quart casserole. Alternate layers of the chili mixture, corn chips, and diced cheese, ending with corn chips.

Bake in moderate oven (350°) 10 minutes, or till heated through. Makes 6 servings. Serve with chilled green salad, oven-hot baked apples, and tall glasses of cold milk.

Gourmet Sausage and Noodles

1 pound bulk pork sausage
4 ounces (2 cups) fine noodles
2 tablespoons chopped pimiento
2 tablespoons chopped green pepper

• • •

¼ cup milk
1 can condensed cream of chicken soup
½ cup (2 ounces) crumbled blue cheese*

• • •

½ cup soft bread crumbs
1 tablespoon butter or margarine, melted

Form sausage in "marbles"; flatten in patties and brown lightly on both sides. (Or, brown sausage, stirring to crumble.) Drain.

Cook noodles in boiling *unsalted* water till tender; drain. Combine patties, noodles, pimiento, and green pepper.

Add milk to soup; heat, stirring constantly. Add blue cheese, heat and stir till cheese melts. Combine sauce with noodle mixture.

Turn into greased 1½-quart casserole. Mix crumbs and butter; sprinkle atop. Bake at 350° 30 to 35 minutes. Makes 6 servings.

*Or, use 1 cup (¼ pound) shredded sharp process cheese. Remove hot soup mixture from heat; add cheese, and stir to melt.

Sausage Polenta

½ cup finely chopped onion
1 clove garlic, minced
2 tablespoons salad oil
1 1-pound can (2 cups) tomatoes
1 6-ounce can (⅔ cup) tomato paste
1 3-ounce can (⅔ cup) broiled sliced mushrooms with liquid
1 teaspoon salt
Dash pepper
½ teaspoon oregano
½ cup grated Parmesan cheese
1 packet or small package corn-muffin mix or 1 package corn-bread mix
1 8-ounce package brown-and-serve sausage
½ cup shredded sharp process cheese

Cook onion and garlic in hot oil till tender but not brown. Add next 6 ingredients and simmer uncovered 5 minutes.

Meanwhile, add Parmesan to corn-muffin or -bread mix and prepare batter following package directions; spread in a greased 10x6x1½-inch baking dish. Slice 3 or 4 sausages over batter; pour hot tomato mixture over all. Bake at 400° for 25 minutes. Arrange remaining sausages on top; bake 15 minutes. Sprinkle with cheese. Serves 5 or 6.

Sausage Macaroni and Cheese

1 pound bulk pork sausage
1 cup chopped onion
3 ounces (about ¾ cup) 7-minute macaroni
1 can condensed cream of celery soup
⅔ cup milk
3 slightly beaten eggs
2 cups shredded sharp process cheese

• • •

½ cup corn-flake crumbs
1 tablespoon butter or margarine, melted

Cook meat and onion till meat is lightly browned; place in ungreased 8x8x2-inch baking pan. Cook macaroni according to package directions; drain; place atop meat.

Combine soup and milk; heat. Stir small amount of hot mixture into eggs; return to remaining hot mixture. Add cheese. Pour over macaroni. Mix corn-flake crumbs and butter; arrange in border. Bake in moderate oven (350°) 40 to 45 minutes. Serves 6.

Quick supper, Italian style It's Sausage Polenta, an appetizing combination of Parmesan-spiked corn bread (from a mix), zippy tomato sauce, cheese, and brown-and-serve sausage.

Sausage Strata

So light and airy that it's almost like souffle; a grand luncheon dish! For ideas, see the meal plan below—

6 slices enriched bread

• • •

1 pound bulk pork sausage
1 teaspoon prepared mustard
1 cup (¼ pound) shredded process Swiss cheese

• • •

3 eggs, slightly beaten
1¼ cups milk
¾ cup light cream
½ teaspoon salt
Dash pepper
Dash nutmeg
1 teaspoon Worcestershire sauce

Trim crusts from bread; fit bread in bottom of 6 greased individual casseroles.*

Brown sausage; *drain off all excess fat.* Stir in mustard. Spoon sausage evenly over bread; sprinkle with cheese.

Combine remaining ingredients; pour over cheese. Bake in moderate oven (350°) 25 to 30 minutes or till puffed and set. Trim with fluffs of parsley. Serve immediately. Makes 6 servings.

*Or put casserole together in a greased 10x6x1½-inch baking dish; bake 30 to 35 minutes or till set.

CASSEROLE LUNCHEON

Melon Cup or Tomato Juice
Sausage Strata
Buttered Green Beans
Cabbage-Celery Slaw   Hard Rolls
Persian Peaches   Hot Tea

To cut last-minute fuss, fix casseroles ahead and chill in refrigerator. (Allow some extra time in oven.)

For *Persian Peaches:* Mix 4 cups sliced peaches, ½ cup orange juice, 3 tablespoons honey, 2 tablespoons finely chopped candied ginger, dash salt. Cover and chill. Spoon over vanilla ice cream. Serves 5 or 6.

Sausage-Stuffing Towers

Peppy apple stuffing is sandwiched between sausage patties; topknot—saucy crab apple—

1½ pounds bulk pork sausage
1 cup packaged herb-seasoned stuffing
1 cup finely chopped pared tart apples
½ cup finely chopped celery
¼ cup minced onion
2 tablespoons snipped parsley
2 tablespoons chili sauce
¼ teaspoon dry mustard
¼ teaspoon pepper
6 spiced crab apples

Shape sausage in 12 thin patties, ¼ inch thick. Prepare stuffing according to package directions, *using ¼ cup water and 2 tablespoons butter.* Add apple, celery, onion, and seasonings; toss to mix. Arrange 6 sausage patties in shallow pan. Top each with ½ cup stuffing, then another patty; toothpick through center to hold. Bake in moderate oven (375°) 45 minutes or till done. Top with crab apples. Makes 6 servings.

Sausage Pilaf

Toasted crumbs hide sausage and rice in bubbly mushroom sauce, flecked with pimiento, green pepper. Rice goes in uncooked!—

1 pound bulk pork sausage
1 cup chopped celery
½ cup chopped onion
½ cup chopped green pepper

• • •

¼ cup chopped pimiento
1 can condensed cream of mushroom soup
1¼ cups milk
½ cup uncooked rice
½ teaspoon poultry seasoning
¼ teaspoon salt

• • •

1 cup soft bread crumbs
2 tablespoons butter or margarine, melted

Brown sausage. *Drain off excess fat.* Add celery, onion, and green pepper; cook till tender but not brown.

Stir in pimiento, soup, milk, rice, and seasonings. Pour into an ungreased 1½-quart casserole. Bake, covered, in moderate oven (350°) 50 minutes, stirring occasionally. Mix crumbs and butter; sprinkle evenly over casserole.

Bake, uncovered, 20 minutes longer. Trim with pimiento cutouts. Makes 6 servings.

Hearty "meat-potato" bakes

Veal-Ham Foldovers

8 ⅛-inch veal cutlets (about 1¼ pounds)
8 thin slices boiled ham
8 thin slices process Swiss cheese
3 tablespoons butter or margarine, melted
½ cup corn-flake crumbs
1 can condensed cream of mushroom soup
½ cup light cream
2 tablespoons cooking sauterne
Hot cooked rice

Pound each cutlet with meat pounder to a very thin rectangle, about 7½x4½ inches.

Cut ham and cheese slices in half. Stack two half-slices of each in center of each cutlet. Fold veal over to cover ham and cheese. Brush with melted butter; roll each Foldover in corn-flake crumbs.

Place Foldovers in an ungreased 11½x 7½x1½-inch baking dish. Bake in moderate oven (350°) for 30 minutes. Combine remaining ingredients; pour over Foldovers. Cover; continue baking 30 minutes longer, or till tender. Serve with rice. Serves 8.

Chopstick Veal and Rice

1½ pounds veal *or* ¾ pound *each* veal and pork
2 tablespoons shortening
1½ cups chopped onion
1½ cups sliced celery
1 cup diced green pepper
¼ cup chopped pimiento
½ cup uncooked long-grain rice
1 can condensed cream of mushroom soup
1 cup milk
2 tablespoons soy sauce
1 3-ounce can (2 cups) chow-mein noodles

Cut meat in strips about 2 inches long and ½ inch wide. Brown meat quickly in hot fat. Add remaining ingredients except noodles.

Turn into a 2-quart casserole. Cover and bake at 325° for 1¼ hours, stirring occasionally. Uncover; sprinkle with chow-mein noodles last 5 minutes of baking. Makes 8 servings.

Spareribs with Caraway Kraut

A delicious old-world dish—spareribs bake with sauerkraut that's flavored with caraway seed, apple, carrot, and tomato juice—

3 pounds spareribs, cut in serving pieces
2 teaspoons salt
¼ teaspoon pepper

. . .

1 No. 2½ can (3½ cups) sauerkraut
2 medium carrots, shredded
1 unpared tart apple, finely chopped
1½ cups tomato juice
2 tablespoons brown sugar
2 to 3 teaspoons caraway seed

Season ribs with salt and pepper; place in Dutch oven. Combine kraut (including liquid) with remaining ingredients and spoon over ribs. Bake, covered, in moderate oven (350°) 2½ to 3½ hours or till ribs are done, basting kraut with juices several times during the last hour. Use spoon to serve ribs and kraut so as to get all the good juices, too. Makes 4 to 6 servings.

Foil-wrapped Steak Supper

Easy oven meal—you don't even have to brown the meat. Onion-soup mix adds rich flavor—

Aluminum foil
1½ pounds chuck steak, 1 inch thick
1 envelope onion-soup mix

. . .

3 medium carrots, quartered
2 stalks celery, cut in sticks
2 to 3 medium potatoes, halved
2 tablespoons butter or margarine
½ teaspoon salt

Tear off 2½-foot length of 18-inch-wide foil. Place meat in center; sprinkle with onion-soup mix; cover with vegetables. Dot vegetables with butter and sprinkle with salt.

Fold foil over and seal securely to hold in juices. Place on baking sheet; bake in very hot oven (450°) 1 to 1½ hours or till done. Makes 4 servings.

Note: To cook Foil-wrapped Steak Supper on a barbecue grill, use a double thickness of foil; cook over *slow* coals.

Round-steak Supper

2 pounds round steak, 1 inch thick, cut in servings
2 teaspoons salt
Dash pepper
Enriched flour

• • •

6 medium onions, sliced
¼ cup fat
3 large potatoes, halved
1 bay leaf
1 can condensed tomato soup
1 1-pound can (2 cups) French-cut green beans, drained

Season meat with salt and pepper; roll in flour. Cook onions in hot fat till tender but not brown; remove onions. Brown meat slowly on both sides. Place meat in 3-quart casserole; add onions, potatoes, and bay leaf; pour soup over. Cover.

Bake in moderate oven (350°) 1 hour and 45 minutes, or till meat is tender. Add green beans; cook 10 to 15 minutes longer. Makes 6 to 8 servings. Pass toasted French bread.

Vegetable-Beef Bake

1½ pounds beef, cut in 1-inch cubes
2 tablespoons fat
2 tablespoons enriched flour
2 teaspoons paprika
1 to 1½ teaspoons chili powder
1 teaspoon salt
¼ teaspoon pepper
1 1-pound can (2 cups) tomatoes
1 cup lengthwise sliced carrots

• • •

1 cup water
4 medium onions, quartered
1 cup sliced celery
1½ cups uncooked mostacciola

Brown beef in hot fat. Mix flour and seasonings; add to meat. Stir in tomatoes, add carrots, cover, and cook over low heat 30 minutes. Add water, onions, celery, and mostacciola; bring to boiling. Pour into ungreased 2-quart casserole. Cover.

Bake in moderate oven (350°), stirring occasionally, 1 hour or till vegetables and meat are tender. Makes 6 to 8 servings.

For "something special," try Tenderloin-Noodle Treat— Noodles are laced with smooth, rich blue-cheese sauce, dotted with pimiento and green pepper. Pork tenderloin slices tuck in atop, make this a company casserole! Serve with buttered green beans, fresh fruit salad, hot French bread slices.

Tenderloin-Noodle Treat

- 6 ounces (about 3 cups) noodles
- 6 slices pork tenderloin, ½ inch thick
- 1 tablespoon shortening
- ½ teaspoon salt
- Dash pepper

• • •

Blue-cheese Sauce:

- 3 tablespoons butter
- 3 tablespoons enriched flour
- ¾ teaspoon salt
- Dash pepper
- 1 cup milk
- 3 ounces blue cheese, crumbled (¾ cup)

• • •

- 3 tablespoons chopped green pepper
- 3 tablespoons chopped pimiento

Cook noodles in boiling salted water; rinse; drain. Brown tenderloin slices slowly on both sides in hot fat (takes about 15 minutes). Season with ½ teaspoon salt, dash pepper.

Make Blue-cheese Sauce: Melt butter; blend in flour, ¾ teaspoon salt, and dash pepper. Stir in milk. Cook and stir till thick. Add blue cheese; stir till cheese melts.

Combine noodles, green pepper, pimiento, and sauce. Place in ungreased 10x6x1½-inch baking dish. Arrange meat on top. Bake at 350° 30 minutes or till done. Serves 6.

Pork-Apple Bake

- 4 pork steaks, about 1 inch thick
- 1½ teaspoons salt
- Dash pepper
- 3 medium unpared apples, cored and cut in thirds
- 3 medium onions, cut in ½-inch slices
- 1 1-pound 2-ounce can sweet potatoes, drained

Trim fat from steaks. Heat fat in skillet; when you have about 2 tablespoons melted fat, remove trimmings. (Or, use salad oil).

Brown chops on both sides; season with salt and pepper. Place in 11½x7½x1½-inch baking dish, overlapping slightly. Place apple and onion slices atop each steak. Add sweet potatoes. Season potatoes and onions.

Pour excess fat from skillet. Pour ½ cup water in skillet; stir in crusty bits on bottom of skillet. Pour over meat and vegetables. Cover with foil or lid.

Bake in moderate oven (350°) 1 hour. Uncover and cook 5 to 10 minutes longer or till tender. Makes 4 servings.

HOMESPUN AND HEARTY

Pork-chop Oven Dinner
Molded Lime-Citrus Salad
or Pineapple Coleslaw
Oven-warm Rolls Butter
Glazed Applesauce Loaf Cake
Coffee Milk

Easy—your oven takes over! Casserole and cake bake at same time; rolls (from the store) heat last few minutes.

Mix ½ cup sifted confectioners' sugar, 1 tablespoon water; glaze warm cake.

Pork-chop Oven Dinner

Wonderful flavor—pork and fresh vegetables bake to perfection in spicy sauce—

- 6 pork chops, about ¾ inch thick
- 3 tablespoons enriched flour
- ¾ teaspoon salt
- Dash pepper
- ¼ teaspoon garlic salt

• • •

- ½ cup water
- ¼ cup cooking sherry
- 1 tablespoon snipped parsley
- ¼ teaspoon ground cloves
- 3 peppercorns
- 1 bay leaf

• • •

- 6 small carrots, pared and halved lengthwise
- 6 small potatoes, pared and halved
- 1 medium onion, thinly sliced

Trim fat from chops. Heat fat in oven-going skillet. When you have about 2 tablespoons melted fat, remove trimmings. Combine flour, salt, pepper, and garlic salt; dip chops in mixture. Brown chops well, about 15 minutes on each side. Remove chops from skillet. Pour off excess fat.

In skillet, combine water with next 5 ingredients. Sprinkle carrots and potatoes generously with salt; place *in the liquid.* Arrange chops atop; add onion slices. Cover. Bake at 350° for 1 to 1¼ hours or till vegetables are tender. Skim off excess fat; remove bay leaf and peppercorns.

Serve in skillet, or arrange chops and vegetables on platter and pass gravy. Trim with parsley. Makes 6 servings. (*See meal plan.*)

Asparagus-Ham Bake

Here's fresh-as-spring flavor—cubes of ham and tender asparagus spears, cheese, peppy onion! Quick sauce is soup, evaporated milk—

Water
1 6-oz. can (⅔ cup) evaporated milk
2 cups cubed cooked or canned ham
2 cups cooked rice
½ cup shredded process cheese
1 can condensed cream of mushroom soup
3 tablespoons finely chopped onion

• • •

1 10-ounce package frozen asparagus spears

• • •

½ cup corn-flake crumbs
3 tablespoons butter or margarine, melted

Add water to evaporated milk to make ¾ cup. Combine with ham, rice, cheese, soup, and onion. Pour boiling water over asparagus spears to separate them; drain.

Spoon *half* of ham mixture into 10x6x1½-inch baking dish; top with the asparagus spears, then with remaining ham mixture.

Combine corn-flake crumbs and butter; sprinkle over top. Bake at 375° for 25 to 30 minutes or till heated through and top is lightly browned. Makes 6 servings.

Ham and Eggs en Casserole

Under crisp crumb topper, ham, eggs, and mushrooms bake in bubbly cheese sauce—

2 to 3 cups diced cooked or canned ham
6 hard-cooked eggs, sliced
1 6-ounce can (1⅓ cups) broiled sliced mushrooms, drained

• • •

1 can condensed cream of celery soup
¼ cup milk
1 cup shredded sharp process American cheese
5 or 6 drops Tabasco sauce

• • •

1½ cups soft bread crumbs

In an ungreased 2-quart casserole, alternate layers of ham, egg slices, and mushrooms, starting and ending with ham.

Combine soup and milk; add cheese and Tabasco sauce. Heat, stirring till cheese is melted. Pour over layers in casserole. Sprinkle the bread crumbs over top.

Bake uncovered in moderate oven (375°) about 25 minutes, or till heated through and crumbs are golden.

If desired, trim with additional hard-cooked egg slices and sprigs of parsley. Makes 6 servings. Round out the meal with leafy green salad, warmed corn-meal muffins.

Ham-Chicken Bake brims with chunks of meat in creamy full-flavored sauce. And—it boasts choice of bonnets, fancy and fast—

When company's coming, choose the fancy topper—Yam Biscuits. These light golden fluffs have a distinctive flavor all their own—the perfect accent for ham and chicken. (See recipe opposite.)

When every minute counts, make *Biscuit Rolls* instead: Shape 6 or 7 refrigerated biscuits (from a package) in 5-inch "logs," by rolling between hands.

Place Rolls crease down, along with remaining biscuits, on ungreased baking sheet. Place in oven with casserole and bake 12 to 15 minutes, or till golden.

Arrange Biscuit Rolls in row down center of casserole as shown. Pass extra biscuits. Serve with fresh relishes, a fruit dessert.

Ham-Chicken Bake

½ cup chopped onion
½ cup chopped celery
¼ cup butter or margarine
¼ cup enriched flour
1½ cups chicken broth
1½ cups light cream or milk
2 cups diced cooked or canned ham
2 cups diced cooked chicken
1 3-ounce can (⅔ cup) broiled
  sliced mushrooms, drained
1 teaspoon poultry seasoning
½ teaspoon monosodium glutamate
¼ teaspoon salt
Dash pepper
Yam Biscuits, *or* Biscuit Rolls, page 16

Cook onion and celery in butter till tender but not brown; blend in flour. Stir in broth and light cream all at once; cook and stir till sauce comes to boil. Add ham, chicken, mushrooms, and seasonings; heat through. Pour into ungreased 11½x7½x1½-inch baking dish.

Top *hot* mixture with Yam Biscuits (or prepare Biscuit Rolls as directed). Bake at 350° 30 to 35 minutes or till biscuits are done and casserole is hot. Makes 6 to 8 servings.

Yam Biscuits

Combine 1 cup mashed cooked yams, ⅓ cup melted butter, and 1 beaten egg.

Sift together 1 cup sifted enriched flour, 2 teaspoons baking powder, and ½ teaspoon salt; blend into yam mixture. Drop by tablespoons around edge of *hot* casserole. Bake as above. Makes 6 to 8 medium biscuits.

Ham and Potatoes au Gratin

¼ cup chopped green onion
¼ cup chopped green pepper
2 cups (1 pound) diced cooked ham
3 cups diced cooked potatoes (3 medium)
¼ cup mayonnaise or salad dressing
¼ teaspoon salt
Dash pepper
1 cup shredded sharp process cheese
¾ cup milk

Cook onion and green pepper in 1 tablespoon hot fat till just tender. Combine with next 5 ingredients. Pour into 10x6x1½-inch baking dish. In saucepan, combine cheese and milk; stir over low heat till cheese is melted. Pour over ham-potato mixture. Bake at 350° 30 to 35 minutes. Makes 4 servings.

Chipped-beef Puff

4 ounces dried beef, coarsely torn
  (2 cups torn)
¼ cup butter or margarine
3 tablespoons enriched flour
Dash pepper
2 cups milk
2 tablespoons diced pimiento
1 3-ounce can (⅔ cup) broiled
  sliced mushrooms, drained

• • •

3 egg whites
¼ teaspoon salt
3 egg yolks
⅓ cup shredded process cheese

Cook dried beef in butter over low heat, stirring till slightly crisp and frizzled. Blend flour into butter; add pepper. Slowly stir in milk; cook and stir till smooth and thickened. Stir in pimiento, mushrooms.

Pour into 10x6x1½-inch baking dish. Keep hot in moderate oven (375°) while you make the topper. Beat egg whites with salt till stiff peaks form. Beat yolks till thick and lemon-colored. Fold yolks into whites; fold in cheese. Pour over hot creamed mixture.

Bake 15 to 20 minutes at 375° or till golden brown. Garnish with frizzled dried beef, if desired. Makes 4 or 5 servings.

Chipped-beef Noodle Bake

4 ounces dried beef, cut up
  (1½ cups cut)
2 tablespoons butter or margarine
2 tablespoons flour
¼ teaspoon pepper
1 14½-ounce can (1⅔ cups)
  evaporated milk
¼ cup diced celery
2 tablespoons diced green pepper
2 hard-cooked eggs, chopped
1 cup (about 2 ounces) medium noodles,
  cooked
1 cup soft buttered bread crumbs

Place beef in strainer; rinse with hot water; drain well. Melt butter in saucepan. Blend in flour and pepper; gradually stir in evaporated milk. Cook and stir till thickened. Mix in remaining ingredients except crumbs.

Place in greased 1-quart casserole, or divide between four 8-ounce individual casseroles. Sprinkle with bread crumbs.

Bake at 350° till bubbly, about 15 minutes for individual casseroles, 20 to 25 minutes for 1-quart casserole. Makes 4 servings.

Wonderful ways with chicken

Chicken Strata

8 slices day-old white bread
2 cups diced cooked chicken or turkey
½ cup chopped onion
½ cup chopped green pepper
½ cup finely chopped celery
½ cup mayonnaise
¾ teaspoon salt
Dash pepper
2 slightly beaten eggs
1½ cups milk

• • •

1 can condensed cream of mushroom soup
½ cup shredded sharp process American cheese

Butter 2 slices bread; cut in ½-inch cubes and set aside. Cut remaining bread in 1-inch cubes; place half of unbuttered cubes in bottom of 8x8x2-inch baking dish. Combine chicken, vegetables, mayonnaise, and seasonings; spoon over bread cubes. Sprinkle remaining unbuttered cubes over chicken mixture. Combine eggs and milk; pour over all. Cover and chill 1 hour or overnight.

Spoon soup over top. Sprinkle with buttered cubes. Bake in a slow oven (325°) 50 minutes or till set. Sprinkle cheese over top last few minutes of baking. Makes 6 servings.

Chicken makes this much when it's diced or sliced

Here's a guide to amount to buy when "chicken for casserole" is on the shopping list:

- 1 3½-pound ready-to-cook chicken will give you about 3 cups diced cooked chicken
- 2 whole chicken breasts (10 ounces each) yield 1½-2 cups diced cooked chicken *or* 12 thin slices cooked chicken

(Cook chicken breasts as for stewed chicken but cook only 30 minutes or till tender.)

To slice cooked chicken breasts: Have them well-chilled (but not frozen). Carefully remove meat from bone (meat will split in half). Lay each piece flat on cutting board. Hold in place; with sharp knife, slice chicken breast lengthwise parallel to board. You should get three thin slices from each half of the breast.

Chicken-Biscuit Pie

1 can condensed cream of celery soup
½ cup milk
1 5-ounce can (⅔ cup) boned chicken
1 8-ounce can peas, drained
2 tablespoons finely chopped onion
½ teaspoon basil
Dash pepper
1 cup biscuit mix
⅓ cup milk

In skillet blend soup and ½ cup milk. Add next 5 ingredients. Heat to boiling, stirring frequently. Pour into 1-quart casserole.

Combine biscuit mix and ⅓ cup milk as directed on package; drop by spoonfuls onto *hot* chicken mixture. Bake in very hot oven (450°) 10 to 15 minutes, or till biscuits are lightly browned. Makes 4 servings.

Classic Chicken Divan

Elegant, delicious! Breast of chicken and tender broccoli are smothered in creamy sauce, broiled at last minute to golden perfection!

2 bunches fresh broccoli *or* 2 10-ounce packages frozen
¼ cup butter
¼ cup enriched flour
2 cups chicken broth
½ cup heavy cream
3 tablespoons cooking sherry
½ teaspoon salt
3 chicken breasts, cooked and thinly sliced (see Tip)
Shredded Parmesan cheese

Cook broccoli in boiling salted water till tender. Drain. Place spears crosswise in 13x9x2-inch baking dish (see page 2).

Melt butter in saucepan; blend in flour. Add chicken broth all at once and cook, stirring constantly, till mixture thickens. Stir in cream, sherry, salt, and dash pepper.

Pour *half* the sauce (1⅔ cups) over the broccoli. Top with chicken slices. To remaining sauce, add ¼ *cup* Parmesan cheese; pour over chicken and sprinkle with additional Parmesan cheese.

Bake at 350° 20 minutes or till hot. Then broil just till sauce is golden brown. Trim with spiced peaches. Makes 6 to 8 servings.

Easy Chicken Divan—old favorite with a new twist

The traditional combination, broccoli spears and slices of chicken, bakes in delicious cheese sauce — but *this* sauce is no-cook. Another surprise: It's seasoned with curry! The topping is crisp buttered crumbs. Remember this dish for a buffet dinner — complete meal with toasty French bread, molded fruit salad, warm upside-down cake. (If dinner goes elegant, substitute Classic Chicken Divan and a handsome torte.

Easy Chicken Divan

2 10-ounce packages frozen broccoli or 2 bunches fresh broccoli
2 cups sliced cooked chicken or 3 chicken breasts, cooked and boned

• • •

2 cans condensed cream of chicken soup
1 cup mayonnaise or salad dressing
1 teaspoon lemon juice
½ teaspoon curry powder
½ cup shredded sharp process cheese

• • •

½ cup soft bread crumbs
1 tablespoon butter or margarine, melted

Cook broccoli in boiling salted water till tender; drain. Arrange stalks in greased 11½x7½x1½-inch baking dish as shown above. Place chicken on top.

Combine soup, mayonnaise, lemon juice, and curry powder; pour over chicken. Sprinkle with cheese. Combine crumbs and butter; sprinkle over all. Bake at 350° 25 to 30 minutes or till thoroughly heated. Trim with pimiento strips. Makes 6 to 8 servings.

Curried Chicken Casserole

A timesaver that's tops—

1 10-ounce package frozen broccoli spears

• • •

1 can condensed cream of chicken soup
1 10½-ounce can chicken a la king
1 teaspoon curry powder
1 teaspoon dry mustard
½ teaspoon Worcestershire sauce
¾ cup shredded sharp process cheese

• • •

2 cups cooked rice

Cook broccoli according to package directions; drain. Combine soup, chicken a la king, and seasonings. Heat through. Add cheese and stir till melted.

In greased 10x6x1½-inch baking dish, place *half* the rice, then *half* the broccoli, and *half* the sauce. Repeat layers. Bake in moderate oven (350°) 25 to 30 minutes or till thoroughly heated. Makes 4 to 6 servings.

Club Chicken

¼ cup butter, margarine, or chicken fat
¼ cup enriched flour
1 cup chicken broth or 1½ chicken bouillon cubes in 1 cup hot water
1 14½-ounce can (1⅔ cups) evaporated milk
½ cup water
1½ teaspoons salt

. . .

2½ cups diced cooked chicken
3 cups cooked rice
1 3-ounce can (⅔ cup) broiled sliced mushrooms, drained
¼ cup chopped pimiento
⅓ cup chopped green pepper
½ cup slivered blanched almonds, toasted

Melt butter; blend in flour. Gradually add broth, milk, and water; cook over low heat till thick, stirring constantly. Add salt.

Add chicken, rice, and vegetables. Pour into greased 11½x7½x1½-inch baking dish. Bake at 350° about 30 minutes. Sprinkle with toasted almonds. Makes 8 to 10 servings.

Creamy Chicken-Rice Casserole

1 cup wild rice
½ cup chopped onion
½ cup butter or margarine
¼ cup enriched flour
1 6-ounce can (1⅓ cups) broiled sliced mushrooms
Chicken broth
1½ cups light cream
3 cups diced cooked chicken
¼ cup diced pimiento
2 tablespoons snipped parsley
1½ teaspoons salt
¼ teaspoon pepper
½ cup slivered blanched almonds

Prepare wild rice according to package directions. Cook onion in butter till tender but not brown. Remove from heat; stir in flour.

Drain mushrooms, reserving liquid. Add enough chicken broth to liquid to measure 1½ cups; gradually stir into flour mixture. Add cream. Cook and stir till thick.

Add wild rice, mushrooms, chicken, pimiento, parsley, salt, and pepper. Place in 2-quart casserole. Sprinkle with almonds. Bake in moderate oven (350°) 25 to 30 minutes. Makes 8 servings.

Casserole Chicken a la King

3 tablespoons butter, margarine, or chicken fat
3 tablespoons enriched flour
1½ cups chicken broth *or* 2 chicken bouillon cubes in 1½ cups hot water
2 cups cooked chicken, cut in pieces
1 cup drained cooked or canned peas
1 3-ounce can (⅔ cup) broiled sliced mushrooms, drained
2 cooked medium carrots, cut in thirds
¼ cup chopped onion
2 tablespoons chopped pimiento
1 teaspoon salt
1 package refrigerated biscuits

Melt butter; blend in flour. Gradually add broth. Cook and stir till thick. Add chicken, vegetables, and salt; heat to bubbling. Pour into 1½-quart casserole.

Make Biscuit Snippets: With scissors, snip 6 refrigerated biscuits in quarters; arrange in ring, rounded side down, atop *hot* chicken. (Bake remaining biscuits on baking sheet.)

Bake casserole at 425° 8 to 10 minutes or till biscuits are done. Makes 5 servings.

Chicken Dinner Bake

1 3-ounce can broiled sliced mushrooms
1 envelope chicken-noodle soup mix
1½ cups water
1 6-ounce can (⅔ cup) evaporated milk
⅓ cup butter or margarine
⅓ cup enriched flour
½ teaspoon salt
Dash pepper
3 5-ounce cans boned chicken, diced
½ 10-ounce package (1 cup) frozen peas, broken up
¼ cup chopped onion
¼ cup chopped pimiento
2 eggs, well beaten
¼ teaspoon salt

Drain mushrooms, reserving liquid. Combine soup mix and water; bring to boil, reduce heat, and simmer 5 minutes. Strain to separate broth and noodles; reserve both.

Combine broth, mushroom liquid, and milk. Melt butter; blend in flour, ½ teaspoon salt, and pepper. Gradually add broth mixture; cook and stir till thick. Add mushrooms, chicken, peas, onion, and pimiento. Pour into greased 1½-quart casserole.

Bake at 350° 25 minutes. Add Topper; bake 5 to 10 minutes longer. Serves 5 or 6.

Topper: Combine eggs, ¼ teaspoon salt, and reserved noodles. Spoon atop casserole.

Chicken with Noodles

6 ounces (about 3 cups)
  medium noodles
1 can condensed cream of chicken soup
1 6-ounce can (⅔ cup) evaporated milk
¼ teaspoon salt
1½ cups shredded process cheese
2 cups diced cooked chicken or turkey
1 cup celery slices
¼ cup diced green pepper
¼ cup diced pimiento
1 cup slivered blanched almonds, toasted
Buttered bread crumbs

Cook noodles in boiling salted water till tender; drain. Form in nest in greased 2-quart casserole. Mix soup, milk, and salt; heat, stirring constantly. Add cheese; stir till melted. Add remaining ingredients *except* ½ cup of the almonds and the crumbs; pour over noodles. Top with crumbs and remaining almonds. Bake uncovered at 400° about 20 minutes. Makes 6 servings.

Chicken and Biscuits

Omit noodles in recipe for Chicken with Noodles. Combine remaining ingredients as directed, but omitting almonds and crumbs. Pour into greased 1½-quart casserole.

Top hot mixture with Pimiento Drop Biscuits. Bake at 450° 15 minutes or till biscuits are done. Makes 5 to 6 servings.

Pimiento Drop Biscuits

1 cup sifted enriched flour
1½ teaspoons baking powder
¼ teaspoon salt
2 tablespoons shortening
½ cup milk
2 tablespoons chopped pimiento

Sift together dry ingredients; cut in shortening till like coarse crumbs. Add milk and pimiento; mix just to moisten flour. Drop from tablespoon around edge of *hot* casserole.

Casserole Chicken a la King —pretty, quick, and good

Plump biscuit wreath (made speedily from snippets of refrigerated biscuits) tops rich sauce that's brimming with big chunks of chicken, mushrooms, tender peas, and carrots. Just right with this homey main dish—crisp coleslaw, hot buttered biscuits, wedges of warm cherry pie. Dad and the kids will really be impressed!

CHICKEN FOR COMPANY

Frosty Pineapple Cubes
Party Chicken-Noodle Bake
Buttered Broccoli with
Lemon Wedges
Hot Rolls Butter
Cranberry Salad Molds
Spice Cake a la Mode Coffee

Dinner for eight can be this easy! The nothing-to-it appetizer is frozen pineapple cubes thawed just enough to eat.

Casserole can be made ahead, stored in the refrigerator. (Allow up to 30 minutes extra time in the oven.) Bake cake, and warm rolls, in same oven. Skip frosting cake; cut wide wedges, scoop ice cream atop each.

Party Chicken-Noodle Bake

One good thing on top of another—that's what this casserole is made of!—

8 ounces wide or lasagne noodles

• • •

1 can condensed cream of mushroom soup
⅔ cup milk
½ teaspoon salt
½ teaspoon poultry seasoning

• • •

2 3-ounce packages cream cheese, softened
1 cup cream-style cottage cheese
⅓ cup sliced stuffed green olives
⅓ cup chopped onion
⅓ cup chopped green pepper
¼ cup minced parsley

• • •

3 cups diced cooked chicken or turkey
1½ cups buttered soft bread crumbs

Cook noodles in boiling salted water till tender; drain; rinse in cold water. Mix soup, milk, salt, and poultry seasoning; heat. Beat cheeses together; stir in green olives, onion, green pepper, and parsley.

Place *half* the noodles in 11½x7½x1½-inch baking dish; spread with *half* the cheese mixture, *half* the chicken, and *half* the soup mixture. Repeat layers. Top with crumbs.

Bake in moderate oven (375°) 30 minutes or till heated through. Trim with pimiento. Let stand 10 minutes. Makes 8 servings.

Bombay Chicken

Really curry in a casserole, with built-in condiments! On top—crisp, tender chicken; beneath—golden rice, wonderfully flavored—

⅓ cup enriched flour
1½ teaspoons salt
Dash pepper
1 2½- to 3-pound ready-to-cook chicken, cut in serving pieces
¼ cup butter or margarine
½ cup thin onion slices
½ cup light raisins
4 cups cooked rice
½ cup flaked coconut
¼ cup coarsely chopped salted peanuts
1½ teaspoons curry powder

Season flour with the salt and pepper; coat chicken pieces with mixture. Brown chicken in butter; remove from skillet.

Cook onion in remaining butter till tender but not brown. Add raisins and heat till they puff. Stir in rice, coconut, and peanuts. Sprinkle with curry powder; mix.

Spoon rice mixture into ungreased 11½x7½x1½-inch baking dish. Top with chicken. Bake at 350° about 1 hour or till chicken is tender. Serve with sliced banana. Serves 4.

Chicken Upside-down Pie

1 10¾-ounce can chicken gravy
1 3-ounce can broiled sliced mushrooms
2 tablespoons chopped pimiento
2 tablespoons sliced stuffed green olives
Dash pepper
2 5-ounce cans (1⅓ cups) boned chicken, diced
2 cups biscuit mix
1 teaspoon sage (optional)

Reserve ⅔ cup gravy. Combine remaining gravy with next 4 ingredients in saucepan; stir in chicken. Bring to boiling; turn into shallow 8- or 9-inch round baking dish.

Add sage to biscuit mix; prepare biscuit dough according to package directions, but using reserved gravy for the liquid. Roll to fit baking dish; place over *hot* sauce.

Bake in very hot oven (450°) 15 minutes. Run knife around edge to loosen. Invert on high-sided plate (sauce will run down sides of biscuit, shortcake-style). Trim with parsley. Cut in wedges. Makes 6 servings.

For more chicken casseroles, see index listing.

Delicious–sea food, fish

Sea Food Fancy

1 6½- or 7½-ounce can (about 1 cup) crab meat, drained and flaked
1 4½- or 5-ounce can (about 1 cup) shrimp, drained
1 cup chopped celery
½ cup chopped onion
½ cup chopped green pepper
1 cup mayonnaise
1½ teaspoons Worcestershire sauce
½ teaspoon salt
Dash pepper

• • •

1 cup soft bread crumbs
2 tablespoons butter or margarine, melted

Combine all ingredients except bread crumbs and butter. Turn into a 1-quart casserole. Combine crumbs and melted butter; sprinkle over top of crab mixture.

Bake in moderate oven (350°) 45 to 50 minutes, or till hot through and crumbs are golden. Makes 6 servings.

Planning a bridge luncheon? Serve Sea Food Fancy with chilled tomato juice, cheese pastry strips and crisp relishes, fluffy wedges of lemon chiffon pie, and iced coffee.

Luncheon Crab Bake

1 6½- or 7½-ounce can (about 1 cup) crab meat, drained

• • •

1 cup soft bread crumbs
1 cup mayonnaise or salad dressing
¾ cup milk
6 hard-cooked eggs, finely chopped
⅓ cup chopped onion
¼ cup sliced stuffed green olives
¾ teaspoon salt
Dash pepper

• • •

½ cup buttered soft bread crumbs

Break crab meat in chunks removing any bony bits. Mix with remaining ingredients except buttered crumbs. Pile in greased individual bakers or 1-quart casserole. Top with buttered crumbs.

Bake in moderate oven (350°) 20 to 25 minutes or till hot through. Trim with stuffed-olive slices. Makes 6 servings.

Lobster en Coquille

1 8-ounce package frozen lobster tails
1 can frozen condensed cream of shrimp soup, thawed*
¼ cup milk
1 3-ounce can broiled sliced mushrooms, drained
½ cup soft bread crumbs
½ cup finely chopped celery
1 tablespoon cooking sherry
¼ cup shredded sharp process cheese

Drop frozen lobster tails into boiling unsalted water to cover. Bring water back to boiling; reduce heat, and simmer 15 minutes. Drain lobster tails, then rinse under cold water till cool enough to handle.

Remove meat from shells; cut in bite-size pieces. Combine with remaining ingredients except cheese. Divide mixture between four shells or individual casseroles. Top with shredded cheese.

Bake at 350° about 25 minutes or till hot through. Trim each with a fluff of parsley; serve with lemon wedges. Makes 4 servings.

*To thaw frozen soup: Let stand in hot water 30 minutes just before using.

Frilly scallop shells give a party air to Luncheon Crab Bake. The ladies will love it! Easy, too—just combine; top with buttery crumbs; bake. There's no sauce to make; it's built in.

STARRING: OUR COMPANY VERSION OF TUNA-AND-NOODLES—IT'S CREAMY TUNA ITALIAN, LACED WITH

MUSHROOMS, RIPE OLIVES, PARMESAN

Tuna Italian

½ cup chopped onion
1 can condensed cream of mushroom soup
1 6-ounce can (⅔ cup) evaporated milk *or* ⅔ cup light cream
⅓ cup grated Parmesan cheese

• • •

1 6½-, 7-, or 9¼-ounce can tuna, drained
1 3-ounce can broiled sliced mushrooms, drained
½ cup chopped ripe olives
2 tablespoons minced parsley
2 teaspoons lemon juice
6 ounces (about 3 cups) noodles, cooked and drained

Cook onion in small amount hot fat till tender but not brown. Add soup, milk, and cheese; heat and stir. Break tuna in chunks; add with remaining ingredients. Pour into greased 2-quart casserole. Sprinkle with additional Parmesan cheese and paprika.

Bake in moderate oven (375°) 20 to 25 minutes. Top with minced parsley and ripe-olive slices as shown. Pass lemon wedges to squirt over. Makes 6 servings.

Tuna-Noodle Casserole

6 ounces (about 3 cups) medium noodles
1 6½, 7-, or 9¼-ounce can tuna, drained
½ cup mayonnaise
1 cup sliced celery
⅓ cup chopped onion
¼ cup diced green pepper
¼ cup pimiento
1 teaspoon salt

• • •

1 can cream of celery soup
½ cup milk
1 cup (¼ pound) shredded sharp process cheese

• • •

½ cup slivered blanched almonds, toasted (optional)

Cook noodles in boiling salted water till tender; drain. Combine noodles, tuna, mayonnaise, vegetables, and salt.

Blend together soup and milk; heat through. Add cheese; heat and stir till cheese melts. Add to noodle mixture.

Turn into ungreased 1½-quart casserole. Sprinkle with toasted almonds. Bake in hot oven (425°) about 20 minutes or till bubbly. Makes 6 servings.

Tuna with Cheese Swirls

1½ cups diced pared potatoes
½ cup diced celery
2 tablespoons chopped onion
1 can condensed cream of celery soup
¼ cup light cream or milk
1 6½- or 7-ounce can (1 cup) tuna
1 cup drained canned or cooked peas
1 canned pimiento, cut in strips
1 recipe Cheese Swirls, page 46

Cook potatoes, celery, and onion in small amount unsalted water till almost tender, about 10 minutes; drain. Add soup and cream; heat. Add tuna (leave in large pieces), peas, and pimiento; bring just to boiling. Pour into ungreased 10x6x1½-inch baking dish. Arrange Cheese Swirls, cut side down, on *hot* tuna mixture. Bake in hot oven (425°) for 15 to 20 minutes, or till biscuits are done. Makes 5 to 6 servings.

Cream-cheese Tuna Bake

4 ounces (1 cup) 7-minute macaroni
1 3-ounce package cream cheese
1 can condensed cream of mushroom soup
1 9¼-ounce can (1½ cups) tuna, drained and flaked
¼ cup chopped onion
¼ cup chopped green pepper
2 tablespoons chopped pimiento
1 tablespoon prepared mustard
¼ teaspoon salt
¼ cup milk
½ cup corn-flake crumbs

Cook macaroni; drain. Soften cream cheese; blend in soup, using electric or rotary beater. Stir in tuna, vegetables, mustard, salt, milk, and macaroni; turn into 1½-quart casserole. Sprinkle crumbs atop. Bake at 375° 20 to 25 minutes or till bubbly. Serves 4 or 5.

Shrimp Pinwheel Casserole has a jaunty bonnet—Pinwheel Biscuits swirled with shredded cheese and pimiento bits! Underneath, casserole is brimful of pink shrimp, tender peas, bubbly tomato-cheese sauce—

Rice and Shrimp Casserole

¼ cup chopped onion
2 tablespoons butter or margarine
2 tablespoons enriched flour
½ teaspoon salt
Dash pepper
1 cup light cream
½ teaspoon Worcestershire sauce
1 3-ounce can (⅔ cup) broiled sliced mushrooms, drained
2 cups cleaned cooked or canned shrimp
2 cups hot cooked rice

• • •

½ cup shredded sharp process cheese
½ cup buttered cracker crumbs

Cook onion in butter till tender but not brown. Blend in flour. Add salt and pepper. Gradually stir in cream and Worcestershire sauce; cook and stir till thick. Add mushrooms and shrimp; heat. Place rice in greased 1½-quart casserole; add shrimp mixture. Top with cheese; border with the cracker crumbs. Bake at 350° 20 minutes. Trim with parsley. Makes 4 servings.

Good to know—how shrimp measures up in ounces, cups—

Number of shrimp in 1 pound depends—

Size	Number of raw shrimp in shell from 1 pound
Jumbo-size	15 to 18
Average-size	26 to 30
Tiny	60 or more

You can buy shrimp in shell or shelled—

Amount needed	Amount to buy
For each 1 cup cleaned cooked shrimp	¾ pound raw shrimp in shell, *or* 7 or 8 ounces frozen shelled shrimp, *or* 1 4½- or 5-ounce can

Shrimp stretches in a casserole or sauce—

Servings	Amount needed
For 4 servings of casserole or creamy sauce (approximate)	1 pound shrimp in shell, *or* 1⅓ cups cleaned cooked shrimp, *or* 1 or 2 4½- or 5-ounce cans (1 or 2 cups) shrimp

Shrimp Pinwheel Casserole

⅓ cup chopped green pepper
¼ cup chopped onion
2 tablespoons enriched flour
½ teaspoon salt
1 1-pound can (2 cups) tomatoes
1½ cups shredded process cheese
1½ cups cooked cleaned shrimp
¾ cup drained cooked or canned peas
1 recipe Pinwheel Biscuits, page 46

Cook green pepper and onion in ¼ cup butter till just tender. Blend in flour, salt, and dash pepper. Add tomatoes; cook and stir till thick. Add cheese; stir till melted. Add shrimp and peas. Pour into greased 2-quart casserole. Top with Pinwheel Biscuits. Bake at 450° 15 to 20 minutes or till biscuits are done. Makes 6 servings.

Shrimp New Orleans

½ cup chopped green pepper
½ cup chopped onion
3 cups cleaned cooked or canned shrimp
1 tablespoon lemon juice
2 cups cooked rice
1 can condensed tomato soup
¾ cup light cream
¼ cup cooking sherry
¾ teaspoon salt
¼ teaspoon nutmeg
¼ cup toasted slivered almonds

Cook green pepper and onion in 2 tablespoons butter till tender but not brown. Stir in remaining ingredients except almonds. Pour into 2-quart casserole. Bake at 350° 30 minutes or till bubbly. Top with almonds. Makes 6 to 8 servings.

Golden Shrimp Bake

Trim, butter, and cube 8 slices slightly dry bread (5 cups cubed). Shred ½ pound sharp process cheese (2 cups shredded).

Place *half* the bread cubes in greased 11x7x1½-inch baking pan. Add 2 cups cleaned cooked or canned shrimp, one 3-ounce can broiled sliced mushrooms, drained, and *half* the cheese. Top with remaining bread cubes and cheese.

Beat together 3 eggs, ½ teaspoon salt, ½ teaspoon dry mustard, dash pepper, and dash paprika; add 2 cups milk; pour over casserole. (May be refrigerated.)

Bake in slow oven (350°) 45 to 50 minutes or till just set. Makes 5 to 6 servings.

Seattle Salmon Pie

2 beaten eggs
½ cup milk
1 tablespoon butter, melted
¼ cup chopped onion
2 tablespoons minced parsley
¾ teaspoon basil
¼ teaspoon salt
1 1-pound can (2 cups) salmon, *or*
  2 6½- or 7½-ounce cans tuna
1 stick packaged pastry mix

Combine eggs, milk, butter, onion, parsley, and seasonings. Break salmon in chunks, removing bones and skin. Stir salmon into egg mixture. Pour into well-greased 8-inch pie plate. Prepare pastry mix according to package directions. Roll ⅛ inch thick. Cut 8-inch circle, then cut circle in 6 wedges. Arrange atop pie. Bake at 425° about 25 minutes. Cut in 6 wedges. Serve immediately. Pass chilled Cucumber Sauce to spoon atop.

Cucumber Sauce

1 medium cucumber, unpared
1 tablespoon grated onion
¼ cup mayonnaise
2 teaspoons vinegar
1 tablespoon minced parsley
½ cup dairy sour cream
Salt and pepper to taste

Cut cucumber in half lengthwise; scoop out seeds. Grate cucumber (you'll need about 1 cup grated); drain. Combine all ingredients; blend well. Chill. Makes about 1½ cups.

SEA-BREEZE SUPPER

Seattle Salmon Pie
Cucumber Sauce Lemon Wedges
Tossed Green Salad
Herbed Chips
Rich Frozen Fruit Squares Coffee

Salad idea: Mix *several* greens, add orange sections for color, thin onion rings for pep! To make Herbed Chips, sprinkle potato chips with majoram, basil, or thyme; heat in oven with casserole last few minutes.

Salmon Florentine

2 10-ounce packages frozen leaf spinach
1 can condensed cream of chicken soup
¼ cup shredded sharp process cheese
¼ cup cooking sherry
2 tablespoons mayonnaise
½ teaspoon Worcestershire sauce
½ teaspoon grated lemon rind
1 1-pound can (2 cups) salmon, drained
1 cup soft bread crumbs
2 tablespoons butter, melted

Cook spinach according to package directions, but using *unsalted* water; drain.

In saucepan, combine soup, cheese, cooking sherry, mayonnaise, Worcestershire, and lemon rind; bring to a boil. Mix ½ *cup* of the sauce with spinach; place in 6 shells or individual casseroles. Break salmon in chunks, removing bones and skin; place on spinach; top with remaining sauce.

Combine crumbs and butter; sprinkle over. Bake in moderate oven (350°) 25 minutes or till bubbly. Makes 6 servings.

Salmon Macaroni

1 cup (4 ounces) 7-minute macaroni

• • •

¼ cup butter or margarine
3 tablespoons enriched flour
½ teaspoon salt
Dash pepper
¼ teaspoon garlic salt
1¾ cups milk

• • •

1 12-ounce carton (1½ cups)
  cream-style cottage cheese
1 cup shredded sharp process cheese
1 1-pound can (2 cups) salmon,
  drained and flaked
2 beaten eggs

• • •

1½ cups soft bread crumbs
2 tablespoons butter, melted

Cook macaroni in boiling salted water till tender; drain.

Melt ¼ cup butter; blend in flour, salt, pepper, and garlic salt. Add milk gradually and cook till thick, stirring constantly. Add cottage cheese, shredded cheese, salmon, and macaroni. Stir in eggs. Pour into greased 11½x7½x1½-inch baking dish.

Toss crumbs in the melted butter; sprinkle over casserole. Bake at 350° about 30 minutes or till set in center. Makes 8 servings.

For sea-food fans, a classic—easy but elegant Scalloped Oysters

1 Crumble crackers into medium-coarse crumbs. Pour melted butter or margarine over crumbs; sprinkle with salt; toss lightly with a fork.

2 Butter round 8-inch shallow baking dish or pan. Spread with ⅓ of the buttered crumbs. Add half the oysters. Dash with pepper. Repeat layers.

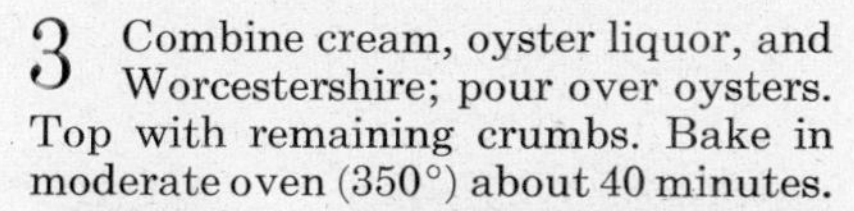

3 Combine cream, oyster liquor, and Worcestershire; pour over oysters. Top with remaining crumbs. Bake in moderate oven (350°) about 40 minutes.

Scalloped Oysters

1 pint fresh oysters, *or* 2 12-ounce cans (about 2 cups) frozen oysters, thawed

• • •

2 cups medium-coarse cracker crumbs
½ cup butter or margarine, melted
½ teaspoon salt

• • •

Pepper

• • •

¾ cup light cream
¼ cup oyster liquor
½ teaspoon Worcestershire sauce

Drain oysters, reserving ¼ cup liquid. Combine cracker crumbs, butter, and salt.

Spread ⅓ of crumb mixture in greased 8-inch shallow round baking dish or pan. Cover with *half* the oysters. Sprinkle with pepper. Using another third of the crumbs, spread a second layer; cover with remaining oysters. Sprinkle with pepper.

Combine cream, oyster liquor, Worcestershire sauce. Pour over oysters. Top with remaining crumbs. Bake in moderate oven (350°) about 40 minutes. Serve immediately. Makes 4 servings.

4 Now to the table! Serve Scalloped Oysters right away while at their very best; puffy and hot. Crispy golden cracker crumbs hide plump oysters, butter-and-cream richness!

Sunny cheese casseroles

Best-ever Macaroni and Cheese

8 ounces (about 2 cups) elbow macaroni

• • •

3 tablespoons butter or margarine
3 tablespoons enriched flour
2 cups milk
½ teaspoon salt
Dash pepper
2 cups shredded process cheese

• • •

Tomato slices

Cook macaroni in boiling, salted water till tender; drain. Melt butter; blend in flour; add milk. Cook and stir till thick. Add seasonings. Add *1½ cups* of the cheese; stir till melted. Place cooked macaroni in greased 10x6x1½-inch baking dish.

Pour sauce over macaroni; salt tomato slices and arrange on top, pushing edge of each slice into macaroni. Top with the remaining cheese.

Bake in moderate oven (350°) about 30 minutes, or till hot and bubbly. Sprinkle with paprika. Makes 6 to 8 servings.

Olive Macaroni-Cheese Bake

4 ounces (about 1 cup) elbow macaroni
2 cups shredded process cheese
⅓ cup milk
½ cup sliced stuffed green olives
Dash pepper

• • •

¼ cup fine dry bread crumbs
1 tablespoon butter, melted

Cook macaroni in boiling, salted water till tender; drain. Combine macaroni, cheese, milk, olives, and pepper. Turn into greased 1-quart casserole. Combine crumbs and butter; sprinkle over top. Bake in moderate oven (350°) 20 to 25 minutes or till crumbs are browned. Makes 4 servings.

Favorite family fare—

← It's Best-ever Macaroni and Cheese—simple and homey, quite delicious. Tender macaroni bakes in rich bubbly cheese sauce, under dashing, flavorful topper of plump tomato slices.

Macaroni-and-Cheese Puff

½ cup small elbow macaroni

• • •

1½ cups milk, scalded
1 cup soft bread crumbs
2 cups (½ pound) shredded sharp process American cheese
3 beaten egg yolks
¼ cup diced pimiento
3 tablespoons butter or margarine, melted
1 tablespoon chopped parsley
1 tablespoon grated onion
½ teaspoon salt

• • •

3 egg whites
¼ teaspoon cream of tartar

Cook macaroni in boiling salted water till tender; drain. Pour the hot milk over bread crumbs. Reserve *½ cup* of the cheese; add the remaining 1½ cups to milk mixture and cover and let stand until cheese melts.

Then add macaroni, egg yolks, pimiento, butter, parsley, onion, and salt. Beat egg whites and cream of tartar until stiff but not dry; fold into the macaroni mixture.

Pour into an ungreased 10x6x1½-inch baking dish. Bake uncovered in slow oven (325°) about 50 minutes or till set. Top with reserved cheese; return to oven for a few minutes until cheese melts. Serve at once. Trim with parsley. Makes 6 servings.

Hurry-up Macaroni and Cheese

This busy-day casserole eats like a prizewinner, yet takes only minutes to fix—

2 15¼-ounce cans macaroni with cheese sauce
¼ cup sliced ripe olives
¼ cup finely chopped onion
2 teaspoons Worcestershire sauce
1 medium tomato, sliced
½ cup shredded sharp process cheese

Combine macaroni with olives, onion, and Worcestershire. Pour into greased 1-quart casserole. Arrange tomato slices atop. Sprinkle with cheese. Bake at 350° till bubbly, 25 to 30 minutes. Makes 4 to 5 servings.

From the world's cheeses—supper dishes full-flavored, rich, hearty

Swiss Onion Bake boasts tender onion, egg slices, and Swiss cheese in rich chicken-flavored sauce. A parade of buttered French bread slices makes the high-hat topper.

Serve with mugs of hot tomato soup, green salad, apple crisp or peppermint ice cream.

Swiss Onion Bake

2 cups sliced onions
2 tablespoons butter or margarine

• • •

5 hard-cooked eggs, sliced
2 cups shredded process Swiss cheese

• • •

1 can condensed cream of chicken soup
¾ cup milk
¼ teaspoon pepper

• • •

8 ½-inch slices French bread, buttered

Cook onions in butter till tender but not brown. Spread in bottom of 10x6x1½-inch baking dish. Top with eggs, then with cheese.

Mix soup, milk, and pepper; heat, stirring till smooth. Drizzle sauce over casserole (be sure some goes to bottom). Overlap bread slices on top. Bake in moderate oven (350°) 20 minutes or till hot. Broil to toast bread. Makes 5 servings.

Framed in a pretty pastry shell, Pizza Supper Pie is a delicious surprise—sausage in cheese custard, a peppy "frosting" of pizza sauce.

To top it off as pictured, arrange triangles of process cheese on hot pie and slide back into the oven just till cheese starts to melt.

Pizza Supper Pie

1 stick packaged pastry mix

• • •

½ pound bulk pork sausage
¾ cup chopped onion
½ teaspoon oregano
¼ teaspoon pepper
4 eggs
½ cup milk
1 cup shredded sharp process cheese
⅔ cup canned pizza sauce

Prepare one 9-inch pastry shell from pastry mix according to package directions. Bake in very hot oven (450°) *only 7 minutes* or just till lightly browned; remove from oven. Reduce oven temperature to 325°.

Slowly brown sausage and onion, breaking up sausage with fork; drain. Add seasonings. Beat together eggs and milk; stir in sausage and cheese. Pour into pastry shell.

Bake in slow oven (325°) 20 minutes or till knife inserted in center comes out clean. Spread top with pizza sauce. Bake 5 minutes longer, trimming as directed at left, if desired. Serve immediately. Makes 6 servings.

Hungarian Noodle Bake

4 ounces (about 2 cups) fine noodles
1 cup cream-style cottage cheese
1 cup dairy sour cream
¼ cup finely chopped onion
1 clove garlic, minced
1 tablespoon Worcestershire sauce
Dash Tabasco sauce
1 tablespoon poppy seed
½ teaspoon salt
Dash pepper

Cook noodles in boiling salted water till tender; drain. Combine noodles with remaining ingredients.* Bake in greased 10x6x1½-inch baking dish at 350° 25 to 30 minutes or till hot. Sprinkle with paprika. Serve with shredded Parmesan cheese. Makes 6 servings.

*Add one 9¼-ounce can (1½ cups) tuna, flaked, if desired. Makes 8 servings.

Parsley Rice Squares with Chicken

3 cups cooked rice
1 cup chopped parsley
¾ cup shredded sharp process cheese
⅓ cup finely chopped onion
1 teaspoon salt
½ teaspoon monosodium glutamate
3 beaten eggs
1½ cups milk
1½ teaspoons Worcestershire sauce
2 10½-ounce cans chicken a la king, heated

Mix first 6 ingredients. Combine eggs, milk, and Worcestershire; add to rice mixture and mix thoroughly. Pour into greased 10x6x1½-inch baking dish.

Bake in slow oven (325°) 40 minutes or just till set. Cut in squares; top with chicken a la king. Makes 6 to 8 servings.

Oven Spanish Rice

Cook ½ cup chopped onion and ½ chopped green pepper in 2 tablespoons hot fat till tender but not brown.

Stir in one 1½-ounce envelope spaghetti-sauce mix, two 1-pound cans (4 cups) tomatoes, 1 cup rice, ½ teaspoon salt, and ½ cup water; simmer 10 minutes.

Pour into a greased 1½-quart casserole; cover and bake in moderate oven (350°) 30 minutes or till rice is done.

Sprinkle with ½ cup shredded sharp process cheese. Makes 4 to 6 servings.

Three-cheese Lasagne

6 ounces (about 3½ cups) wide noodles

• • •

1 1½-ounce envelope spaghetti-sauce mix
1 6-ounce can (⅔ cup) tomato paste
1 beaten egg
1½ cups large-curd, cream-style cottage cheese
1 teaspoon salt
1 6- or 8-ounce package sliced Mozzarella cheese
¼ cup grated Parmesan cheese

Cook noodles in boiling salted water till tender; drain. Prepare spaghetti-sauce mix according to package directions, using the tomato paste. Combine egg, cottage cheese, and salt; mix well.

In greased 10x6x1½-inch baking dish, alternate layers of *half* each of the noodles, sauce, cottage cheese, Mozzarella, and Parmesan. Repeat layers. Bake in moderate oven (375°) 30 minutes. Let stand 15 minutes before serving. Makes 6 servings.

tips ***Cheese—how to melt it; how to measure it***

When the casserole starts with cheese sauce, get it off to a smooth start—this easily:

Process cheese melts easily and quickly. Slice it into a saucepan of milk, broth, or sauce—either hot or cold. Heat only till cheese melts, stirring frequently.

Using *natural cheese?* See tip on page 112.

When planning the grocery list, allow ¼ pound cheese for each 1 cup shredded cheese.

Light for luncheon—versatile eggs

Swiss Cheese-Onion Pie

1 cup finely crushed rusk
2 tablespoons poppy seed
¼ cup butter or margarine, melted

• • •

3 cups thinly sliced onions
(3 to 4 medium onions)
¼ cup butter or margarine
2 cups (½ pound) shredded process Swiss cheese
1 tablespoon enriched flour
1 teaspoon salt
Dash pepper
3 eggs, slightly beaten
1 cup milk, scalded
Chopped chives

Combine first 3 ingredients; press firmly into a 9-inch pie plate. Bake in moderate oven (350°) 8 to 10 minutes. Cool.

Cook onions in ¼ cup butter till tender but not brown; place in crumb crust. Combine cheese with flour, salt, and pepper; add eggs and milk. Pour over onions. Bake in slow oven (325°) 40 minutes or till set. Top with chives. Let stand 5 to 10 minutes before serving. Makes 6 servings.

Swiss Pies

(A favorite from Sun Valley)

6 slices bacon
1 cup chopped onion (about 2 medium)
2 eggs, slightly beaten
¾ cup dairy sour cream
½ teaspoon salt
Dash pepper
2½ cups (12 ounces) Swiss cheese, cut in ½-inch cubes
6 unbaked 4-inch tart shells

Fry bacon till crisp; drain on paper towels. Drain off all but 2 tablespoons bacon fat; add onion and cook till just tender.

Combine eggs, sour cream, onions, salt, pepper, cheese, and crumbled bacon. Pour into tart shells.

Bake in moderate oven (375°) till knife inserted halfway between outside and center of filling comes out clean, 25 to 30 minutes. Garnish with chopped chives, if desired. Serve at once. Makes 6 servings.

Deviled Egg-Ham Casserole

Deviled Eggs:

6 hard-cooked eggs
¼ cup mayonnaise
1 teaspoon prepared mustard
½ teaspoon salt
Dash pepper

• • •

¼ cup butter or margarine
¼ cup enriched flour
2 cups milk
1 cup shredded process cheese
1 cup diced cooked or canned ham
½ 10-ounce package (about 1 cup) frozen peas, broken up
½ cup dry bread crumbs
2 tablespoons butter, melted

Deviled Eggs: Halve eggs. Remove yolks; mash with next 4 ingredients; refill whites.

Arrange eggs in ungreased 10x6x1½-inch baking dish. Melt butter; blend in flour. Gradually stir in milk; cook and stir till thick. Stir in cheese, ham, and peas. Pour over eggs. Combine crumbs and butter; sprinkle over. Bake at 375° 15 minutes. Makes 6 servings.

Eggs in Spanish Sauce

3 tablespoons butter
3 tablespoons enriched flour
1 No. 2½ can (3½ cups) tomatoes
½ cup chopped onion
2 teaspoons sugar
1¼ teaspoons salt
Dash pepper
6 hard-cooked eggs, *deviled**
½ cup bread crumbs
2 tablespoons butter, melted

Melt butter; blend in flour. Add tomatoes, onion, sugar, salt, and pepper; cook till thick, stirring constantly. Pour into ungreased 10x6x1½-inch baking dish.

Arrange deviled eggs in sauce. Combine crumbs and butter; sprinkle atop. Bake at 425° for 10 minutes or till hot. Serve over toast or buttered noodles. Makes 6 servings.

*Follow your favorite recipe, *or* prepare Deviled Eggs using first 5 ingredients listed in recipe above.

Ham 'n Egg Divan

1 10-ounce package frozen broccoli, cooked and drained

• • •

6 hard-cooked eggs
3 tablespoons salad dressing
1 tablespoon minced onion
1 teaspoon prepared mustard
½ teaspoon Worcestershire sauce
1 4½-ounce can deviled ham

• • •

2 tablespoons butter or margarine
2 tablespoons enriched flour
1 cup milk
½ teaspoon salt
¼ pound sharp process American cheese, diced (1 cup)

Arrange broccoli in 10x6x1½-inch baking dish. Cut eggs in half lengthwise; remove yolks and mash; mix with salad dressing, onion, mustard, Worcestershire, and *half* the ham; add salt and pepper to taste.

Place small amount of deviled ham in egg whites; fill with yolk mixture and top with remaining ham. Arrange on broccoli.

Melt butter; blend in flour. Gradually add milk; cook, stirring constantly, till thick; add salt. Add cheese; stir till melted. *Cover* eggs with sauce. Bake in moderate oven (350°) 20 to 25 minutes.

Makes 6 servings.

Ham 'n Egg Divan is doubly deviled, doubly good—spicy deviled ham zips up egg stuffing. Then broccoli and eggs bake in zesty cheese sauce. Handy—fix ahead; bake at last minute.

Curried Eggs in Shrimp Sauce

8 hard-cooked eggs
⅓ cup mayonnaise or salad dressing
½ teaspoon salt
½ teaspoon curry powder
½ teaspoon paprika
¼ teaspoon dry mustard

• • •

Shrimp Sauce:

2 tablespoons butter or margarine
2 tablespoons enriched flour
1 can frozen condensed cream of shrimp soup
1 soup can milk
½ cup shredded sharp process cheese

• • •

1 cup soft bread crumbs
2 tablespoons butter or margarine, melted

Cut eggs in half lengthwise; remove yolks and mash; mix with mayonnaise and seasonings. Refill egg whites; arrange eggs in 10x6x1½-inch baking dish.

Make *Shrimp Sauce:* Melt 2 tablespoons butter; blend in flour. Stir in soup and milk; cook and stir till sauce thickens. Add cheese; stir till melted.

Cover eggs with sauce. Mix crumbs and melted butter; sprinkle around edge.

Bake in moderate oven (350°) 15 to 20 minutes or till heated through. Trim with parsley. Makes 6 to 8 servings.

Sunday-Supper Egg Cups

⅔ cup mayonnaise or salad dressing
¼ teaspoon salt
Dash pepper
1 teaspoon Worcestershire sauce
¼ cup milk
1 cup shredded process cheese
6 eggs

Combine mayonnaise, salt, pepper, and Worcestershire sauce. Gradually add milk, stirring till smooth. Add cheese. Cook over low heat, stirring constantly, till cheese melts and mixture is thick and smooth, about 5 minutes.

Put 2 tablespoons cheese mixture in bottom of each of 6 custard cups. Break an egg into each cup, then add another 2 tablespoons of cheese mixture to each. Sprinkle additional cheese on top, if desired.

Place cups in shallow pan, filling pan to 1 inch with hot water. Bake in moderate oven (350°) 25 to 30 minutes.

Gifts from the garden row

Vegetable-Meat Pie

¾ pound ground beef
¾ cup coarse dry bread crumbs
¼ cup finely chopped onion
1 tablespoon chopped green pepper
1 teaspoon salt
½ medium bay leaf, crushed
Dash thyme
1 egg, beaten
1 8-ounce can seasoned tomato sauce
1 1-pound can (2 cups) mixed vegetables, drained, *or* 1 10-ounce package frozen mixed vegetables
1 teaspoon garlic salt

Combine first 7 ingredients; mix well. Combine egg and ½ *cup* tomato sauce; blend into mixture. Press into greased 8-inch pie plate; build up edges. Bake at 350° for 10 minutes.

Pour boiling water over frozen vegetables to separate; drain. Season vegetables with garlic salt; pour into meat shell. Spoon on remaining tomato sauce. Bake 25 minutes. Let stand 5 minutes; cut in 4 or 5 wedges.

Scalloped Eggplant Italian

1 large eggplant, pared and sliced thin
2 eggs, well beaten
1½ cups finely crushed cracker crumbs
Salad oil
1 8-ounce package sliced sharp process American cheese
2 8-ounce cans (2 cups) seasoned tomato sauce
½ teaspoon Worcestershire sauce
1 teaspoon oregano

Dip eggplant slices into beaten egg, then in crumbs. Brown slowly in hot oil.

Place *one-fourth* of the eggplant slices in bottom of 2-quart casserole; top with *one-fourth* of the cheese slices. Combine tomato sauce, Worcestershire, and oregano; spoon *one-fourth* of the sauce (about ½ cup) over cheese. Repeat layers till all ingredients are used, ending with sauce.

Cover and bake in moderate oven (350°) about 1 hour or till eggplant is tender. Snip parsley over top. Makes 6 to 8 servings.

Calico Bean Bake

1 cup chopped onion
1 clove garlic, minced
1 tablespoon shortening

• • •

½ cup catsup
2 tablespoons brown sugar
1 teaspoon dry mustard
1 teaspoon salt
1 to 2 tablespoons vinegar

• • •

1 1-pound can (2 cups) pork and beans
1 1-pound can (2 cups) kidney beans, drained
1½ cups baby Limas (or 1 10-ounce frozen package), cooked and drained

• • •

6 ¼-inch slices Canadian bacon

Cook onion and garlic in shortening till tender but not brown. Add catsup, brown sugar, mustard, salt, and vinegar. Combine beans; stir in catsup mixture.

Place about ¾ of mixture in ungreased 1½-quart casserole. Arrange bacon slices on top; cover with remaining bean mixture.

Bake in moderate oven (350°) 1 hour. Just before serving, bring bacon slices to the top of casserole. Makes 6 servings.

Limas and Franks

1 pound (2½ cups) large dry Limas
2 teaspoons salt

• • •

1 8-ounce can (1 cup) seasoned tomato sauce
½ cup finely chopped onion
⅓ cup catsup
3 tablespoons brown sugar
2 tablespoons vinegar
1 tablespoon Worcestershire sauce
2 to 3 teaspoons prepared mustard

• • •

1 pound (8 to 10) frankfurters
¼ pound sharp process American cheese cut in strips

Rinse beans; add to 1½ quarts boiling water. Cover; simmer till tender, about 1½ hours, adding salt after 1 hour. Drain. Place beans in 11½x7½x1½-inch baking dish.

Combine tomato sauce, onion, catsup, brown sugar, vinegar, Worcestershire, and mustard; pour over beans.

Slit franks lengthwise, almost to ends. Insert strip of cheese in each and arrange atop beans. Bake uncovered in moderate oven (375°) 20 to 25 minutes or till hot. Makes 6 to 8 servings.

Sturdy main dishes, homespun and colorful— from plump squash, a rainbow of beans, and crisp pepper cups

The autumn bounty of your garden or the grocer's bins is worth pure gold when it comes to table in these wonderful casseroles.

While the weather outside is chilly, concoct appetizing Squash-Sausage Bake, brimming with spicy hot applesauce, plump pork-sausage balls. See recipe, page 41.

Busy day? Slide easy Calico Bean Bake and mix cake into the oven; combine chilled canned fruits for salad. Casserole boasts *three* kinds of beans—with a Boston accent of sweet-spicy sauce, a flavor boost from Canadian bacon.

When Dad's corn and green peppers are ready, whip up Old-time Stuffed Peppers, penny-wise, delicious. Kids will go for the hearty hamburger-cheese-corn filling—and so will you! Recipe is on page 40.

Wonderful tradition—Boston bean supper! Pop Boston-style Beans into the oven right after lunch—they'll be full-flavored and fragrant by supper time. Serve with crisp slaw, warm brown bread, corn relish and piccalilli, mince pie!

Boston-style Beans

1 pound (2 cups)
dry navy beans
⅓ cup brown sugar
1 teaspoon salt
1 teaspoon dry mustard
¼ cup molasses
1 medium onion, sliced
¼ pound salt pork, sliced

Rinse navy beans; add to 6 cups cold water. Bring to boiling and simmer 2 minutes. Remove from heat. Cover; let stand 1 hour. (Or soak beans overnight in the water.) Add 1 teaspoon salt to beans and soaking water; cover, and simmer till *tender*, about 1 hour.

Drain, reserving liquid. Measure 1¾ cups bean liquid (add water if needed). To it add brown sugar, salt, dry mustard, and molasses.

In 2-quart bean pot or casserole, alternate 2 layers each of beans, onion, salt pork, and the sauce. Cover; bake in slow oven (300°) 5 to 6 hours, adding more liquid, if necessary, as beans bake. Makes 8 servings.

Bean-pot Limas

1 pound (2½ cups)
large dry Limas
¼ pound salt pork
2 cups hot bean liquor
1 medium onion, sliced
2 teaspoons salt
½ teaspoon dry mustard
⅓ cup dark molasses
⅓ cup chili sauce
1 tablespoon vinegar

Rinse beans, soak in 6 cups water overnight. Don't drain. Cover; simmer over low heat (do not boil) until just tender, about 30 minutes. Drain, reserving bean liquor.

Cut salt pork in half; grind one piece, score the other in squares. Combine all ingredients but scored salt pork. Pour into 2-quart bean pot or casserole. Top with salt-pork slice. Cover and bake in slow oven (300°) 2½ hours, uncovering last 30 minutes. (If necessary, add more bean liquor or hot water during baking.) Makes 8 servings.

From tender sweet corn—golden casseroles

Indian Corn Casserole

3 eggs, well beaten
¼ cup enriched flour
2 tablespoons sugar
2 cups (½ pound) shredded sharp process cheese
2 1-pound cans (4 cups) whole kernel corn, drained
10 slices (about ½ pound) bacon, cooked and crumbled

Combine eggs, flour, and sugar; beat well. Add shredded cheese and corn. Stir in about ¾ of the bacon. Turn mixture into an ungreased 10x6x1½-inch baking dish; sprinkle remaining bacon over top.

Bake in moderate oven (350°) 30 minutes or till knife inserted in center comes out clean. Makes 8 servings.

Timesaver—casserole doubles as a bowl

When you're making a mix-in-one-bowl main dish, stir it up right in the greased casserole—saves an extra bowl in the after-dinner suds.

Corn Puff

2 tablespoons butter or margarine
2 tablespoons enriched flour
1 cup milk
¾ teaspoon salt
Dash pepper
1 1-pound can (2 cups) whole kernel corn, drained
1 3-ounce can (⅔ cup) broiled chopped mushrooms, drained
3 well-beaten egg yolks
3 stiff-beaten egg whites

Melt butter, blend in flour. Gradually stir in milk; add seasonings. Cook, stirring constantly, till sauce is thickened. Stir in corn and mushrooms. Stir a small amount of the hot mixture into the egg yolks; pour yolk mixture into sauce. Fold in egg whites and pour into ungreased 1½-quart casserole. Bake in slow oven (325°) 1 hour, or till knife, inserted halfway between outside and center comes out clean. Makes 6 servings.

Jumbo Cornburger

1 pound ground beef
1 egg, slightly beaten
½ cup seasoned tomato sauce
1 teaspoon Worcestershire sauce
1 teaspoon salt
Dash pepper

• • •

1 1-pound can (2 cups) whole kernel corn, drained
½ cup medium coarse cracker crumbs
1 egg, slightly beaten
¼ cup diced green pepper
¼ cup chopped onion
2 tablespoons chopped pimiento
½ teaspoon salt
¼ teaspoon sage
½ cup shredded sharp process cheese

Combine beef, egg, sauces, and seasonings. Spread half of mixture in 8-inch shallow round baking dish. Combine remaining ingredients except cheese; spoon over meat. Cover with remaining meat mixture. Bake in moderate oven (350°) 40 minutes. Last 5 minutes, sprinkle with cheese. Trim with parsley. Makes 6 servings.

Vegetables doubly good—with stuffings!

Creole Stuffed Peppers

The rosy shrimp filling is topped with tangy tomato sauce. Perfect for your next buffet—

6 medium green peppers
• • •
2 cups diced cooked cleaned shrimp
2 cups cooked rice
1 cup salad dressing
2 tablespoons chopped onion
Salt and pepper
Dash Tabasco sauce
• • •
1 8-ounce can (1 cup) seasoned tomato sauce

Cut off tops of green peppers; remove seeds and membrane. Precook pepper cups in small amount boiling, salted water 5 minutes; drain. Sprinkle inside with salt. Combine shrimp, rice, salad dressing, and onion. Add salt, pepper, and Tabasco to taste. Fill peppers and place upright in 10x6x1½-inch baking dish. Pour tomato sauce around peppers. Bake in moderate oven (350°) 30 minutes. Spoon the tomato sauce over filling before serving. Makes 6 servings.

Fancy fare—Creole Stuffed Peppers

Old-time Stuffed Peppers

If you like pepper shells crisp, don't precook—

8 medium green peppers
1 pound ground beef
½ cup chopped onion
1½ cups fresh corn (3 to 4 ears) *or* 1 12-ounce can whole-kernel corn, drained
1 8-ounce can seasoned tomato sauce
1 teaspoon Worcestershire sauce
¾ teaspoon salt
½ teaspoon monosodium glutamate
2 cups shredded sharp process cheese
1 cup soft buttered bread crumbs

Cut off tops of green peppers; remove seeds and membranes. Precook pepper cups in boiling salted water about 5 minutes; drain. Sprinkle insides with salt.

Brown meat and onion; add next 5 ingredients; simmer till hot through, about 5 minutes. Add cheese and stir till melted.

Stuff peppers; stand upright in 11x7x1½-inch baking dish. Sprinkle tops with crumbs. Fill baking dish to ½ inch with water.

Bake uncovered at 350° for 40 minutes or till hot through. Makes 8 servings.

Curried Chicken in Pepper Cups

6 medium green peppers
1 4⅝-ounce package (1⅓ cups) precooked rice
2 cups diced canned or cooked chicken
1 cup chopped celery
¼ cup minced onion
2 tablespoons chopped pimiento
¾ cup mayonnaise
¼ cup salad dressing
1 teaspoon curry powder
½ teaspoon salt
Dash pepper

Remove tops and seeds from peppers; precook in boiling salted water 5 minutes; drain.

Prepare rice according to package directions; mix with chicken, celery, onion, and pimiento. Combine remaining ingredients; add to rice mixture and toss lightly.

Fill peppers; place in 10x6x1½-inch baking dish. Fill dish to ½ inch with water. Bake at 350° 30 minutes. Trim each with pimiento cross. Makes 6 servings.

Artichokes With Crab Stuffing

Leafy cups hold a luscious hot salad—

2 6½-ounce cans (2 cups) crab meat, drained
1 cup cubed process Swiss cheese
⅓ cup chopped green pepper
¼ cup finely chopped onion
1 teaspoon salt

• • •

½ cup mayonnaise or salad dressing
2 teaspoons lemon juice

• • •

5 cooked medium artichokes

Break crab meat in chunks; toss with cheese, green pepper, onion, and salt. Blend mayonnaise and lemon juice; add to crab mixture and toss lightly. Remove small center leaves of each artichoke, leaving a cup. Carefully remove choke. Fill artichokes with crab salad; place in large casserole or baking dish. Pour hot water around artichokes to depth of 1 inch. Cover and bake in moderate oven (375°) about 35 minutes or until heated thoroughly. Makes 5 servings.

To eat artichokes: You eat the leaves, too! Tear off one leaf at a time and dunk it in melted butter or peppy sauce. Then, you eat just the tender base of the leaf—turn it upside down, bite, and pull. Under stuffing, you'll find the heart—eat it with a fork.

Hash-stuffed Onions

A hearty meat-and-vegetable dish for cool evenings—

6 medium Bermuda onions

• • •

1 1-pound can corned-beef hash
1 tablespoon Worcestershire sauce
1 tablespoon chopped sweet pickle

• • •

1 8-ounce can (1 cup) seasoned tomato sauce

Peel onions; cook in large amount of boiling, salted water 30 minutes; drain and cool. Cut each onion in fourths, cutting only ¼ way down from top. Scoop out centers.

To corned beef, add Worcestershire sauce and sweet pickle. Stuff onions with meat mixture. Set upright in baking dish.

Combine chopped onion centers and tomato sauce; pour over stuffed onions. Bake in moderate oven (350°) 30 minutes or till onions are tender. Makes 6 servings.

Artichokes take to cold shower, a brush with lemon

How to prepare: Give artichokes a shower of cold running water. With sharp knife, cut off about 1 inch from top. Chop off stem even with base or leave about 1 inch.

Pull off any loose leaves around bottom. With kitchen scissors, snip sharp leaf tips off artichoke. Brush cut edges with lemon juice.

How to cook: Place artichokes upright in small amount boiling salted water. (Add ¼ cup olive oil, 3 or 4 garlic cloves, or a few lemon slices to water, if you wish.)

Cover; simmer artichokes 25 to 30 minutes or till you can pierce stalk easily with fork or pull out a leaf readily.

Remove vegetable with tongs; turn upside down to drain. Cut off any stem left on.

Squash-Sausage Bake

Whole meal in a squash "cup"—see page 37—

2 medium acorn squash
1 pound bulk pork sausage
2 cups sweetened applesauce
Cinnamon to taste (optional)

Cut squash in half lengthwise; remove seeds. Bake uncovered, cut side down, in shallow baking pan in moderate oven (350°) till almost tender, about 35 to 40 minutes.

Meanwhile, form sausage in small balls; brown slowly, about 15 minutes; drain. Season applesauce with cinnamon, then add to sausage balls; cover and simmer 15 minutes.

Turn squash cut side up and sprinkle with salt; fill with applesauce and sausage. Continue baking till squash is tender, about 15 to 20 minutes. Tuck in crisp red apple slices for trim, if desired. Makes 4 servings.

Honey-baked Squash

2 medium acorn squash
Melted butter
¼ cup honey
1 dozen sausage links, browned

Cut squash in half lengthwise; remove seeds. Bake uncovered, cut side down, at 350° 35 to 40 minutes. Turn. Brush insides with butter. Drizzle 1 tablespoon honey over each. Fill center of each with 3 browned sausage links. Bake 20 minutes longer. Serves 4.

Hearty favorites—full of rich flavor

FAMILY FARE

Hot Potato Salad with Franks
Buttered Spinach
Crisp Relishes
French Bread Parmesan
Apple Crisp with Cream
Milk Coffee

While oven's on for Hot Potato Salad, slip in Apple Crisp. Cut French Bread diagonally in 1-inch slices, almost through. Butter slices; sprinkle with Parmesan cheese. Heat in oven.

Hot Potato Salad with Franks

6 to 8 slices bacon, chopped
¼ cup chopped onion
1 tablespoon enriched flour
1 tablespoon sugar
1½ teaspoons salt
Dash pepper
⅓ cup vinegar
¼ cup water
3 tablespoons salad dressing
4 cups sliced or diced cooked potatoes
1 pound frankfurters, halved crosswise
2 hard-cooked eggs, sliced
1 tablespoon minced parsley
½ teaspoon celery seed

Cook bacon till crisp, add onion, cook till tender but not brown. Blend in next 4 ingredients. Add vinegar and water; cook and stir till thick. Remove from heat; stir in salad dressing. Sprinkle potatoes with ¾ teaspoon salt, pour dressing over, toss lightly.

Stand frankfurter halves upright around sides of 8-inch shallow round baking dish; fill center with salad. (Or, to hold frankfurters in place, put part of salad in center first.) Bake at 350° 20 minutes, or till hot through. Trim with egg slices. Sprinkle with parsley and celery seed. Makes 6 or 7 servings.

Scalloped Potatoes With Sausage

½ cup finely chopped onion
2 tablespoons butter or margarine
1 can condensed cream of celery soup
⅓ cup milk

• • •

3 cups diced cooked potatoes
¼ cup chopped green pepper
2 tablespoons chopped pimiento
1 12- or 16-ounce package ready-to-eat smoked sausage links

• • •

¾ cup shredded process American cheese

Cook onion in butter till tender but not brown. Stir in soup and milk; heat. In 1½-quart casserole, combine potatoes, green pepper, and pimiento. Slice *half* the sausage links; add to potato mixture. Pour soup over; top with cheese. Arrange remaining sausage on top. Bake in moderate oven (350°) about 30 minutes. Makes 6 servings.

Ham and Potato Scallop

1 can condensed cream of mushroom soup
¼ cup milk
Dash pepper

• • •

5 cups thinly sliced pared potatoes (about 5 medium potatoes)
1 pound cooked or canned smoked ham, cut in ½-inch cubes (about 2 cups)
½ cup chopped onion
¼ cup chopped green pepper

• • •

1 tablespoon butter or margarine

Blend soup, milk, and pepper. Add potatoes, diced ham, onion, and green pepper. Mix. Turn into ungreased 2-quart casserole. Dot top with butter or margarine.

Bake uncovered in moderate oven (350°) for 1 hour. Cover and continue baking 45 minutes or till potatoes are done. Trim top of casserole with parsley. Makes 6 servings.

Note: To match picture opposite, use individual casseroles. Bake uncovered 50 minutes. Cover and bake 10 to 20 minutes longer or till potatoes are done.

Club Mushroom Casserole

1 pound fresh mushrooms, sliced
½ cup butter or margarine
⅓ cup enriched flour
3 cups milk
2 teaspoons Worcestershire sauce
1½ teaspoons salt
¼ teaspoon pepper
2 cups shredded process cheese
4 hard-cooked eggs, sliced
½ cup diced green pepper
1 4-ounce can pimiento, drained, diced

Cook mushrooms in butter till tender but not brown. Push to one side; blend in flour. Stir in milk gradually; cook and stir till thick. Add remaining ingredients. Turn into greased 10x6x1½-inch baking dish.

Bake at 350° for 30 minutes or till lightly browned. Top with cheese crescents. Serve with hot rice or toast. Makes 6 to 8 servings.

Sausage and Sweets

This always-favorite goes into the oven in jig time, comes out glazed, flavorful—

1 pound bulk pork sausage
6 medium cooked sweet potatoes, sliced *or* 2 1-pound cans
2 tablespoons soft butter or margarine
⅓ cup brown sugar

Form sausage into 6 thin patties. Brown lightly on both sides; drain well. Arrange sweet potatoes in greased 9x9x2-inch baking dish. Dot with butter; sprinkle with brown sugar. Arrange sausage patties on top.

Bake in moderate oven (350°) for 30 to 35 minutes or till done. Makes 6 servings.

Ham and Potato Scallop is a supper special

Old-fashioned goodness with a modern touch—ham and thinly sliced potatoes bake in quick mushroom-soup sauce, flavored with green pepper, onion, butter!

Party-going casserole—with bells on! Steal the idea—top cheese triangles with *Salami Bells:* For every pair of bells, cut a large thin salami slice to the center. Twist one cut side one way, the other opposite way. Add parsley clappers.

For the final touch, add trims

Parsley is a natural, of course—just a fluff atop the casserole adds personality to a tasty, but plain-Jane dish. And this is only a start! Your refrigerator and pantry shelf offer the beginnings for *dozens* of easy, colorful garnishes.

A *border* adds crispness and a pretty frame to a deserving main dish. Experiment with bread crumbs or cracker crumbs (plain, buttered, or mixed with shredded cheese), potato chips whole or crushed, canned shoestring potatoes, crushed corn chips, chow mein noodles.

Or, transform the "border" into diagonal stripes, spokes, or a whirligig.

Try a topper of canned or frozen *French-fried onions.* Place on casserole just long enough to heat through.

Meat may double as ingredient *and* garnish. In recipes containing shrimp, crumbled bacon, luncheon-meat or ham strips, reserve some for trim. Parade sausages or franks in rows or whirls. Cut Canadian-bacon slices in half, arrange in "scallops." Roll salami slices in cornucopias; fasten with toothpicks. Tuck parsley into ends; arrange spoke-style.

Firecracker-red *pimiento* adds dash to a casserole. Cut crescents; line up with stuffed-olive slices. Or whirl crescents in a star, center with parsley or water cress. Crisscross pimiento strips atop individual casseroles or line up in a row.

Tumble *olive slices* in center of casserole, or in dizzy rows. Turn *olive halves* cut side down in daisy effect. Add parsley.

Round-up of garnishes—quick and easy, smart-looking and good

Vegetable toppers—flavorful and picture-pretty

Use pinwheel of hot cooked asparagus (on ham, chicken bakes), overlapped green pepper and onion rings, or mushroom slices (with meat), tomato slices alternated with cheese triangles.

Bacon Curls—crisp and pretty

Cook bacon till about half done and still flexible. Use two forks. Insert tines of first fork in one end of bacon strip; turn fork to wind bacon around it, using second fork as a guide.

Remove fork; let curl finish cooking. Place curls atop hot casserole, or garnish each serving. Bacon's good with corn, eggs, cheese.

The golden touch—melty cheese in fancy shapes

Cut square process cheese slices in half on the diagonal. Make a whirligig on *hot* casserole, as shown, or overlap along sides of baking dish.

Slice a roll of cheese food; cut each slice in half. Zigzag or make chevrons on hot dish.

Before baking, sprinkle shredded process cheese on casserole; dash with paprika.

Slice an olive or a pickle for speedy finish—

Wreath—Sprinkle circle of snipped parsley atop casserole. Add olive-slice "berries," as shown.

Pickle fans—Slice pickle lengthwise almost to stem end, making thin slices. Spread each fan and press uncut end so fan will hold shape. Swirl several fans from center of casserole.

To delight folks—a ring of Thimble Biscuits!

Prepare biscuit mix according to package label. Roll to ½ inch; cut in 1½-inch rounds. Place biscuits atop *hot* casserole 15 minutes before it's done (or heat mixture, pour in baker, add biscuits). Bake at 450° (turn up heat if necessary) 15 minutes or till biscuits are done.

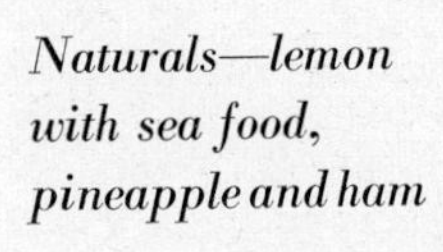

Naturals—lemon with sea food, pineapple and ham

Lemon wedges—Whirl in a star or line up. More color: Dip edges in paprika or snipped parsley.

Lemon slices—Overlap in a row and poke tiny parsley fluff into each slice.

Pineapple—Brush rings or sticks with melted butter; broil 3 inches from heat 5 minutes. Arrange rings with maraschino-cherry halves. Form a daisy of sticks; center with parsley.

Toast bonnets to add at the very last minute

Spread hot toast with butter, margarine, or sharp spreading cheese. For extra zest, sprinkle with seasoned or garlic salt. Cut in small cubes; place on hot casserole just before serving.

Cut toast with doughnut cutter, butter, top with shredded cheese. Broil to melt cheese. Place on baked casserole. On holiday, use toast trees decked with pimiento, snipped parsley.

tips **For casseroles—flaky, tender biscuit bonnets**

• Mix-match these baked-on toppers! On Hamburger Pie, use Onion Biscuits one time, Cheese Pretzels the next. Pinwheels dress up tuna, chicken, or hamburger casseroles.

• Put biscuits on top of *hot* mixture—no soggy bottoms.

Heat casserole in hot oven (425°) 15 to 20 minutes,* *or* heat mixture in skillet; turn into casserole. *Then* top with biscuits; bake as directed in biscuit recipe.

*If casserole bakes longer than 30 to 35 minutes, bake according to casserole recipe; then, last 15 or 20 minutes, add biscuits and finish baking as directed for biscuits.

• Try these toppers too: Biscuit Rolls, page 16; Yam Biscuits, page 17; Pimiento Drop Biscuits, page 21.

Cheese Swirls

1 cup sifted enriched flour
2 teaspoons baking powder
¼ teaspoon salt
2 tablespoons shortening
⅓ cup milk
½ cup shredded sharp process cheese

Sift together flour, baking powder, and salt. Cut in shortening till mixture resembles coarse crumbs. Add milk all at once; stir just till dough follows fork around bowl.

Turn out on lightly floured surface and knead gently ½ minute. Roll in rectangle ¼ inch thick. Sprinkle with cheese and roll as for jelly roll, starting at narrow end; seal edge. Cut in ½-inch slices.

Place atop *hot* casserole. Bake at 425° 15 to 20 minutes or till biscuits are done.

Note: For speed, use 1 cup biscuit mix in place of first 4 ingredients.

Pinwheel Biscuits

2 cups sifted enriched flour
3 teaspoons baking powder
½ teaspoon salt
¼ cup shortening
⅔ cup milk
1½ cups shredded process cheese
¼ cup chopped pimiento
1 tablespoon butter, melted

Sift together dry ingredients. Cut in shortening till mixture resembles coarse crumbs. Add milk all at once, stir just till dough follows fork around bowl. Turn out on lightly floured surface and knead gently ½ minute.

Roll in rectangle ½ inch thick. Sprinkle with cheese and pimiento and roll as for jelly roll. Cut in 1-inch slices. Place atop *hot* casserole; brush with melted butter. Bake at 450° 15 to 20 minutes or till biscuits are done and golden brown. (Bake remaining biscuits on greased baking sheet.)

Cheese Pretzels: Combine dry ingredients and cut in shortening as for Pinwheel Biscuits. Stir in ½ cup shredded process cheese; add milk. Omit remaining ingredients.

On lightly floured board, roll to ⅜ inch thick. Cut with doughnut cutter. For pretzel snip through one doughnut and link it through another. Place on *hot* casserole. Bake in hot oven (425°) for 12 to 15 minutes or till biscuits are done and golden brown.

Onion Biscuits

¾ cup finely chopped onion
1½ cups sifted enriched flour
1½ teaspoons baking powder
½ teaspoon salt
1 teaspoon celery seed
¼ cup shortening
1 slightly beaten egg
⅓ cup milk

Cook onion in hot fat till just tender. Sift together flour, baking powder, and salt; stir in celery seed. Cut in shortening till mixture resembles coarse crumbs. Stir in onion. Combine egg and milk; add all at once, stir just till dough follows fork around bowl.

Turn out on lightly floured surface and knead gently ½ minute. Roll ½ inch thick and cut with doughnut cutter. Place "doughnuts" and "holes" atop *hot* casserole mixture; bake at 450° 10 to 15 minutes or till biscuits are done. (Bake remaining biscuits on ungreased baking sheet.)

When you freeze main dishes

Make your dinner casserole a "double header." Freeze half—and you'll have a main dish already to heat and eat on a busy, busy day.

You can take advantage of peak-of-season vegetables and plentiful meats, too. Buy in quantity, whip up a batch of a la king, stew, or casseroles; freeze in family-size portions.

When you fix food for the freezer, brush up on these do's and don'ts:

- Don't oversalt *or* overseason—it's better to add more later if needed.
- Don't overcook foods to be frozen.
- Cool quickly before packaging. The best way is to set the pan of cooked food in a bowl, pan, or sink containing cold water with ice. When cooled to room temperature, ladle immediately into freezer containers.
- Label each container with contents, date.
- Store at 0°. Use frozen cooked foods within 1 or 2 months. Don't refreeze cooked foods.

Quick tips: Freeze casseroles in foil containers. To heat—remove lid, slide into oven.

Or, line skillet or casserole with heavy foil, leaving long ends. Fill. Fold ends of foil together over food to seal. Place container in freezer. When food is frozen, remove from container neatly packaged! (Be sure foil is tightly sealed.) Simply place in same skillet or casserole, foil and all, to reheat.

These main dishes take to a stay in the freezer—

Foods	Preparation for freezing	Thawing and cooking
Meat and fish dishes Meat balls in sauce Chop suey Corned-beef hash Spanish rice Hamburger bakes Fish in creole or cheese sauce Fish-rice bakes Lobster thermidor	Don't overcook. Cool quickly to room temperature. Pack in freezer containers or foil containers that can be sealed airtight. For liquid foods, allow head space. Seal tightly, label, and date. Freeze immediately.	Heat over low heat, in top of double boiler, or in casserole or foil pan in the oven.
Beef and veal stews	Use highest quality ingredients. Omit potatoes. Shorten cooking time. Cool quickly and package.	Heat in casserole or foilware pan in oven, or in top of double boiler.
Creamed dishes Chicken or turkey Fish or sea food	Freeze any except those containing hard-cooked egg white. Don't overcook. Use fat sparingly when making sauce—helps prevent separation of sauce on reheating. Cool rapidly by setting pan on ice. Package in wide-mouth freezer containers. Freeze.	Heat in top of double boiler. Or heat and stir over low heat. If sauce separates, beat with fork or spoon during reheating.

Casseroles for the crowd

There's no trick to cooking for 25 or 50 people —if you plan ahead, and pick foods that are easy to fix with the equipment at hand.

Simplest and thriftiest large-size meal starts with a casserole or other main dish. It replaces meat *and* vegetable, can be fixed ahead and heated at mealtime, is simple to serve. We give 10 *big* main dishes that look good, taste grand!

Just add a salad (see our recipes for salads that serve 24), maybe a bread, dessert, and coffee. Before you order groceries, check the tables, pages 52-53, that suggest amounts to buy.

These recipes are tailored to serve 24 or a few more. If you're serving a group of 50 or 100, ask several helpers to make one recipe apiece.

Our casseroles bake in two 13x9x2-inch pans. If you're lucky enough to own one of the large casseroles designed to hold a jumbo recipe, allow it to bake till hot through (check in the center)—it may take longer than a standard pan.

When you're the only chef, plan make-ahead salad and dessert; put casseroles together early, refrigerate. (Allow an extra 20 to 30 minutes in the oven when casserole goes in cold.)

Slip bread in the oven to warm alongside casserole. At serving time, put main course on buffet table; let guests serve themselves. Dessert, coffee go on side table for pick-up later.

When there's plenty of help, you can go fancy with last-minute salad, hot rolls, dessert that's served. If using a large coffee maker, know how long it takes; start in plenty of time.

For a large crowd, plan two buffet lines—speediest with hostesses to do the dishing-up. Put dessert at places ahead of time or serve it, along with coffee, so guests needn't juggle.

Let's have everybody over!—

← Your back yard makes a delightful dining room, your picnic table the buffet. Use red-hanky napkins; corral silverware in sturdy relish baskets.

Serve a take-it-easy meal like this: Hamburger Pie, Cabbage Slaw, brown-bread sandwiches. Dessert is warm apple pie or ice-cream sundaes, coffee.

Hamburger Pie

4 medium onions, chopped
4 pounds ground beef
3 teaspoons salt
Dash pepper
2 No. 2½ cans (7 cups) cut green beans, drained
4 cans condensed tomato soup

• • •

5 pounds medium potatoes, cooked*
2 cups warm milk*
4 eggs, beaten
Salt and pepper
½ pound process cheese, shredded

Cook onion in small amount hot fat till tender but not brown. Add meat and seasonings; brown lightly. Spoon off excess fat. Add drained beans and soup; pour into two ungreased 13x9x2-inch pans.

Mash potatoes while hot; add milk, egg, and seasonings. Drop in fluffs over meat. Sprinkle potatoes with shredded cheese.

Bake at 350° 30 minutes or till hot through. Makes 24 servings.

*Or, use instant mashed potatoes (for 24 servings) and add milk as directed on package. Add eggs and seasonings as above.

Hamburger-Corn Casserole

4 pounds ground beef
3 medium onions, chopped (3 cups)
3 12-ounce cans whole-kernel corn, drained
3 cans condensed cream of chicken soup
3 cans condensed cream of mushroom soup
3 cups dairy sour cream
¾ cup chopped pimiento
2 teaspoons salt
1½ teaspoons monosodium glutamate
¾ teaspoon pepper

• • •

9 cups medium noodles, cooked, drained
3 cups soft bread crumbs
½ cup butter or margarine, melted
¾ teaspoon paprika
¾ cup chopped parsley

Brown meat. Add onion; cook till tender but not brown. Add next 8 ingredients. Blend well. Add noodles.

Pour into two ungreased *13x9x2 5/8*-inch cake pans. Combine soft crumbs, butter, and paprika. Sprinkle across casseroles in diagonal stripes. Bake in moderate oven (350°) about 45 minutes, or till hot through. Sprinkle with parsley. Makes 24 servings.

Lasagne

2 pounds Italian or bulk pork sausage
2 cloves garlic, minced
2 tablespoons parsley flakes
2 tablespoons basil
1 tablespoon salt
2 1-pound cans (4 cups) tomatoes
4 6-ounce cans (2⅔ cups) tomato paste

• • •

20 ounces lasagne or wide noodles

• • •

6 cups cream-style cottage cheese
4 beaten eggs
1 tablespoon salt
1 teaspoon pepper
¼ cup parsley flakes
1 cup grated Parmesan cheese

• • •

2 pounds Mozzarella or American cheese, sliced *very thin*

Brown meat slowly. Spoon off excess fat. Add next 6 ingredients. Simmer uncovered about 30 minutes, stirring occasionally.

Cook noodles in boiling salted water till tender; drain; rinse in cold water.

Meanwhile, combine cottage cheese, eggs, seasonings, and Parmesan cheese. Place *half* the noodles in two 13x9x2-inch pans; spread *half* the cottage cheese mixture over; add *half* the Mozzarella cheese and *half* the meat sauce. Repeat layers.

Bake at 375° 30 minutes. *Let stand* 10 to 15 minutes before cutting in squares—filling will set slightly. Makes 24 servings.

Ham-and-Potato Scallop

12 pounds potatoes, pared and thinly sliced (5 quarts)
4 pounds cooked ham, sliced thin
4 cans condensed cream of mushroom soup
1 cup milk
2 medium onions, chopped (2 cups)
1 large green pepper, chopped (1 cup)
1½ teaspoons salt
½ teaspoon pepper
Butter or margarine
Minced parsley

Place potatoes in two greased 13x9x2-inch pans. Cut ham in serving pieces, bury in potatoes. Combine soup, milk, onion, green pepper, and seasonings; pour over potatoes. Dot casserole with butter.

Bake at 350° 1 hour. Then cover pans with foil and bake 1½ hours longer, or till done. Sprinkle with parsley. Makes 24 servings.

Macaroni and Cheese

2 pounds (8 cups) elbow macaroni
¾ cup butter or margarine
¾ cup enriched flour
2 quarts milk
2 teaspoons salt
¼ teaspoon pepper
2 pounds process cheese, shredded
24 to 32 tomato slices
(one for each serving)

Cook macaroni in boiling salted water till tender; drain.

Melt butter; blend in flour; add milk. Cook and stir over low heat till thick. Season. Add *6 cups* of the cheese; stir till melted.

Place cooked macaroni in two greased 13x9x2-inch pans. Pour sauce over.

Salt tomato slices; arrange atop in rows, pushing edges into macaroni. Top with remaining cheese. Bake in moderate oven (350°) 30 minutes or till hot and bubbly. Sprinkle with paprika. Makes 24 to 32 servings.

Italian Spaghetti Sauce

4 pounds ground beef
2 large onions, chopped (2 cups)
8 cloves garlic, minced
2 6-ounce cans (2⅔ cups) broiled
sliced mushrooms

• • •

1 cup chopped parsley
4 No. 2½ cans plus 1 1-pound can
tomatoes (16 cups) *or* 8 1-pound cans
8 8-ounce cans seasoned tomato sauce
4 6-ounce cans tomato paste
2 tablespoons oregano
4 teaspoons salt
2 teaspoons monosodium glutamate
1 teaspoon thyme
½ teaspoon pepper
4 bay leaves, crumbled
1 quart water

• • •

1 tablespoon sugar
2 pounds spaghetti, cooked, drained

In two large heavy kettles, cook ground beef, onion, and garlic till meat is lightly browned. Add sliced mushrooms with liquid.

Combine remaining ingredients except sugar and spaghetti; pour into kettles. Bring to boil; turn down heat, simmer uncovered 2 to 2½ hours or till of desired consistency; stir occasionally. Add sugar. Serve over hot spaghetti. Pass Parmesan cheese. Makes 24 servings, of 1 cup sauce each.

Church-supper Tuna Bake

¾ cup diced green pepper
3 cups sliced celery
2 medium onions, chopped (2 cups)
¼ cup butter
3 cans condensed cream of
mushroom soup
1½ cups milk
3 cups shredded process cheese
24 ounces medium noodles, cooked
and drained
3 9¼-ounce cans tuna, drained
1½ cups mayonnaise
¾ cup chopped pimiento
1 cup slivered blanched
almonds, toasted

Cook green pepper, celery, and onion in butter for 5 minutes. Blend together soup and milk; add and heat through. Add cheese; heat and stir till cheese melts.

Combine noodles, tuna, mayonnaise, and pimiento. Pour cheese sauce over; mix. Turn into two greased 13x9x2-inch pans. Sprinkle almonds over top.

Bake at 425° for 30 to 35 minutes or till hot and bubbly. Makes 24 servings.

Chicken Strata

32 slices white bread
8 cups diced cooked chicken
(3 3-pound chickens)
2 large onions, chopped (2 cups)
2 large green peppers, chopped (2 cups)
2 cups finely chopped celery
2 cups mayonnaise
1 tablespoon salt
¼ teaspoon pepper
6 eggs, slightly beaten
6 cups milk
4 cans condensed cream of mushroom
soup
2 cups shredded sharp process cheese

Dry out bread slightly in oven. Butter *8* slices; cut in ½-inch cubes; set aside. Cut remaining bread in 1-inch cubes; place half of unbuttered cubes in bottom of two ungreased 13x9x2-inch pans.

Combine next 7 ingredients; spoon over bread cubes. Sprinkle remaining unbuttered cubes over chicken mixture.

Combine eggs and milk; pour over all. Cover and chill 1 hour or overnight.

Spoon soup over top. Sprinkle with buttered cubes. Bake at 325° for 50 to 60 minutes or till set. Sprinkle cheese over top last few minutes of baking. Makes 24 servings.

Chili Con Carne for 24

6 cups (about 2½ pounds) dry red chili or kidney beans*
4 large onions, sliced
4 medium green peppers, chopped
4 pounds ground beef
4 1-pound cans (8 cups) tomatoes
4 8-ounce cans seasoned tomato sauce
2 tablespoons salt
½ teaspoon paprika
4 bay leaves, crumbled
3 to 4 tablespoons chili powder

Rinse beans; soak in 6 quarts cold water overnight. Add 1 tablespoon salt to beans and water; cover, simmer till *tender*, about 1 hour. Drain; reserve liquid.

Brown onion, green pepper, and meat in hot fat in two heavy kettles. Mix beans, remaining ingredients; add. Cover; simmer 2 hours. Add bean liquid, water if needed.

*Or use six 1-pound cans red or kidney beans. Drain beans; add with tomatoes.

Roaster Baked Beans

16 1-pound cans (32 cups) pork and beans in tomato sauce*
1½ cups brown sugar
2 tablespoons dry mustard
2 14-ounce bottles (2½ cups) catsup

• • •

1 pound bacon, cut in pieces
Bacon strips

Preheat electric roaster to 300°. Into inset pan in roaster, empty *8 cans* of the beans.

Combine brown sugar and mustard; sprinkle *half* of mixture over the beans. Drizzle with *one bottle* of the catsup.

Top with remaining beans, brown sugar mixture, and catsup. Sprinkle bacon pieces over. Top with bacon strips for trim.

Cook covered at 300° for 3½ to 4 hours. Keep hot when cooking is done at 150°. Makes 30 one-cup servings.

*Or use five 46-ounce cans plus one No. 2½ can pork and beans, if available.

When you shop for 24

First—how many servings will you provide, and for how many? These casserole recipes make *one serving apiece* for 24 people—no seconds. For two dozen hearty eaters, plan more. (For 50 people or 100, simply multiply recipes and foods listed on tables by 2 or 4.)

Then how much coffee, how many rolls? Use this table as a guide. We've indicated whether these amounts provide only 1 serving apiece for 24, or more.

The large cans listed are most apt to be available from a wholesale grocer. He may also carry institution-size packages of frozen vegetables and fruits.

Last, double-check your list for essentials like paper towels and soap or detergent—especially if using church or club kitchen.

Food	Amount for 24
Beverages	*(1 serving each)*
Milk	6 quarts
Coffee, ground	½ pound
Coffee, instant	A 2-ounce jar makes 25 to 30 cups
Tea leaves	½ cup or 24 bags
Tea, instant	½ cup
Breads	*(1-2 servings each)*
French bread	2 18-inch loaves
Nut bread	2 8x4- or 9x4-inch loaves, sliced thin
Rolls, biscuits	2-3 dozen
Desserts	*(1 serving each)*
Cake	2 8- or 9-inch 2-layer cakes 1 15x10-inch sheet 2 9x9-inch cakes
Fruits, canned	4 No. 2½ cans (makes 28 servings) *or* 1 No. 10 can
Fruits, frozen	
Cherries	6 20-ounce cans
Peaches	8 pounds
Strawberries	7 pounds
Ice cream	1 gallon
Pie	5 8-inch or 4 9-inch

Cabbage Slaw

10 cups (about 1⅔ pounds) shredded cabbage
2 cups (⅔ pound) shredded carrot
⅔ cup finely chopped green pepper

• • •

2 cups salad dressing
¼ cup sugar
¼ cup vinegar
4 teaspoons prepared mustard
2 teaspoons salt
2 teaspoons celery seed

Combine chilled vegetables. Combine remaining ingredients for dressing. Just before serving, combine slaw and dressing; toss lightly. Makes 24 ½-cup servings.

Serve in leafy cabbage bowl, if desired: Select a large cabbage head with curling leaves. Loosen leaves and spread out, petal fashion. With sharp knife, hollow center to within 1 inch of sides and bottom. (Use center for the slaw.) See picture, page 49.

Tossed Green Salad for 50

3 heads lettuce
1 pound spinach
¾ pound radishes, sliced (2 cups)
1 pound cucumbers, thinly sliced (2 cups)
2 large green peppers, chopped (2 cups)
1 medium onion, chopped (1 cup)

• • •

1 1-pint jar garlic French dressing
1 cup sweet pickle relish
½ cup chopped pimiento
⅓ cup vinegar
1 tablespoon salt

Break lettuce in bite-size chunks. Tear spinach. Make several layers each of greens, radishes, cucumbers, green pepper, and onion in large salad bowl. Refrigerate.

Combine remaining ingredients for dressing. Pour over vegetables *just before serving*. Toss lightly. Makes 50 ½-cup servings *or* 32 ¾-cup servings.

Food	Amount for 24
Relishes	*(combine several)*
Carrot strips	1 med. bunch carrots
Cauliflowerets	1 head cauliflower
Celery curls	1 med. bunch celery
Green pepper rings	1 large pepper
Olives	1 quart
Pickles	1 quart
Soup, condensed	8 10½- to 11-ounce cans or 2 50- to 54-ounce cans
Vegetables	*(½-cup servings)*
All canned	6 1-pound cans or 4 No. 2½ cans (28 servings) *or* 1 No. 10 can
Asparagus, frozen	6¼ pounds
Beans (all), frozen	4½-5 pounds
Beans, Green, fresh	5 to 6 pounds
Carrots, fresh	5 medium bunches
Corn, frozen, cut	5 pounds
Mixed vegetables, frozen	5½ pounds
Peas, frozen	5 pounds
Potatoes—to mash	7½ pounds
—to scallop	6½-7 pounds
Squash, frozen	7 pounds

Food	Amount to buy
Extras	
Butter	½ pound (24 squares)
Catsup	2 bottles
Cream for coffee	1 to 2 pints
Jam or preserves	1½ to 2 pounds
Juice	2 46-ounce cans
Potato chips	1½ pounds

Measure after preparation

Food	Measure
Cheese, shredded	1 pound—4 cups
Cracker crumbs	1 pound—6½ cups
Macaroni, uncooked	1-1¼ cups (¼ pound)—2¼ cups cooked
Noodles, uncooked	1½-2 cups (¼ pound)—2¼ cups cooked
Rice, uncooked	1 cup—3 to 3½ cups cooked
Rice, precooked	1 cup—2 cups cooked
Spaghetti, uncooked	1-1¼ cups (¼ pound)—2½ cups cooked
Vegetables, olives	
Celery, diced	1 pound—4 cups
Green pepper, diced	1 large—1 cup
Olives, sliced	4 ounces—⅔ to 1 cup
Onion, chopped	1 pound—2 to 3 cups

Quick, colorful Sweet-Sour Tuna

Take your pick!

These one-dish meals are delicious, handy, *and* easy on the budget.

Here are samples: Veal chops and potatoes with an exciting cheese topper; super-speedy tuna sauce Oriental style; durable favorites in new dress—chicken and rice, glazed ham and squash.

Spanish-style Chicken Skillet

Ham and Squash Skillet

Veal-chop Dinner

Skillet meals

Easy! Brown, braise, stew, serve—all in the skillet! Penny-wise! Ham, shrimp, chicken goes a long way when sauced, served on noodles or rice. All-occasion! Meat-and-potato specials, ladies'-luncheon fare, Saturday-night suppers—

Popular quick suppers

Skillet cooking is simple—you brown meat or vegetables, then go ahead and simmer the whole main course in the same pan.

Most skillet meals cook quickly with little fuss, come directly to the table. Dishwashing is minimum. No wonder the popularity of these top-of-range casseroles has skyrocketed!

Here are meat sauces to serve over buns and noodles, meat-vegetable dinners, creamed turkey or sea food dramatized in a rice ring, eggs in fancy ways for luncheon.

Remember chafing-dish specialties, too—most will work just as well in an electric skillet. (See chapter: Chafing-dish classics.)

Off with the cover—it's suppertime!

Show off the first tender spring vegetables in this Meat-ball Garden Skillet—or, serve it to brighten a mid-winter meal. (Use onion slices then, and cut up potatoes and carrots.)

Inexpensive and nourishing for the family, this skillet specialty is so tempting you'll serve it sometimes to company.

Meat-ball Garden Skillet

You'll treasure this ground-meat fix-up for its easy ways, its party look—

Meat Balls:

¼ cup chopped onion
1 tablespoon butter or margarine
½ pound ground beef
½ pound ground veal
2 tablespoons flour
1½ teaspoons salt
½ teaspoon pepper
1 egg
¼ cup milk

• • •

Butter
2 tablespoons flour
1 can condensed consomme

• • •

"Garden:"
6 to 10 small potatoes *or*
6 medium potatoes, quartered
12 small carrots, *or*
6 medium carrots, halved lengthwise and crosswise
2 cups fresh peas*
1 bunch green onions, cut in 1-inch lengths
1 teaspoon salt
¼ teaspoon pepper

To prepare Meat Balls: Cook onion in 1 tablespoon butter till it's tender but not brown. (Use same large skillet you'll need later; save washing two skillets.) Combine ground beef and ground veal with next 5 ingredients. *Beat thoroughly.* (This mixture should be light and fluffy.) Add cooked onion and form into 1-inch balls.

In large skillet, brown balls lightly in a little additional butter or margarine. Shake skillet to turn the meat balls as they brown. Push the balls aside.

Blend 2 tablespoons flour into fat in skillet. Add the consomme. Cook, stirring constantly, till the mixture thickens.

To complete Garden Skillet: To meat balls in skillet, add potatoes, carrots, peas, and onions, arranging attractively. Sprinkle vegetables with 1 teaspoon salt and ¼ teaspoon pepper. Cover skillet and simmer till vegetables are tender, about 30 minutes.

Garnish with fluff and snippets of parsley just before serving. Makes 6 servings.

*Or, use one 10-ounce package frozen peas. Pour boiling water over, to separate them; drain; and add to skillet the last 5 minutes of cooking time.

Stroganoff Beefburgers

Sour cream, crisp bacon bits make this good—

1 to 1½ pounds ground beef
3 slices bacon, diced
½ cup chopped onion
1½ tablespoons enriched flour
¾ teaspoon salt
¼ teaspoon paprika
Dash pepper

• • •

1 can condensed cream of mushroom soup
1 cup dairy sour cream

• • •

8 to 10 hamburger buns, split and toasted

Brown ground beef and bacon. Add onion; cook until tender but not brown. Drain off the excess fat. Blend flour and seasonings into meat mixture. Stir in soup. Cook slowly, uncovered, 20 minutes, stirring frequently. Stir in sour cream and heat through.

Serve in toasted buns or over hot toast points. Makes 8 to 10 servings.

Ground Beef and Noodles in Sour-cream Sauce

1 cup chopped onion
2 tablespoons fat
1 pound ground beef

• • •

3 cups medium noodles
3 cups tomato juice
1 teaspoon salt
1½ teaspoons celery salt
Dash pepper
2 teaspoons Worcestershire sauce

• • •

¼ to ½ cup chopped green pepper

• • •

1 cup dairy sour cream
1 3-ounce can (⅔ cup) broiled sliced mushrooms, drained

Cook onion in hot fat until tender but not brown. Add beef; brown lightly. Place noodles in layer over meat. Combine tomato juice and seasonings; pour over the noodles. Bring to boiling; cover, and simmer over low heat for 20 minutes.

Add green pepper; cover and continue cooking 10 minutes or till noodles are tender. Stir in sour cream and mushrooms; heat just to boiling. Season to taste. Top with green-pepper rings.

Makes 6 servings.

Texas Straw Hats

1 cup chopped onion
⅔ cup chopped celery
⅔ cup chopped green pepper
3 tablespoons fat
2 pounds ground beef

• • •

2 to 3 teaspoons chili powder
2 teaspoons salt
½ teaspoon thyme
¼ teaspoon pepper
2 6-ounce cans (1⅓ cups) tomato paste
½ cup catsup
2 cups water
2 teaspoons Worcestershire sauce
Dash Tabasco sauce

• • •

2 6-ounce packages corn chips
2 cups shredded sharp process American cheese

In large skillet, cook onion, celery, and green pepper in hot fat till tender but not brown. Add ground beef; brown lightly.

Add remaining ingredients except corn chips and cheese; simmer uncovered 1 hour, stirring occasionally.

Serve the meaty sauce on corn chips; top generously with shredded cheese. Makes 6 or 7 servings.

Texas Straw Hats are a happy combination of crisp corn chips, colorful burger-tomato sauce, and sharp cheese. Serve with relishes, cold milk. Give dessert a ranch-style touch: Tie up cookies and fruit in bright red bandannas.

Burger-Q Buns

When the kids are cooking, suggest this skillet special—with relishes, big sundaes—

1 pound ground beef
1 tablespoon fat
1½ cups chopped onion
1½ cups chopped celery

• • •

1 8-ounce can (1 cup) seasoned tomato sauce
1 can condensed tomato soup
Few drops Tabasco sauce
1 teaspoon salt
½ teaspoon monosodium glutamate
¼ teaspoon chili powder
Dash pepper

• • •

5 or 6 hamburger buns, split and toasted

Brown meat in hot fat. Add onion and celery; cook until tender but not brown. Add tomato sauce, soup, and seasonings.

Simmer uncovered about 20 minutes or until of the consistency you like. Spoon over toasted bun halves. Makes 6 servings.

Bow-tie Noodles with Meat Sauce

¾ pound ground beef
¼ pound bulk pork sausage
¼ cup chopped onion
¼ cup chopped celery
1 clove garlic, minced

• • •

2 1-pound cans (4 cups) tomatoes
2 6-ounce cans (1⅓ cups) tomato paste
¼ cup shredded Parmesan cheese
2 tablespoons parsley flakes
1½ teaspoons salt
1 teaspoon oregano
½ teaspoon monosodium glutamate

• • •

6 ounces (3 cups) bow-tie noodles (farfalline)*, cooked and drained

Lightly brown ground beef and sausage. Add onion, celery, and garlic; cook till tender but not brown. Pour off excess fat.

Add tomatoes and tomato paste, Parmesan cheese, parsley flakes, and seasonings. Cover; simmer about 1½ hours.

Serve over hot noodles, saving some "bow ties" for border and center trim; sprinkle with shredded Parmesan cheese.

Makes 6 servings.

*Or use 8 ounces elbow macaroni.

Saucy Franks

5 slices bacon, diced
½ cup chopped onion
1 cup unsweetened pineapple juice
¾ cup catsup
⅛ teaspoon chili powder
12 frankfurters
¼ cup chopped green pepper

Cook bacon but do not crisp. Add onion and cook till tender but not brown. Stir in juice, catsup, and chili powder. Score franks diagonally every 1 inch; add. Cover; bring to boil; add green pepper, simmer 8 to 10 minutes. Serve with hot cooked rice. Serves 6.

Sausage with Parsley Noodles

1 pound pork sausage
⅔ cup chopped onion
2 cans condensed tomato soup
2 teaspoons Worcestershire sauce
½ teaspoon salt
Dash pepper
6 ounces lasagne noodles
1 tablespoon chopped parsley

Brown sausage in skillet. Drain off excess fat. Add onion, soup, Worcestershire sauce, and seasonings. Simmer 30 minutes.

Cook noodles in boiling, salted water until tender; drain, butter, and sprinkle with parsley. Serve with border of meat sauce. Makes 8 servings. *See meal plan below.*

SAVORY SAUSAGE DINNER

Sausage with Parsley Noodles
Hot Buttered Beets
Citrus-Avocado Salad
Bread Sticks
Butter Pecan-Peach Sundaes
Milk Coffee

For salad, alternate sections of orange and grapefruit on lettuce; add strips of avocado (dip first in citrus juice to keep bright). Dessert is butter-pecan ice cream topped with warm peach slices and maple syrup.

Sausage Creole

1 8-ounce package brown-and-serve sausages

• • •

2 8-ounce cans (2 cups) seasoned tomato sauce
½ cup water
½ cup chopped onion
½ cup chopped green pepper
1 tablespoon brown sugar
1 teaspoon Worcestershire sauce

• • •

Salt to taste

• • •

3 cups hot cooked rice (1 cup uncooked)

Brown sausage according to package directions. Remove sausage and pour off drippings.

In same skillet, combine tomato sauce, water, onion, green pepper, brown sugar, and Worcestershire sauce. Simmer uncovered about 20 minutes or till thick. Add sausage links; heat through. Salt to taste.

Serve over hot rice. Makes 5 servings.

Hawaiian Sausage Platter

1 pound sausage links
8 canned pineapple slices, drained, cut in half

• • •

1 tablespoon cornstarch
½ teaspoon curry powder
Pineapple syrup plus water to make 1 cup
Salt and pepper

• • •

1 4⅝-ounce package (1⅓ cups) precooked rice
½ teaspoon salt
1½ cups boiling water

Place sausage and 2 tablespoons water in skillet. Cover; steam 5 minutes. Drain. Brown sausage and pineapple slices lightly in skillet, then remove.

Blend cornstarch, curry powder, and syrup mixture; add to fat in skillet; cook, stirring constantly, till thick. Season with salt and pepper to taste.

Add rice and salt to boiling water in saucepan; mix just to moisten all rice. Cover; remove from heat; let stand 13 minutes.

Arrange hot sausage, pineapple, and rice on platter; pour sauce over rice. Makes 5 or 6 servings.

SOUTHERN SUPPER

Ham and Squash Skillet
Buttered Green Beans
Perfection Salad Hot Corn Bread
Speedy Apple Pie Coffee

Bake corn bread and pie in same oven.

For pie—Fill 8-inch shell (pastry mix) with No. 2 can sliced pie apples. Top with mixture of ⅓ cup *each* brown sugar, granulated sugar, broken walnuts; ½ teaspoon cinnamon.

Drizzle with 3 tablespoons maple syrup. Bake at 425° 10 minutes, cover with foil, bake 15 minutes more.

Ham and Squash Skillet

1 pound cooked ham, ground
1 egg
½ cup soft bread crumbs
½ cup finely chopped onion
2 tablespoons prepared mustard
1 medium acorn squash, cut in 5 rings
½ cup brown sugar
2 tablespoons soft butter

Combine first 5 ingredients; form in 5 patties; brown lightly in hot fat; push aside.

Cut squash rings in half; season. Add to skillet. Add 2 tablespoons water. Combine brown sugar and butter; dot over squash.

Cover, cook till squash is tender, 15 to 20 minutes. Uncover, cook 5 minutes, basting often. Turn patties before serving. Serves 5.

Spanish Tomato Rice

Cook 8 slices bacon till crisp; drain. Pour off half bacon fat; in remaining fat, fry 1 cup finely chopped onion and ¼ cup chopped green pepper till tender but not brown.

Add one 1-pound can tomatoes, 1½ cups water, ¾ cup long-grain rice, ½ cup chili sauce, 1 teaspoon salt, dash pepper, 1 teaspoon brown sugar, ½ teaspoon Worcestershire sauce. Cover and simmer 45 minutes.

Serve with the bacon crumbled on top. Trim with parsley. Makes 6 to 8 servings.

Pork-chop Spanish Rice

5 pork chops, ½ inch thick

• • •

1½ teaspoons salt
½ to 1 teaspoon chili powder
1 teaspoon monosodium glutamate
Dash pepper

• • •

¾ cup long-grain rice*
½ cup chopped onion
¼ cup chopped green pepper
1 No. 2½ can (3½ cups) whole tomatoes

• • •

4 green pepper rings
Shredded sharp cheese

Trim excess fat from chops; heat fat in heavy skillet. When you have about 2 tablespoons melted fat, remove trimmings. (Or, use salad oil instead of melting fat.) Brown chops slowly in hot fat; drain off excess.

Combine seasonings and sprinkle over meat. Add rice, onion, and green pepper. Pour tomatoes over. Cover and cook over low heat about 30 to 35 minutes, stirring occasionally.

Add green pepper rings and continue cooking, 5 minutes longer, or till rice and meat are tender. Before serving, sprinkle with shredded cheese. Makes 5 servings.

*Or use packaged precooked rice, but add rice last 10 minutes of cooking.

Hawaiian Sweet-Sour Ham

2 cups cooked ham in julienne strips

• • •

1 9-ounce can (1 cup) pineapple tidbits
2 tablespoons brown sugar
1½ tablespoons cornstarch
1 teaspoon monosodium glutamate
3 to 4 teaspoons vinegar
2 teaspoons prepared mustard

• • •

¾ cup water

• • •

1 green pepper, cut in strips

• • •

2 cups cooked rice

Brown ham in small amount hot fat. Drain pineapple, reserving syrup. Mix next 5 ingredients; stir in syrup and water; add to skillet. Cook and stir till mixture thickens. Cover; simmer 10 minutes.

Add pineapple tidbits and green pepper strips; simmer 5 to 8 minutes. Salt to taste. Serve with hot cooked rice. Makes 4 servings.

Man-style beef, veal combos

Steak 'n Potato Dinner

1½ pounds round steak, ½ inch thick
¼ cup enriched flour
2 teaspoons salt
¼ teaspoon pepper

• • •

2 tablespoons fat
1 can condensed beef broth

• • •

4 medium potatoes, pared, cut in ¼-inch slices
2 medium onions, thinly sliced

Cut steak in serving-size pieces. Combine flour, salt, and pepper; coat the meat with flour mixture. In skillet*, brown meat *slowly* in hot fat—this should take 20 to 30 minutes. Add the broth. Cover skillet tightly and simmer (*don't boil*) 30 minutes or until almost tender. (Add a little water if needed.)

Place potato and onion slices over the meat. Season vegetables with salt and pepper. Cover tightly and cook *slowly* about 35 minutes longer or until potatoes are done. Snip parsley atop. Makes 6 servings.

Round out meal with buttered carrots, fresh fruit salad, gingerbread with whipped cream, hot coffee.

*When you're using an electric skillet, follow the manufacturer's directions as to correct temperature settings for browning and simmering the meat.

Curried Beef Cubes

Like sauces with snap? Use the 3 teaspoons of curry powder—

2 pounds beef chuck, cut in ¾-inch cubes
⅓ cup flour
⅓ cup salad oil

• • •

1 large onion, sliced (1 cup)
1 clove garlic, minced
1 teaspoon salt
¼ teaspoon pepper
2 8-ounce cans (2 cups) seasoned tomato sauce
1½ cups water

• • •

2 to 3 teaspoons curry powder
1 10-ounce package (2 cups) frozen French-style green beans

• • •

Hot cooked rice *or* buttered noodles

Roll beef cubes in flour and brown in hot oil. Combine onion, garlic, salt, pepper, tomato sauce, and water; pour over meat.

Cover and cook slowly over low heat till meat is fork-tender, about 1½ hours. Stir in the curry powder.

Add green beans and cook till tender, about 15 minutes, separating beans with fork as they heat. Serve over hot rice or noodles. Makes 6 to 8 servings.

Curried Beef Cubes—a meaty mainstay that's most of meal

Beef cubes simmer in zesty tomato sauce till fork-tender. Then you dash in curry, add crisp colorful green beans at next-to-last minute.

Serve this peppy meat sauce over buttered noodles *or* hot cooked rice. Pass a crisp apple-nut salad, toasted French bread. For dessert—warm spice cake, cider.

Beef Goulash—Poppy-seed Noodles

2 pounds beef chuck, cut in ¾-inch cubes
⅓ cup fat
1 cup chopped onion
1 tablespoon enriched flour
1½ teaspoons salt
1 tablespoon paprika
1 8-ounce can (1 cup) seasoned tomato sauce
1 1-pound can (2 cups) tomatoes
1 to 2 cloves garlic, minced
Bouquet garni*

• • •

6 ounces noodles
2 tablespoons poppy seed
2 tablespoons butter

Brown beef cubes in hot fat; add onion. Stir in flour, salt, and paprika. Add tomato sauce, tomatoes, garlic, and bouquet garni. Cover, simmer over low heat till meat is tender, about 1½ hours. Remove bouquet garni.

Cook noodles in boiling salted water; drain. Add poppy seed and butter. Serve goulash over noodles. Makes 6 to 8 servings.

****Bouquet garni:*** In a piece of cheesecloth, tie 1 bay leaf, 1 stalk celery and leaves, 2 tablespoons chopped parsley, and ¼ teaspoon leaf thyme.

Savory Beef and Spaghetti

1 pound round steak, cut in ¾-inch cubes
Flour
2 tablespoons fat
½ cup chopped onion
1 clove garlic, minced
2 3-ounce cans (1⅓ cups) broiled chopped mushrooms
1 cup dairy sour cream
1 can condensed tomato soup
1 tablespoon Worcestershire sauce
6 to 8 drops Tabasco sauce
½ teaspoon salt
Dash pepper

• • •

7 ounces spaghetti, cooked and drained
Shredded Parmesan cheese

Dip beef cubes in flour; brown in hot fat. Add onion, garlic, and mushrooms with liquid. Combine sour cream, soup, and seasonings; pour over meat. Cover; simmer till tender, about 1¼ hours.

Serve over hot spaghetti. Sprinkle with Parmesan cheese. Makes 6 servings.

Veal-chop Dinner

4 veal chops, ½ inch thick
2 tablespoons enriched flour
2 tablespoons shortening
⅓ cup grated Parmesan cheese
½ teaspoon salt
¼ teaspoon pepper
4 medium potatoes, sliced thin (about 4 cups)
2 medium onions, sliced thin (2 cups)
3 beef bouillon cubes
¾ cup hot water
1 tablespoon lemon juice

Coat veal chops with flour; in large skillet brown slowly on both sides in hot shortening. Combine Parmesan cheese, salt, and pepper. Sprinkle *2 tablespoons* of the mixture over meat. Cover with potato slices; sprinkle with 2 tablespoons more cheese. Add onion slices and sprinkle with remaining cheese.

Dissolve bouillon cubes in hot water; add lemon juice and pour over meat. Cover; simmer about 40 minutes, or till meat and vegetables are done. Makes 4 servings.

Veal Parmesan

¼ cup fine dry bread crumbs
¼ cup grated Parmesan cheese
½ teaspoon salt
½ teaspoon garlic salt
½ teaspoon paprika
Dash pepper

• • •

4 veal chops, ¾ inch thick
1 beaten egg
3 tablespoons olive or salad oil
1 pound (about 12) tiny new potatoes, scraped, *or* 4 medium potatoes, peeled and quartered
1 8-ounce can seasoned tomato sauce
½ cup water
1 teaspoon oregano
4 thin slices Mozzarella cheese

Combine bread crumbs, Parmesan cheese, seasonings. Dip chops in egg, then in crumb mixture. Brown slowly on both sides in hot oil; arrange potatoes around meat. Combine tomato sauce and water. Pour around meat and potatoes; sprinkle with oregano.

Cover; simmer 45 to 50 minutes or till meat and potatoes are done. Last five minutes place a slice of Mozzarella cheese atop each chop. If desired, sprinkle with additional oregano. Makes 4 servings.

Sunday-best chicken skillets

Gourmet Chicken with Noodles

⅓ cup chopped onion
1 tablespoon butter
• • •
3 cups fine noodles
2¾ cups chicken broth
½ teaspoon grated lemon peel
½ teaspoon monosodium glutamate
1 teaspoon salt
• • •
2 tablespoons cooking sherry
1 cup dairy sour cream
2 cups diced cooked or canned chicken
¼ cup slivered almonds, toasted
3 tablespoons snipped parsley

Cook onion in butter till tender but not brown. Add noodles, broth, lemon peel, monosodium glutamate, and salt; bring to boiling. Cover; cook over *low* heat 25 minutes or till noodles are done.

Stir in cooking sherry, sour cream, and chicken; heat through. Sprinkle with almonds and parsley. Makes 4 servings.

Spanish-style Chicken Skillet

1 2- to 3-pound ready-to-cook chicken, cut up
2 teaspoons salt
¼ teaspoon pepper
½ teaspoon monosodium glutamate
3 tablespoons shortening
½ cup chopped onion
1 clove garlic, minced
1 cup tomato juice
2 cups chicken broth
1 cup long-grain rice
1 10-ounce package (2 cups) frozen peas, broken apart
¼ cup pimiento, coarsely chopped

Season chicken with salt, pepper, and monosodium glutamate. Brown in melted shortening. Add onion and garlic; cook till onion is just tender. Add tomato juice and ½ *cup* of broth. Cover; simmer 20 minutes.

Add rice and remaining 1½ cups broth. Simmer covered 20 minutes. Add peas and pimiento. Simmer 5 minutes more or till peas are tender. Makes 4 or 5 servings. (*See meal plan at right*).

Company Chicken and Potatoes

2 chicken bouillon cubes
1 cup hot water
1 2½- to 3-pound chicken, cut up
2 tablespoons enriched flour
1 medium onion, sliced
1 clove garlic, minced
1 1-pound can tiny potatoes, drained
3 tablespoons cooking sherry

Dissolve bouillon cubes in water; cool. Slowly brown chicken in ¼ cup butter, 10 to 15 minutes. Push chicken to one side; blend in flour; slowly stir in bouillon. Cook and stir till mixture thickens. Add onion and garlic. Cover; cook 30 minutes or till tender. Add potatoes; heat. Stir in sherry and dash pepper. Makes 3 or 4 servings.

Chicken Livers Stroganoff

Cook 2 cups thinly sliced onion in ¼ cup butter till tender but not brown. Add ½ pound halved chicken livers. Season with 1 tablespoon paprika, ½ teaspoon salt, dash pepper. Brown livers. Cover, cook over low heat 10 minutes or till livers are tender.

Add 1 cup dairy sour cream; heat through. Serve over hot cooked rice. Trim with parsley. Makes 4 servings.

CHICKEN AND BISCUITS

Spanish-style Chicken Skillet
Avocado Fruit Toss
Hot Buttered Biscuits
Strawberry Ice Cream   Cookies
Milk   Hot Tea

While skillet simmers, pop biscuits in oven; make salad of curly endive, lettuce, avocado slices, orange and grapefruit sections, French dressing.

Easy-does-it elegance —chicken in rice ring Confetti Rice Ring is the glamour touch—and it's molded in a minute, complete with polka dots of pimiento and peas. In center—Creamed Chicken. Could be ham, sea-food sauce.

Creamed Chicken or Turkey

½ cup finely chopped onion
⅓ cup butter or margarine
¼ cup enriched flour
1½ cups canned chicken broth or turkey broth
1½ cups light cream
2 teaspoons salt
1 teaspoon monosodium glutamate
2 slightly beaten egg yolks
3 cups diced cooked chicken or turkey
1 6-ounce can (1⅓ cups) broiled sliced mushrooms, drained

Cook onion in butter till tender but not brown. Blend in flour. Slowly stir in broth and cream. Add seasonings. Cook and stir over medium heat till mixture thickens.

Stir small amount of hot mixture into egg yolks; return to hot mixture; cook and stir over low heat about one minute. Add chicken and mushrooms; heat just till hot through. Serve in Confetti Rice Ring or over hot biscuits. Makes 8 servings.

Confetti Rice Ring

1⅓ cups long-grain rice, cooked (4 cups cooked)
1 10-ounce package (2 cups) frozen peas, cooked and drained
3 tablespoons diced pimiento
2 tablespoons butter, melted

Combine all ingredients. Press into 5½-cup ring mold. Unmold at once onto hot serving plate. (See tip at right.) *Or*, cover with foil and set in pan of hot water, in very slow (250°) oven, till ready to serve. Place bowl in center; fill with creamed chicken or sea food. Makes 8 servings.

Parsley Rice Ring

4 cups hot cooked rice
⅔ cup finely chopped parsley
3 tablespoons finely chopped onion

Combine ingredients. Press firmly into 5-cup ring mold; unmold as directed for Confetti Rice Ring. Makes 5 to 6 servings.

Over rice or noodles— a sea-food sauce

Honolulu Shrimp and Rice

4 strips bacon, diced
½ pound ground beef
1 cup finely chopped onion (1 medium)
3 cups cooked rice
2 cups cleaned cooked or canned shrimp
⅓ cup minced celery leaves
1 teaspoon salt
¼ teaspoon dry mustard
Dash pepper
2 tablespoons soy sauce
3 tipped-with-green bananas

Cook bacon crisp; add ground beef, onion. Cook and stir till onion is tender but not brown. Add remaining ingredients except bananas; mix, heat through.

Slice bananas. Brown lightly in butter. Serve shrimp mixture in bowl; border with banana slices. Makes 6 servings.

For quick party look, mold rice in ring or one-apiece cups—

Pack hot cooked rice (see variations opposite) into ring mold *or* into custard cups; turn out on hot platter. Center ring with bowl for sauce.

Shrimp Creole

½ cup chopped onion
½ cup chopped celery
1 clove garlic, minced
1 1-pound can (2 cups) tomatoes
1 8-ounce can seasoned tomato sauce
1½ teaspoons salt
1 teaspoon sugar
½ to 1 teaspoon chili powder
1 tablespoon Worcestershire sauce
Dash Tabasco sauce
1 teaspoon cornstarch
2 teaspoons cold water
¾ pound raw cleaned shrimp
½ cup chopped green pepper

Cook onion, celery, and garlic in hot fat till tender but not brown. Add tomatoes, tomato sauce, and seasonings. Simmer uncovered 45 minutes. Mix cornstarch with water; stir into sauce; cook and stir till mixture thickens. Add shrimp, green pepper. Cover; simmer till done, about 5 minutes. Serve in Parsley Rice Ring. Serves 5 or 6.

Sweet-Sour Tuna

1 No. 2 can (2½ cups) pineapple chunks
¼ cup sugar
2 tablespoons cornstarch
1 chicken bouillon cube in
 1 cup hot water
2 tablespoons vinegar
2 teaspoons soy sauce
½ teaspoon salt
2 cups green-pepper strips,
 ½ inch wide
2 6½- or 7-ounce cans tuna, drained
 and broken in chunks
2 tablespoons butter or margarine
2 6-ounce cans chow-mein noodles

Drain pineapple, reserving syrup. Combine sugar, cornstarch; stir in bouillon, pineapple syrup, vinegar, soy sauce, and salt. Cook and stir till mixture thickens.

Add pineapple, green pepper, tuna, butter. Heat 5 minutes, stirring occasionally. Serve over noodles. Pass soy sauce. Serves 6 to 8.

With toast-egg, cheese specials

Curried-egg Biscuit Topper

Over oven-hot biscuits, a peppy golden sauce—

1 package refrigerated biscuits

• • •

¼ cup shortening
1 tablespoon minced onion
3 tablespoons enriched flour
1 teaspoon salt
1 teaspoon curry powder
½ teaspoon sugar

• • •

2½ cups milk

• • •

1 1-pound can (2 cups) peas, drained
6 hard-cooked eggs, sliced
½ teaspoon lemon juice

Bake biscuits as directed on package.

Meanwhile, melt shortening in saucepan. Add onion and cook till tender but not brown. Blend in flour, salt, curry powder, and sugar, stirring till smooth. Add milk all at once. Cook, stirring constantly, till mixture thickens and boils. Add peas, egg slices, and lemon juice. Heat through.

Split hot biscuits. Spoon curried mixture over. Makes 5 or 6 servings.

SPRING SPECIAL

Eggs a la King over Toast
Hot Buttered Broccoli
Lettuce Wedges,
Blue-cheese Dressing
Whole-wheat Rolls
Rhubarb Cobbler Cold Milk

Slide brown-and-serve rolls into the oven with cobbler. Top lettuce with bottled dressing, *or* blend 1 cup mayonnaise, 3 tablespoons chili sauce, and ⅓ cup crumbled blue cheese.

For a party, serve Eggs a la King from chafing dish, into toast cups.

Eggs a la King

1 cup chopped celery
¼ cup chopped green pepper
¼ cup finely chopped onion
2 tablespoons salad oil

• • •

1 can condensed cream of celery soup
½ cup milk
1 cup (¼ pound) diced process American cheese

• • •

4 hard-cooked eggs
6 stuffed green olives, sliced

• • •

Hot buttered toast

Cook celery, green pepper, and onion in hot salad oil till tender but not brown. Stir in cream of celery soup, milk, and cheese; heat and stir till cheese melts.

Slice eggs; reserve several slices for garnish. Chop remaining eggs and add to sauce along with green olives; heat. Serve on hot buttered toast; garnish with reserved egg slices. Makes 4 or 5 servings.

Creamed Eggs a la Asparagus

3 tablespoons butter or margarine
3 tablespoons enriched flour
1¾ cups milk
½ teaspoon salt
Dash pepper
½ cup shredded sharp process American cheese

• • •

5 hard-cooked eggs, sliced
1 10-ounce package frozen asparagus spears, cooked and drained
Paprika

• • •

Toast points

In skillet, melt butter over low heat (or at about 220°, if using electric skillet); blend in flour. Gradually stir in milk; cook, stirring constantly, till mixture thickens.

Add salt and pepper. Add cheese; stir till melted. Fold in egg slices. Arrange the hot asparagus spears on top, as shown. Sprinkle with paprika. Serve over the hot toast. Makes 3 or 4 servings.

Chipped Beef-Egg Patties

¼ cup butter or margarine
¼ cup enriched flour
½ teaspoon salt
1 cup milk
6 hard-cooked eggs, chopped
½ cup chopped dried beef
1 tablespoon finely chopped onion
1 egg, beaten
1 tablespoon milk
½ cup dry bread crumbs

Melt butter in saucepan; blend in flour. Add salt. Add milk all at once, and cook, stirring constantly, till thickened. Remove from heat. Add chopped eggs, dried beef, and onion. Chill mixture about 1½ hours.

Blend beaten egg and milk. Shape chilled mixture in 3-inch patties. Dip in milk-egg mixture, then in crumbs. Cook patties in hot fat till browned, about 5 minutes, turning once. Makes 6 servings.

Egg and Cheese Scallop

¾ cup ½-inch bread cubes
¼ cup butter or margarine
6 eggs, beaten
⅓ cup milk
1 cup diced sharp process cheese
¾ cup shredded carrots
2 tablespoons finely snipped parsley
½ teaspoon salt
Dash pepper

Toast bread cubes in butter in a skillet, stirring frequently. Combine remaining ingredients and pour over bread cubes.

Cook over low heat till done, stirring occasionally. Makes 4 to 6 servings.

Creole Rabbit

It's tomato rabbit, New Orleans style. For a Lenten main dish, omit the bacon and serve over fluffy rice—

4 slices bacon, diced
½ cup chopped onion
½ cup diced green pepper

• • •

1 1-pound can (2 cups) tomatoes
1 teaspoon salt
Dash pepper
1 teaspoon Worcestershire sauce

• • •

2 tablespoons butter
  or margarine
3 tablespoons enriched flour
⅔ cup milk
⅔ cup shredded sharp process
  American cheese

• • •

4 to 6 slices hot toast

Cook bacon till crisp; add onion and green pepper and cook till tender but not brown. Add tomatoes, salt, pepper, and Worcestershire sauce; simmer uncovered for 15 minutes.

Meanwhile make cheese sauce: melt butter; blend in flour. Gradually stir in milk. Cook, stirring constantly, till thick. Add cheese to white sauce and stir till cheese is melted. Remove from heat.

Slowly stir hot tomato mixture into cheese sauce. Serve rabbit over hot buttered toast. Makes 4 to 6 servings.

Complete the meal with hot buttered broccoli, chilly relishes, and baked ripe pears with crisp cookies.

Fancy eggs, bacon hit the spot for brunch, late snack

Here Creamed Eggs a la Asparagus team up with *two* kinds of bacon, crisp toast, perky spiced crab apples, *lots* of hot coffee!

Whole meal is cook-at-the-table, if you use electric helpers and call on guests to butter toast, flip bacon, "pour" coffee.

In Turkey, the word for vegetables is "stuffed." Try tasty Zucchini Dolmas!

Shells, too, go in Spain's intriguing Paella, famous sea-food-chicken stew

Japan's Sukiyaki is picture-pretty, delicious! Everybody gets to cook!

Traveler's choice

Here are prize souvenirs of a world-wide cook's tour—an array of famous recipes from fourteen countries! Some are homespun as Hungarian Gulyas (wonderful goulash!); others exotic (but easy!) as India's curries. Few take fancy ingredients—eggs, bacon, and cheese turn into fabulous Quiche Lorraine! Leftovers? They'll taste better than ever in extravagant Danish Smorrebord. And for party meals you'll want to repeat again and again, choose from Paella, Sukiyaki, Pizza "to order," Chinese Hot Pot. Wonder how to do it, what goes with what? The answers are all here. Adventure away!

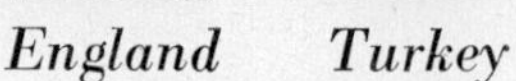

England *Turkey* *Sweden* *Denmark*

Favorites of the old world

English Beefsteak and Kidney Pie

This sturdy main dish is traditionally served with parsleyed potatoes, brussels sprouts. You might add molded or fresh fruit salad, too. For dessert—rich pastries, and tea, of course!

¾ pound (6 medium) lamb kidneys*
1 pound round steak, in ½-inch cubes
1 medium onion, sliced
2 cups water
¼ cup flour
⅓ cup cold water
1 teaspoon salt
Dash pepper

• • •

1 cup sifted enriched flour
½ teaspoon salt
⅓ cup shortening
3 to 4 tablespoons cold water

Remove membrane of kidneys; cut in ½-inch pieces, removing excess fat and tubules. Roll cubed kidney and steak in flour; brown in hot fat. Add onion when meat is partially browned. Add 2 cups water; cover; cook over low heat till tender, about 30 minutes.

Blend ¼ cup flour with ⅓ cup cold water; stir into hot mixture. Add 1 teaspoon salt and the pepper. Pour into an 8-inch shallow round baking dish.

Make plain pastry of remaining ingredients. Roll in circle ½ inch larger than casserole. Place over *hot* meat mixture; cut design in center so steam can escape. Turn under edge of pastry; flute.

Bake pie in very hot oven (450°) 20 minutes or till crust is golden. Makes 6 servings.

*Or, use 1 small beef kidney (about ¾ pound). Soak in lukewarm salted water (1 tablespoon salt to 1 quart water) 1 hour. Drain.

Remove skin and tubes. Cover with cold water; bring to boil; simmer 20 minutes. Drain. Cut in ½-inch cubes, removing fat.

Turkish Zucchini Dolmas

1 pound ground beef
½ cup chopped onion
⅓ cup precooked rice
¾ cup milk
2 teaspoons salt
½ teaspoon pepper
1 teaspoon chopped fresh mint leaves, *or* ¼ teaspoon dried mint
1 teaspoon chopped fresh dill, *or* ¼ teaspoon dried dill
8 medium zucchini squash
2 8-ounce cans seasoned tomato sauce

Combine first 8 ingredients; mix well. Cut both ends from zucchini; with apple corer, scoop out centers. (Chop centers and reserve.) Fill zucchini loosely with meat mixture.

Heat tomato sauce in skillet; add zucchini, the chopped centers, and any leftover meat mixture rolled into balls. Cover, simmer 30 minutes or till squash are tender. Serve with the sauce. Makes 8 servings.

With Dolmas, you might serve rice pilau; figs, grapes, peaches; coffee, flaky pastry.

Swedish Cabbage Rolls

For a starter—herring and cheese, buttered bread; dessert—fruit soup, Swedish coffee—

1 egg
2 teaspoons salt
¼ teaspoon pepper
1 teaspoon Worcestershire sauce
¼ cup finely chopped onion
⅔ cup milk
½ pound ground beef
½ pound ground pork
¾ cup cooked rice
6 large cabbage leaves
1 can condensed tomato soup
1 tablespoon brown sugar

Combine first 6 ingredients; mix well. Add meat and rice; beat together.

Steam cabbage leaves 3 minutes or just till limp; drain. Slit heavy vein of leaf about 2½ inches. Place ½ cup meat mixture on each leaf; fold in sides and roll ends over meat.

Place rolls in ungreased 11½x7½x1½-inch baking dish. Blend together soup, 1 soup-can water and the brown sugar; pour over cabbage rolls.

Bake at 350° for 1¼ hours or till done. Makes 6 servings. Serve with boiled potatoes

Danish Smorrebrod

The Danes serve a marvelous variety of these elaborate open-face sandwiches. For topping, almost anything goes—as long as it looks and tastes delicious. Try our combinations, create your own. Make them beautiful, pile them high; then eat with knife and fork!

Start off with *very* thin-sliced bread. Spread each slice to the edges with butter (whipped, if you like). Now for the toppers:

Shrimp Pyramid: Top firm buttered white bread with a lettuce leaf, then pile up row on row of tiny shrimp. Serve with mayonnaise, and a lemon wedge.

Salami-Potato Tower: On buttered rye bread, alternate thin slices of salami and cooked potato. For trim, fill a salami cornucopia with mayonnaise and dot with capers, as shown below. Snip chives over all.

Chicken-Tomato Whirl: Spread pumpernickel with mayonnaise; add slices of chicken, asparagus spear, olive rings, a tomato whirl.

Sardine Special: Top rye bread with slices of hard-cooked egg and tomato, then sardines.

Garnishes for Smorrebrod

Spirals: Corkscrews of pickle, cucumber, or carrot often trim Smorrebrod.

Hold pickle at bottom in left hand. With sharp paring knife at an angle, make cut at top, going almost to center. Continue cutting in one motion, turning pickle around as you cut down entire length.

Whirls: Slice tomato, lemon, or orange in thin circles. Cut each slice to center. Pull one cut end toward you, the other end away. Place on sandwich so uncut portion is standing upright—as shown below.

Danish specialty—open-face sandwiches

They're perfect light-buffet fare. Create a variety; serve with hot coffee, fruit. Customarily, three sandwiches make a meal—Danes choose one fish, one meat, one "salad." Smorrebrod below: Shrimp Pyramid, Salami-Potato Tower, Chicken-Tomato Whirl.

Hungary

France

Hungarian Gulyas

Hungarians give top honors to goulash, make it in endless variety. Sun Valley has imported this version, with tiny puffy dumplings—

2½ pounds veal, beef, or pork, cut in ½-inch cubes
1 cup chopped onion
1 clove garlic, minced
¼ cup enriched flour
1½ teaspoons salt
¼ teaspoon pepper
1½ tablespoons paprika
2 bay leaves
¼ teaspoon thyme
1 No. 2½ can (3½ cups) tomatoes
1 cup dairy sour cream

Brown veal in hot fat. Reduce heat; add onion and garlic and cook till onion is tender but not brown. Blend in flour and seasonings. Add tomatoes, cover; simmer till veal is tender and sauce is thick, about 1 to 1¼ hours. Stir often toward end of cooking.

Stir in sour cream; remove from heat. Serve over hot buttered Spaetzels. Makes 6 servings. Serve with hot red-cabbage-and-apple, lettuce with sour-cream dressing, strudel.

Spaetzels

2 cups sifted enriched flour
2 eggs
2 egg yolks
⅔ cup milk
1½ teaspoons salt
Dash pepper
Dash nutmeg
1 tablespoon minced parsley
¼ cup butter or margarine
½ cup fresh bread crumbs
Minced parsley

Mix first 8 ingredients. Place mixture in coarse-sieved colander over large kettle of rapidly boiling salted water (2 to 3 quarts); press through colander with heavy-bottomed glass, greased to prevent sticking.

When all mixture has been pressed through, cook about 5 minutes, stirring occasionally. Wash under cold water; drain. Melt butter; add bread crumbs and brown lightly. Stir in Spaetzels and brown lightly over low heat, about 10 minutes. Sprinkle with minced parsley. Makes 6 servings.

Quiche Lorraine

1 9-inch unbaked pastry shell
8 slices bacon, diced
½ pound Swiss cheese, shredded
1 tablespoon enriched flour
½ teaspoon salt
Dash nutmeg
3 eggs, beaten
1¾ cups milk

Bake pastry shell in very hot oven (450°) *only 7 minutes*, or just till lightly browned. Remove from oven; reduce oven temperature to 325°.

Fry bacon till crisp; drain and crumble. Reserve 2 tablespoons bacon for trim. Place remaining bacon in pie shell; add cheese. Combine remaining ingredients; pour over. Sprinkle reserved bacon atop in circle.

Bake at 325° for 35 to 40 minutes or till almost set in center. *Let cool 25 minutes* before serving. Serves 6.

French Veal Stew

To be very French, start with anchovy-deviled eggs, crisp relishes. End meal with fruit tarts, or fruit and cheese—

2 pounds veal shoulder, cut in ¾-inch cubes
¼ cup enriched flour
1 teaspoon salt
¼ teaspoon pepper
2 cups hot water
½ cup cooking sherry
1 large whole onion, studded with 2 whole cloves
2 carrots, cut in 1-inch pieces
2 cloves garlic, crushed
Bouquet garni*
½ teaspoon basil
½ teaspoon thyme
½ teaspoon nutmeg
3 egg yolks, beaten
2 tablespoons lemon juice
1 tablespoon cream

Roll veal in flour seasoned with salt and pepper. Brown well in hot fat. Add next 9 ingredients. Cover; simmer one hour. Discard bouquet garni.

Combine egg yolks, lemon juice, and cream. Add some of hot mixture to yolks, blend, add to stew. Heat through, stirring constantly. Serve over rice. Makes 6 to 8 servings.

**Bouquet garni:* Tie together celery stalk, few sprigs parsley, bay leaf.

Quiche Lorraine—

Pride of the French—a main-dish pie! The rich custard filling is chock-full of melted Swiss cheese and bacon bits, framed in the flakiest of crusts!

To accent the mellow cheese flavor—ham-onion roll-ups and French green salad; then demitasse coffee, Petits Fours.

Mexico

Brazil

Spain

Specialties from sunny coast countries

Mexican Eggplant Skillet

You never knew eggplant could be so good! Pass crisp green salad, tortillas. For a pleasant ending—caramel-sauced custard, coffee!

1 pound ground lean beef
¼ cup chopped onion
1 tablespoon flour

• • •

1 8-ounce can (1 cup) seasoned tomato sauce
¼ cup chopped green pepper
1 teaspoon oregano
½ to 1 teaspoon chili powder
½ teaspoon salt

• • •

1 small eggplant, cut in ½-inch slices (pared or unpared)
1 cup shredded sharp process American cheese

• • •

Shredded Parmesan cheese

Cook beef and onion in small amount hot fat till meat is browned. Spoon off excess fat. Sprinkle flour over meat; stir.

Add tomato sauce, green pepper, oregano, chili powder, and salt; mix well. Season eggplant slices with salt and pepper; arrange slices over the meat sauce. Cover and simmer till eggplant is tender, 10 to 15 minutes. Top with shredded process cheese. Pass Parmesan cheese. Makes 4 servings.

Mexican Tamale Pie

1 cup chopped onion
1 cup chopped green pepper
1 tablespoon fat
¾ pound ground beef
2 8-ounce cans seasoned tomato sauce
1 12-ounce can (1½ cups) whole-kernel corn, drained
1 cup chopped ripe olives
1 clove garlic, minced
1 tablespoon sugar
1 teaspoon salt
2 to 3 teaspoons chili powder
Dash pepper
1½ cups shredded sharp process cheese

• • •

Corn-meal Topper:
¾ cup yellow corn meal
½ teaspoon salt
2 cups cold water
1 tablespoon butter or margarine

Cook onion and green pepper in hot fat till just tender. Add meat; brown lightly. Add next 8 ingredients. Simmer 20 to 25 minutes, till thick. Add cheese; stir till melted. Pour in greased 10x6x1½-inch baking dish.

Make Corn-meal Topper: Stir corn meal and ½ teaspoon salt into cold water. Cook and stir till thick. Add butter; mix well. Spoon over meat mixture, making 3 lengthwise stripes. Bake casserole in moderate oven (375°) 40 minutes, or till top is lightly browned. Before serving, sprinkle top with ripe-olive slices. Makes 6 servings.

For a Mexican meal, serve with refried beans, lettuce and tomato salad, crisp tortillas, jam-filled turnovers, and hot coffee.

Jiffy Tamale Chili

You get real Mexican flavor fast with this combination of canned specialties, onion and green pepper, sharp cheese—

¼ cup minced onion
¼ cup chopped green pepper
1 tablespoon butter or margarine
1 1-pound can (2 cups) chili con carne with beans
1 11-ounce can tamales
½ cup shredded sharp process cheese

Cook onion and green pepper in butter till tender but not brown. Add chili.

Remove shucks from tamales; arrange spoke-fashion on top. Cover and heat 10 to 15 minutes. Sprinkle with shredded cheese before serving. Makes 4 or 5 servings.

Brazilian Shrimp Pie

3 large potatoes, cooked
½ cup milk
2 tablespoons enriched flour
2 egg yolks
¼ cup grated Parmesan cheese
1 teaspoon salt
Dash nutmeg
½ pound cleaned raw shrimp
¼ cup salad oil
5 canned artichoke hearts, halved
¼ cup chopped ripe olives
2 hard-cooked eggs, sliced
1 teaspoon capers
1 egg yolk

Mash potatoes; gradually add milk. Beat in next 5 ingredients. Line a greased 9-inch pie plate with ⅔ of the mixture; reserve remainder for top.

Cook shrimp in oil till tender and pink, about 5 minutes; drain; arrange on potatoes. Top with artichoke hearts, olives, hard-cooked egg slices, and capers.

Cover with remaining potato mixture, smoothing surface with a knife. Beat egg yolk; brush over top crust. Bake pie at 400° about 20 minutes or till top is lightly browned. Serve hot. Makes 6 servings.

Serve with chilly marinated green beans, orange-avocado salad, coconut pudding, coffee (or cocoa-coffee, with cream).

SPANISH FEAST

Chilled Tomato-Cream Soup
Spanish Olives Radishes
Paella
Escarole with
Vinegar-Oil Garlic Dressing
Ripe Melon *or* Banana Cake
Coffee Almond-Honey Candies

In place of Spain's traditional, but complicated, *Gazpacho* salad-soup, try this spicy chilled tomato soup:

In blender or shaker, combine 1 can condensed tomato soup, 1 cup light cream, ½ teaspoon nutmeg, and ¼ teaspoon salt. Blend or shake till smooth. Chill. Serve in 6 small chilled glasses or bowls. Trim Spanish-style with cucumber slices.

Spanish Paella

Whatever the fisherman brings home goes into this famous dish. You might vary it, too, with chorizos (hot sausage), artichokes, tomato—

1 3-pound ready-to-eat chicken, cut up
5 cups water
2 carrots, sliced lengthwise
2 onions, quartered
1 celery stalk with leaves
2½ to 3 teaspoons salt
¼ teaspoon freshly ground black pepper

• • •

⅔ cup long-grain rice
2 cloves garlic, crushed
¼ cup olive oil
¼ cup diced pimiento
½ teaspoon oregano
¼ teaspoon Spanish saffron

• • •

1 cup frozen peas, broken apart
⅔ pound shelled raw shrimp (1 pound in shell)
1 dozen clams *in shell**, or 1 10½-ounce can clams

Place chicken pieces in Dutch oven; add water and next 5 ingredients. Bring to boil, reduce heat, cover, and simmer 1 hour or till just tender. Remove chicken from stock; bone, cut up meat. Strain stock; save 4 cups.

Fry rice and garlic in olive oil over medium heat, stirring constantly till rice is browned, about 10 minutes. Add reserved chicken stock, pimiento, oregano, and saffron. Cover, cook over low heat 15 minutes.

Add chicken, peas, shrimp, and clams. Bring to boil, cover, then cook over very low heat 15 minutes. Makes 6 servings.

*To prepare clams in shell, see page 82.

Spanish Fried Rice

(from Spanish Kitchen at Farmers Market)

Soak 1 cup long-grain rice in 1½ cups hot water for ½ hour; drain well; spread in big shallow pan to dry a little, about 1 hour.

Cook 6 slices bacon till crisp; crumble; set aside. Add rice to drippings and cook till rice is lightly browned. Add crumbled bacon, 1 can condensed beef broth, 1 8-ounce can seasoned tomato sauce, ¼ cup chopped green pepper, ¼ cup chopped onion, 1 clove garlic, minced, and ½ teaspoon cumin seed.

Cover, cook over low heat, stirring now and then, till rice is done and liquid absorbed, about 30 minutes. (Add extra water if needed.) Makes 4 to 6 servings.

Good Italian pasta sauces—

In Italy, *spaghetti*, *macaroni*, and *noodles* are names for whole families of pasta products. And more and more of these styles are becoming available on *our* grocery shelves.

You'll find macaroni big enough to stuff (*manicotti*); spaghetti thick and thin, and in spirals (*rotini*); noodle bow ties; shells and stars and alphabets, to name just a few.

Pick a sauce, try it on several pasta styles —each shape seems to have its own flavor!

The Italians are past masters of pasta cookery. This is how *they* do it:

How to cook: Use a large pan so there's plenty of room for the strands or pieces to cook separately and for the water to bubble briskly. Use lots of water for cooking—3 to 4 quarts water for 8 ounces of pasta (best even for a handful!). Add about 1 teaspoon salt for each quart water. Have water boiling vigorously before adding pasta.

Prize import—Spaghetti and Meat Balls

The tomato sauce has the richness that long simmering gives; the spaghetti is cooked *al dente* (just tender, but firm).

To sauce spaghetti: Place drained spaghetti in warm serving bowl, add part of sauce. With two forks, lift spaghetti so sauce coats strands—almost as you would toss a salad. Toss with remaining sauce. Sometimes serve over other pastas, too.

You might also add a teaspoon of olive or salad oil to the water—it helps prevent sticking. This is especially wise when cooking large pasta—like *lasagne, manicotti.*

Instead of breaking *long spaghetti*, hold a handful at one end, dip the other into the bubbling water. As spaghetti softens, curl it round in pan till whole length is dunked.

Don't cover; stir at the start of cooking to prevent sticking. Cook till tender, but firm (*al dente*). The thinner or finer the pasta, the faster it cooks—be a pot watcher. Drain immediately when done.

Spaghetti and Meat Balls

¾ cup chopped onion
1 clove garlic, minced
3 tablespoons olive or salad oil
2 1-pound cans (4 cups) tomatoes
2 6-ounce cans tomato paste
1 cup water
1 tablespoon sugar
1½ teaspoons salt
½ teaspoon pepper
1 bay leaf
1½ teaspoons crushed oregano
1 recipe Italian Meat Balls
Hot cooked spaghetti

Cook onion and garlic in hot oil till tender but not brown; add the next 8 ingredients. Simmer uncovered 30 minutes; remove bay leaf. Add Italian Meat Balls and continue cooking about 30 minutes longer. Serve over hot spaghetti. Pass bowl of grated Romano or shredded Parmesan cheese for folks to help themselves. Makes 6 servings.

Italian Meat Balls

4 slices dry bread
1 pound ground beef
2 eggs
½ cup grated Romano cheese
2 tablespoons chopped parsley
1 clove garlic, minced
1 teaspoon crushed oregano
1 teaspoon salt
Dash pepper
2 tablespoons olive or salad oil

Soak bread in water 2 or 3 minutes, then squeeze out moisture. Combine soaked bread with remaining ingredients except oil, mixing well. Form in small balls (about 20). Brown slowly in hot oil. Cook in sauce as directed in recipe above.

This is the way for Spaghetti and Meat Balls

Dip one end spaghetti in boiling water. As it softens, curl in whole length.

Cook sauce at long *lazy* bubble for rich flavor. Remove bay leaf after ½ hour.

Brown meat balls on *all* sides; then cook 30 minutes in the spicy sauce!

Italian Meat Sauce

½ cup onion slices
2 tablespoons olive oil or salad oil
1 pound ground beef
2 cloves garlic, minced
1 3-ounce can broiled sliced mushrooms
2 1-pound cans (4 cups) tomatoes
2 8-ounce cans seasoned tomato sauce
1 6-ounce can (⅔ cup) tomato paste
¼ cup chopped parsley
1½ teaspoons oregano or sage
1 teaspoon salt
½ teaspoon monosodium glutamate
¼ teaspoon thyme
1 bay leaf
1 cup water

In large skillet, cook onion in hot oil till almost tender, but not brown. Add meat and garlic; brown lightly, Add mushrooms with liquid. Stir in the remaining ingredients.

Simmer, uncovered, 2 to 2½ hours or till thick. Remove bay leaf. Serve over Italian Green Noodles or hot spaghetti. Pass bowl of shredded Parmesan cheese. Makes 6 servings.

Italian Green Noodles

2 cups sifted enriched flour
½ teaspoon salt
2 beaten eggs
¼ cup strained spinach
2 tablespoons butter, melted

Sift together flour and salt. Combine remaining ingredients; add to flour. Mix well.

Knead gently ½ minute on lightly floured surface. Divide dough in half; roll *very* thin. Let stand about 45 minutes (dough must not be sticky or too dry).

Roll like jelly roll; cut ¼-inch slices. Cook in boiling salted water 8 to 10 minutes. Rinse with hot water; drain. Serves 6.

tips *To keep spaghetti hot—butter; steam in colander*

Drain spaghetti in colander and set colander over pan containing small amount boiling water. Coat spaghetti with 3 or 4 tablespoons butter (for 6 servings) to keep strands from sticking together. Cover colander.

Or, for a short time, you may return drained spaghetti to the empty cooking pan, add butter, then cover to keep it warm.

Fine Spaghetti with Green Sauce

The no-cook sauce is parsley-flecked cream cheese, the spaghetti is dainty size. Flavor is robust and luscious—

8 or 10 ounces *spaghettini* (or *capellini*, *fideline*, or *vermicelli*)

• • •

2 tablespoons basil
2 tablespoons parsley flakes
¼ cup soft butter or margarine
1 8-ounce package cream cheese, softened
⅓ cup grated Parmesan cheese
¼ cup olive oil or salad oil
1 clove garlic, minced
½ teaspoon pepper
⅔ cup boiling water

Cook spaghettini in boiling salted water till just tender (*don't overcook*); drain.

Make sauce: Add basil and parsley flakes to butter. Blend in cream cheese, Parmesan cheese, olive oil, garlic and pepper. Stir in boiling water; blend well.

Arrange hot spaghettini on warm platter and serve with the sauce. Pass Parmesan cheese. Serve with bowl of crisp Italian green salad. Makes 6 servings.

To eat spaghetti: Spear only a few strands, then twirl the fork against your plate (or a spoon if you prefer)—come the ends; you have a neat bite!

Mushroom Pasta Sauce

1 3-ounce can (⅔ cup) broiled sliced mushrooms

• • •

1 large onion, chopped
1 clove garlic, minced
2 tablespoons olive or salad oil

• • •

3 tablespoons chopped parsley
2 6¼-ounce cans (1½ cups) concentrated tomato juice
1½ cups water
1 tablespoon sugar
1½ teaspoons salt
1 teaspoon basil

Drain mushrooms, reserving liquid. Cook onion and garlic in hot oil till tender but not brown. Add parsley, mushroom liquid, tomato juice, water, and seasonings.

Simmer uncovered 35 minutes or till of desired consistency. Add mushrooms. Serve over hot spaghetti or other pasta. Pass shredded Parmesan cheese. Makes 4 or 5 servings.

For snack or supper—pizza

Homemade Pizza Crust

1 package active dry yeast
1 cup warm water
3½ cups sifted enriched flour
1 tablespoon olive oil
1 teaspoon salt

Soften yeast in water. Beat in *1½ cups* of the flour; mix in olive oil and salt. Stir in remaining flour. Knead till smooth and elastic, about 12 minutes (will be firm). Place in lightly oiled mixing bowl; turn oiled side up.

Cover. Let rise in warm place till more than double, 1½ to 2 hours. Punch down, cover, refrigerate till cold.

Cut dough in 2 parts. On lightly floured surface, roll each in 12-inch circle, about ⅛ inch thick. Place on greased cooky sheets or two 12-inch pizza pans, turning edges of dough up slightly. With knuckles, dent dough here and there to prevent bubbles. Brush each circle with 1 tablespoon olive oil.

Fill. Bake at 425° for 20 to 25 minutes or till crust is done. Makes two 12-inch crusts.

Jiffy Pizza Crust

Prepare 1 package hot roll mix according to package, but using *1 cup* warm water and *no egg. Do not let rise.* Cut in 2 parts.

With oiled hands, pat each part into 12-inch circle on an oiled baking sheet. Clip edge at 1-inch intervals; press so it stands up. Brush circles with olive oil. Fill.

Bake at 450° 15 to 20 minutes, or till crust is done. Makes two 12-inch crusts.

Biscuit Pizza Crust

Soften 1 cake compressed yeast in ¾ cup lukewarm water. Add 2½ cups biscuit mix; beat vigorously for 2 minutes. On surface dusted with biscuit mix, knead till smooth, 25 strokes. Divide dough in fourths.

Roll each piece to a 10-inch circle; place on greased cooky sheets, and crimp edge. Brush dough with olive oil. Fill crusts.

Bake at 425° for 15 minutes or till crusts are done. Makes four 10-inch pizza crusts.

Patsy's Pizza

(*From Patsy's Pizza place, Farmers Market*)

1 pound Italian sausage
2 fresh tomatoes, peeled and cut in thin slices
2 12-inch pizza-dough circles
1 6-ounce package Mozzarella cheese, *thin-sliced* and cut in pieces
1 6-ounce can (⅔ cup) tomato paste
2 cloves garlic, minced
2 tablespoons crushed oregano
1 tablespoon parsley flakes
Salt and fresh-ground pepper
About ¼ cup olive oil
¼ cup grated Romano cheese

Break sausage in small bits in skillet; fry slowly till evenly and lightly browned, about 10 minutes, stirring occasionally. Drain.

Place layer of tomato slices on pizza-dough circles; cover with *half* the Mozzarella.

Mix tomato paste and garlic; spread over cheese. Sprinkle with seasonings. Drizzle with some of the olive oil. Top with sausage and remaining Mozzarella. Sprinkle with Romano cheese; drizzle with remaining olive oil. Dash with salt and pepper. Bake as directed for crust. Makes two 12-inch pizzas.

Pepperoni Pizza

8 ounces pepperoni, thinly sliced
4 10-inch pizza-dough circles*
2 8-ounce cans seasoned tomato sauce
¾ cup chopped onion
1 tablespoon oregano
1 teaspoon aniseed
½ teaspoon salt
Dash pepper
2 cloves garlic, minced
2 6-ounce packages Mozzarella cheese, *thin sliced* and cut in pieces

Scatter pepperoni slices over dough circles, reserving some pepperoni for trim.

Mix next 7 ingredients; spread over pepperoni. Add cheese. Top with reserved pepperoni slices. Bake according to directions for crust. Makes four 10-inch pizzas.

*Or use two 12-inch pizza-dough circles; cut Mozzarella cheese to 1 package.

Sausage Pizza

1 pound Italian or bulk pork sausage
2 cloves garlic, crushed
1½ tablespoons crushed oregano
1 tablespoon basil
2 12-inch pizza-dough circles
2 6-ounce cans (1⅓ cups) tomato paste
1 6-ounce can (1⅓ cups) broiled sliced mushrooms, drained
2 6-ounce packages Mozzarella cheese, *sliced thin,* cut in pieces

Break sausage in small bits in skillet; fry slowly till browned, pouring off fat as it accumulates. Drain. Add garlic, seasonings.

Spread each dough circle with 1 can tomato paste; cover with sausage mixture, mushrooms, then Mozzarella cheese. Bake according to directions for pizza crusts. Makes two 12-inch pizzas.

Mushroom Pizza

Using two 6-ounce packages sliced Mozzarella cheese, cut each slice in 4 triangles. Reserve 16 triangles for trim; layer remainder over four 10-inch pizza-dough circles.

Top with 1 cup chopped onion, ½ cup chopped green pepper, and 1 6-ounce can broiled sliced mushrooms, drained. Dash with salt, pepper. Drizzle with two 5½-ounce cans pizza sauce. Top each pizza with four Mozzarella triangles, centered with pieces of pickled banana pepper. Bake as directed for crust. Makes four 10-inch pizzas.

Pizza On The Run

Prepare refrigerated or packaged pizza mix according to package directions. Place in pizza pans. Then add your own toppers.

Anchovy Pinwheel: Top filling with pieces of Mozzarella cheese, then pinwheel of anchovy fillets centered with ripe-olive half. Bake.

Pepperoni: On circle of Mozzarella triangles, arrange ring of pepperoni slices; bake.

Cheese Wheels: Arrange strips of Mozzarella cheese spoke-fashion on pizza. After baking, center each pizza with trio of green pickled peppers.

← ***In all its glory—Sausage Pizza!***

Just a whiff of the savory aroma—from oregano, basil, spicy sausage—will bring folks to the table in a hurry! Stylish trim—salami cornucopias (fasten with toothpicks), stuffed olives. Serve with crisp Italian salad, espresso coffee.

Spicy specialties, Roman-style

Baked Lasagne

1 pound Italian sausage, bulk pork sausage, or ground beef
1 clove garlic, minced
1 tablespoon parsley flakes
1 tablespoon basil
1½ teaspoons salt
1 1-pound can (2 cups) tomatoes
2 6-ounce cans (1⅓ cups) tomato paste
• • •
10 ounces lasagne or wide noodles
• • •
3 cups cream-style cottage cheese
2 beaten eggs
2 teaspoons salt
½ teaspoon pepper
2 tablespoons parsley flakes
½ cup grated Parmesan cheese
• • •
1 pound Mozzarella cheese, sliced *thin*

Brown meat slowly; spoon off excess fat. Add next 6 ingredients. Simmer uncovered 30 minutes to blend flavors, stirring occasionally.

Cook noodles in boiling salted water till tender; drain; rinse in cold water. Meanwhile combine cottage cheese with eggs, seasonings, and Parmesan cheese.

Place *half* the noodles in 13x9x2-inch baking dish; spread *half* the cottage-cheese mixture over; add *half* the Mozzarella cheese and *half* the meat sauce. Repeat layers.

Bake at 375° for 30 minutes. Garnish with triangles of Mozzarella cheese. Let stand 10 to 15 minutes before cutting in squares—filling will set slightly. Makes 12 servings.

tips ***For Italian taste adventures, try these seasonings, foods***

Sauces take on Italian flair when you add oregano or basil, a dash of thyme or marjoram.

Experiment with olive oil for real Italian cooking and in salad dressings.

Try appetizers like canned minestrone soup or *antipasto*, oil-cured olives, pepper salad.

Pass grated Parmesan and Romano cheeses in handy shakers. Sometimes try Scamorse or smoky Provolone cheese in place of Mozzarella.

Cioppino (*Italian Fish Stew*)

It's scrumptious—and simple! Make zesty tomato sauce; all at once add lobster, shrimp, fish, clams in shell. Folks will rave!

¼ cup minced onion (½ medium onion)
3 cloves garlic, minced
1 tablespoon snipped parsley
¼ cup olive oil
• • •
1 No. 2½ can (3½ cups) tomatoes
2 8-ounce cans (2 cups) seasoned tomato sauce
1½ cups water
1 teaspoon salt
Dash pepper
½ teaspoon crushed oregano
½ teaspoon marjoram
• • •
½ cup cooking sherry
• • •
2 ¾-pound uncooked rock-lobster tails, cut in serving pieces, shell and all
1½ pounds white fish (sole, haddock, halibut, cod, etc.), cut up
⅔ pound raw cleaned shrimp (1 pound in shell)
2 dozen clams in shell*, *or* 2 10½-ounce cans clams

In Dutch oven, cook onion, garlic, and parsley in hot oil, till onion is tender but not brown. Add tomatoes, tomato sauce, water, and seasonings. Cover and bring to boiling; reduce heat and simmer uncovered ½ hour, adding sherry the last 10 minutes. (This sauce may be made the day before.)

Add fish and sea food to hot sauce, adding clams last; cover tightly, bring to boil and cook over very low heat for 15 minutes. (Clam shells will pop open during cooking.)

Serve in large hot soup bowls—be sure each person has a sample of every kind of fish and sea food. Pass Italian bread, crisp green salad. Makes 6 servings.

**To prepare clams in shell:* Scrub shells. Allow clams to stand in cold salted water (⅓ cup salt to 1 gallon water) 15 to 20 minutes. Repeat twice. Store in refrigerator till ready to use.

Lasagne, Short-cut Style

1 pound ground beef
1 No. 2½ can (3½ cups) tomatoes
1 8-ounce can (1 cup) seasoned tomato sauce
1 or 2 envelopes spaghetti-sauce mix
2 cloves garlic, minced
8 ounces lasagne or wide noodles
1 6- or 8-ounce package thin-sliced Mozzarella cheese
1 cup cream-style cottage cheese
½ cup grated Parmesan cheese

Brown meat slowly; spoon off excess fat. Add next 4 ingredients. Cover and simmer 40 minutes, stirring occasionally. Salt to taste. Cook noodles in boiling salted water till tender; drain; rinse in cold water.

Place *half* the noodles in an 11½x7½x 1½-inch baking dish; cover with a *third* of the sauce; add *half* the Mozzarella, then *half* the cottage cheese. Repeat layers, ending with sauce. Top with Parmesan cheese.

Bake in moderate oven (350°) 25 to 30 minutes. Let stand 15 minutes; cut in squares. Makes 6 to 8 servings.

Polenta with Meat Sauce

1 pound Italian sausage
½ cup chopped onion
1 1-pound can (2 cups) tomatoes
1 6-ounce can (⅔ cup) tomato paste
1 cup water
1 teaspoon salt
1 tablespoon minced parsley
1 tablespoon grated Parmesan cheese

• • •

1½ cups corn meal
1½ cup cold water
1 teaspsoon salt
2½ cups boiling water

Make Meat Sauce: Slowly brown sausage; add next 7 ingredients. Simmer uncovered 1½ hours or till thick, stirring occasionally. Skim off excess fat.

For *Polenta*, combine corn meal, cold water, and salt; gradually stir into boiling water. Cook and stir till thick. Cover; cook over *low* heat about 45 minutes, stirring occasionally. Pour into 9-inch pie plate. Cool 5 minutes. Cut in 6 wedges. Serve Sauce over. Makes 6 servings.

Company-perfect—Baked Lasagne for 12. It's hearty, flavorful!

Ruffly noodles (*lasagne ricce*) and *three* kinds of cheese bake layer on layer in a meaty full-bodied tomato sauce!

Trim with big fluff of parsley and pass the Parmesan!

Flavor adventures from the exotic Orient

Dinner is dramatic, and definitely "company," when you serve these Chinese and Japanese specialties. The surprise: There's a minimum of last-minute fuss. Almost all Oriental dishes require a certain amount of chopping and slicing ahead of time—but the results are worth it! Small pieces get done presto, flavor is exotic, and often guests can cook their own!

Chinese Hot Pot is a meal in itself, perfect to serve four people after the show or for a leisurely evening of dinner-and-conversation. Eight guests? Plan two sets of everything; use two small tables for easy reaching.

You slice the foods, make sauces early. When guests are hungry, just heat up the broth, set out sauces and artistically-arranged tidbits, hand out the chopsticks.

Everything on the tray is raw, of course. You pick out a few choice tidbits at a time—with chopsticks, bamboo tongs, or long-handled fork—and drop them in the lazily bubbling broth. In a few minutes, fish them out, dip into the zesty sauces on your plate, and eat with fluffy rice.

Traditionalists poach eggs in the broth at the very last, when it's subtly flavored from all the foods simmered in it. As a final fillip to this delicious dinner, you may dash cooking sherry into the broth, pass it in dainty no-handle teacups.

Skip dessert, or serve fruit and candied ginger with hot tea.

We show an honest-to-goodness Mongolian cooker, but any chafing dish or electric skillet will work.

To use Mongolian cooker: Fill chimney of cooker with charcoal and add charcoal starter. Pour cold broth into "moat" of cooker. Cover cooker, then light charcoal. When broth is hot, you're ready to cook.

Chinese Hot Pot

1 pound raw cleaned shrimp
2 chicken breasts, skinned, boned, and sliced *very thin* across grain
½ pound beef sirloin, sliced *very thin* across grain
½ head Chinese cabbage *or* 1 lettuce heart, coarsely cubed
1 cup cubed eggplant *or* 1 5-ounce can (⅔ cup) water chestnuts, drained and sliced thin
1½ cups halved fresh mushrooms
4 cups small spinach leaves, with stems removed

• • •

3 14-ounce cans chicken broth
3 chicken bouillon cubes
1 tablespoon monosodium glutamate
½ tablespoon grated gingerroot *or* ½ teaspoon ground ginger

• • •

Chinese Mustard*
Ginger Soy*
Peanut Sauce*
Red Sauce*
Hot cooked rice

Shortly before cooking time, arrange meats and vegetables on large tray or platter and fill bowl with spinach.

Set out little bowls of the dunking sauces. Provide bamboo tongs, chopsticks, or long-handled forks as cooking tools for guests.

Heat broth to simmering in electric skillet or chafing dish (or use Mongolian cooker as directed at left). Add bouillon cubes and stir to dissolve; add monosodium glutamate and ginger. Heat to *barely* bubbling for cooking.

Each guest picks up desired foods with chopsticks or whatever, drops them into the bubbling broth. When his tidbits are cooked, he lifts them out and dips into the sauces on his plate. (Add more broth if needed.)

Serve with hot fluffy rice and Chinese tea. Makes 4 servings.

*See sauce recipes, next page.

For a wonderful cook-your-own party, plan Chinese Hot Pot!

China *Japan*

Ginger Soy (*for Chinese Hot Pot*)

½ cup soy sauce
1½ teaspoons ginger

Combine soy sauce and ginger. Bring to boiling and serve hot.

Chinese Mustard
(*for Chinese Hot Pot*)

¼ cup boiling water
¼ cup dry English mustard
½ teaspoon salt
2 teaspoons salad oil

Stir boiling water into dry mustard. Add salt and salad oil. For yellower color, add a little turmeric. Makes about ⅓ cup.

Peanut Sauce (*for Chinese Hot Pot*)

½ cup chunk-style peanut butter
1½ tablespoons soy sauce
1 tablespoon water
½ teaspoon sugar
2 drops Tabasco sauce
1 clove garlic, minced
½ cup water

Thoroughly combine first 6 ingredients; slowly stir in the ½ cup water, mixing till smooth. Makes about 1 cup sauce.

Red Sauce (*for Chinese Hot Pot*)

3 tablespoons catsup
3 tablespoons chili sauce
1½ tablespoons prepared horseradish
1 teaspoon lemon juice
Dash Tabasco

Combine all ingredients, mixing well. Season to taste. Makes about ½ cup sauce.

Chinese Fried Rice

Delicious with Chicken Almond—

Fry ½ cup finely diced cooked ham, chicken, or pork lightly in 2 tablespoons hot oil. Add 3 finely sliced fresh mushrooms, 1 quart *cold* cooked rice, 1 finely chopped green onion, and 2 tablespoons soy sauce.

Fry over low heat 10 minutes. Add 1 well-beaten egg; fry and stir 5 minutes more. If color isn't dark enough, add a little more soy sauce. Makes 6 to 8 servings.

Chicken Almond

(*Specialty of Trader Vic's, San Francisco*)

2 cups finely sliced raw
 breast of chicken
¼ cup peanut or salad oil
3 5-ounce cans (2 cups) diced
 bamboo shoots, drained
2 cups diced celery
1 cup diced bok choy (Chinese chard)
 or romaine
2 5-ounce cans (1⅓ cups)
 water chestnuts, drained and sliced
½ cup blanched almonds
2 tablespoons soy sauce
2 teaspoons monosodium glutamate
3 cups chicken broth

• • •

¼ cup cornstarch
½ cup cold water

Fry the chicken in the oil in a preheated, heavy, large pan; add rest of ingredients except cornstarch and water; mix thoroughly. Cover and steam 5 minutes.

Blend cornstarch and cold water; add to chicken and cook, stirring constantly, till mixture thickens. Salt to taste. Garnish with extra almonds. Serve immediately with Chinese Fried Rice. Makes about 8 servings.

Note: High heat and quick stirring are essential. The secret is to avoid overcooking.

What to serve with Chicken Almond? For appetizers, heat packaged frozen egg rolls and fried shrimp; serve with some of the Hot Pot sauces. Serve cucumber slices in vinegar as salad; fruit sherbet and green tea for dessert.

Try chopsticks—they're fun to use!

Hold top stick above center, between *tips* of index and middle fingers; anchor with thumb. Wiggle up and down. Slip lower stick into position shown; rest on ring finger. (Lower stick *never moves.*) Use sticks like tweezers.

A Sukiyaki party can be all-evening dinner *and* entertainment, with everyone getting into the act. The host or hostess starts things off by cooking the first four servings, then continues with the next four or lets a guest take over. Everyone will want to try a hand at the wok* (really your electric skillet), before the evening's over.

Folks add a few bites more to the cooking sauce at whim of appetite. Seconds taste like firsts, tempting and hot. And tardy guests fare as well as early arrivals.

For the beauty of a still-life picture, line up the raw foods in stark simplicity—see tray pictured on page 69. Fill pretty bottles with soy sauce and broth, a tiny dish with sugar, a Japanese soup spoon with monosodium glutamate. Place all near the "wok" and you're ready to begin.

Pocket change buys plain wood chopsticks for the crowd. Afraid of fumbling? Oh, come on, see our directions, give them a try. Your guests will have the time of their lives!

*If your Sukiyaki party's outside, you may want to cook in a real wok. You can find these basin-shaped saucepans in some Oriental shops. To cook, place the wok on its base over an hibachi or other grill. (See wok at back of picture, page 69.)

Sukiyaki

2 to 4 ounces dry bean threads* (optional)

• • •

Few small pieces of beef suet
1 pound beef tenderloin, sliced paper-thin across the grain

• • •

2 tablespoons sugar
1 teaspoon monosodium glutamate
½ cup soy sauce
½ cup beef stock *or* canned condensed beef broth

• • •

2 cups 2-inch length bias-cut green onions
1 cup 2-inch bias-cut celery slices
½ cup thinly sliced fresh mushrooms

• • •

1 5-ounce can (⅔ cup) water chestnuts, drained and thinly sliced
1 5-ounce can (⅔ cup) bamboo shoots, slivered or diced, drained
5 cups small spinach leaves or 2-inch lengths (stems removed)
1 1-pound can bean sprouts, drained
12 to 16 ounces bean curd, cubed* (optional)

Prepare bean threads ahead by soaking 2 hours in cold water; drain.

Just before cooking time, arrange meat and vegetables attractively on large platter or tray. Have small containers of sugar, monosodium glutamate, soy sauce, and beef stock handy. For "toss-stirring" you'll want to use two tools at once—chopsticks or big spoon and fork.

Preheat large (12-inch) skillet or Oriental saucepan; add suet and rub over bottom and sides to grease; when you have about 2 tablespoons melted fat, remove suet. Add beef and cook briskly, turning it over and over, 1 or 2 minutes or just till browned.

Now sprinkle meat with sugar and monosodium glutamate; pour soy sauce and beef stock over. Push meat to one side. Let the soy-sauce mixture bubble.

Keeping in separate groups, add onions, celery, and mushrooms. Continue cooking and toss-stirring *each group* over high heat about 1 minute; push to one side.

Again keeping in separate groups, add remaining vegetables in order given, bean curd, and bean threads. Cook and toss-stir each food just till heated through.

Let guests help themselves to some of everything, including sauce. Serve with rice. Pass cruet of soy sauce. Makes 4 servings.

For more batches of Sukiyaki, leave remaining sauce in pan and add soy sauce, beef stock, and seasonings by guess. Let guests cook as they please.

*Dry bean threads (*shirataki*) are also called "cellophane" noodles or Japanese vermicelli. This product and bean curd (*tofu*) may be found at Japanese food shops, or may be obtained from American mail-order houses that specialize in Oriental foods.

With Sukiyaki, serve hot fluffy rice (for fun, serve in rice bowls or mold individual servings in a custard cup and turn out). Offer cups of green tea with Sukiyaki and afterward pour tea again to go with crisp almond cookies.

Etiquette: Use one set of chopsticks for cooking and fishing out morsels of Sukiyaki; use a second set for eating. (This goes for Chinese Hot Pot, too.) If only one set is provided for each guest, simply reverse your chopsticks (large ends down) when you cook or help yourself to food.

Handy manners—when eating rice with chopsticks, it's polite to hold the rice bowl under your chin!

Pakistan *India*

Colorful, zesty • curries

Chicken Curry

4 tiny ripe pineapples or 1 large
¼ cup sugar
½ cup water
1½ teaspoons curry powder
1 tablespoon butter or margarine
⅓ cup minced onion
⅓ cup diced celery
¼ cup sliced mushrooms
½ cup light cream
½ cup milk
¼ cup chicken broth
1 tablespoon cornstarch
1 tablespoon cold water
1 cup cubed cooked chicken
½ teaspoon monosodium glutamate
¼ teaspoon salt

Leaving green crown intact, cut slice off top of each pineapple; set aside. Scoop out fruit, leaving shells ½ inch thick. Dice ½ cup pineapple (discard core); combine with sugar and water; cook, covered, about 8 minutes. Drain and set aside. Just before cooking curry sauce, heat pineapple shells in very hot oven (450°) about 10 minutes.

Brown curry powder lightly in butter; add vegetables and mix well. Stir in cream, milk, and broth; bring to boil. Combine cornstarch and cold water; stir into hot mixture and cook and stir till sauce thickens.

Add chicken, cooked pineapple, and seasonings; heat through. Serve in hot pineapple shells, placing leafy crowns alongside for trim. Pass condiments. Makes 4 servings.

Saffron Rice

To 2 cups boiling water, add 1 teaspoon salt and 15 grains saffron. Stir in 1 cup long-grain rice; return to boiling, then lower heat, cover and cook over *low* heat till tender and water is absorbed, about 25 minutes. Serve hot with curried chicken, shrimp, or lamb. Makes 3 cups, about 6 servings.

Note: For speed, used packaged yellow rice, preparing according to label directions.

Curried Shrimp

2 tablespoons butter or margarine
1½ cups finely chopped, pared tart apples
2 tablespoons enriched flour
2 to 2½ teaspoons curry powder
2 cups milk
1 teaspoon salt
2 to 3 cups cleaned canned or cooked shrimp (1½ to 2 pounds in shell)
Saffron Rice

Melt butter; add apples and cook 5 minutes. Mix flour and curry powder; stir into apples. Slowly stir in milk. Cook, stirring constantly, till mixture thickens. Add salt. Add the shrimp, and heat through. Serve with fluffy Saffron Rice. Offer choice of condiments from list at right. Makes 5 or 6 servings.

Shrimp Curry In A Hurry

Cook ⅓ cup chopped onion, ¼ cup chopped green pepper, and 1 clove garlic, minced, in butter till tender but not brown.

Stir in 1 cup dairy sour cream, 1 teaspoon curry powder, ¼ teaspoon salt, and dash pepper. Add 1 cup cleaned cooked shrimp. Heat slowly, stirring often, till hot. Serve over hot raisin rice. Makes 4 servings.

Curried Lamb

2 pounds lean lamb breast or shoulder, cubed
1½ teaspoons salt
1 bay leaf
6 whole black peppers
1 medium onion, sliced
1 teaspoon chopped parsley
¼ cup enriched flour
1 teaspoon curry powder
3 tablespoons cold water
Hot cooked rice or Saffron Rice

Brown meat slowly in hot fat; cover meat with boiling water (about 2 cups); add salt, bay leaf, whole peppers, onion, and parsley. Cover and cook slowly 1½ hours, or until meat is tender. Remove meat, and measure 2 cups stock, adding water if necessary.

Mix flour and curry powder; slowly stir in cold water and blend. Stir into stock; cook, stirring constantly, until mixture thickens. Add meat, heat through. Serve with fluffy rice. Offer little bowls of curry condiments—see list at right. Makes 6 servings.

Curry of Shrimp, Suzanne

The Chalet Suzanne, in Lake Wales, Florida, has imported curry, added its own personal touches to this exotic dish. Result—superb!

⅓ cup butter or margarine
3 tablespoons enriched flour
1 to 2 tablespoons curry powder
½ teaspoon salt
¼ teaspoon paprika
Dash nutmeg

• • •

2 cups light cream

• • •

3 cups cleaned cooked shrimp
1 tablespoon finely chopped candied ginger
1 tablespoon lemon juice
1 teaspoon cooking sherry
1 teaspoon onion juice
Dash Worcestershire sauce
Salt to taste

Melt butter; blend in flour, curry powder, salt, paprika, and nutmeg. Gradually stir in cream; cook and stir till mixture thickens.

Add remaining ingredients; heat through. (To match picture, pour into individual casseroles; bake in hot oven (400°) about 10 minutes or until top is lightly browned.)

Serve with Orange Rice and condiments: Currant Chutney, finely shredded orange peel, flaked coconut, chopped roasted peanuts, watermelon pickles. Makes 4 servings. Dessert might be carrot or rice pudding.

Orange Rice

2 cups water
1 tablespoon grated orange peel
½ cup orange juice
1 teaspoon salt
1 cup uncooked long-grain rice

Combine water, orange peel, orange juice, salt; bring to boiling. Stir in rice, return to boiling, then lower heat, cover and cook over *low* heat till tender and liquid is absorbed, about 25 minutes. Serve hot. Makes 3½ cups, about 6 or 7 servings.

Currant Chutney

½ cup chutney, cut in smaller pieces
½ cup red currant jelly
3 tablespoons dried currants
2 tablespoons cooking sherry

Combine all ingredients. Serve as a condiment with Curry of Shrimp, Suzanne.

A famous curry—magnificent!

This one is Curry of Shrimp, Suzanne—pink shrimp nestled in a creamy sauce, seasoned with curry powder, candied ginger, and lemon juice, plus a whiff of nutmeg! Complements are Orange Rice with a baked-tomato bonnet, quartet of condiments.

Condiments add to the fun of serving any curry. Choose from chutney, chopped peanuts and hard-cooked egg, sliced green onions, flaked coconut, plumped raisins, preserved kumquats, and watermelon pickles.

*Cheese Souffle—
the kind you dream
about! It's light
as a cloud, tangy
with sharp cheese.*

Souffles and omelets

Turn out a puffy, golden souffle, a tender omelet and you've made your reputation as a really good cook! Souffles and omelets are easier than you think! We give all the techniques for a successful souffle, along with step-by-step picture directions for both French omelets and fluffy omelets. Special bonus: Scrambled eggs, all ways! Make them extra tasty with herbs, toss in Vienna sausages, or serve scrambled eggs Mexican style. Get out your skillet or souffle dish and take your choice of our good recipes. Mealtime in your house suddenly becomes a big event!

tips *These pointers assure you a puffy souffle*

- Yolks aren't as likely to break if you separate them from the whites while still cold from refrigerator.
- If you let egg whites warm to room temperature before beating, they'll fluff up better.
- Till "thick and lemon-colored" is the word on beating egg yolks. Egg whites are beaten till stiff but still glossy—never till dry.
- Stir the ready-and-waiting hot sauce slowly into the beaten yolks.
- Fold sauce mixture into beaten whites; gently lift up-and-over in high strokes. Take your time.
- Never keep a souffle waiting! Whisk it right from oven to table. Treat this airy dish tenderly—break apart into servings with two forks.

Paper collar: Measure waxed paper to go around top of casserole and overlap 1 inch. Fold in thirds lengthwise.

Butter one side. Letting collar extend 2 inches above casserole, fasten around dish (buttered side in) with cellophane tape or pins. Bake souffle. Gently remove collar before serving.

Cheese Souffle

Feathery light, flavor-rich. With a little sleight of hand, the top of the souffle goes "poof" while baking—

¼ cup butter or margarine
¼ cup enriched flour
1 cup milk
½ teaspoon salt
Dash cayenne
½ pound sharp process American cheese, thinly sliced
4 egg yolks
4 stiff-beaten egg whites

Melt butter; blend in flour. Gradually add milk and cook over low heat until thick, stirring constantly. Add seasonings and cheese; stir till cheese melts. Remove from heat. Beat egg yolks until thick and lemon-colored. Slowly add cheese mixture to egg yolks, stirring constantly. Cool mixture slightly, then pour slowly into beaten egg whites, folding together thoroughly. Pour into *ungreased* 1½-quart casserole or souffle dish.

With the tip of a spatula or spoon, trace a circle through the top of the mixture 1 inch from the edge and about 1 inch deep—see picture on next page.

Bake in slow oven (300°) about 1 hour and 15 minutes, or till mixture doesn't adhere to knife. Serve. Makes 4 servings.

Parsley Cheese Souffle

3 tablespoons butter
3 tablespoons flour
1 cup milk
2 cups shredded sharp process cheese
1 cup cooked rice
¼ cup snipped parsley
½ teaspoon salt
4 egg yolks
4 stiff-beaten egg whites

Melt butter and blend in flour. Add milk; cook and stir till thick. Remove from heat; add shredded cheese; stir to melt. Add rice, parsley, and salt.

Beat egg yolks till thick and lemon-colored; slowly add the hot mixture, stirring constantly. Pour mixture slowly into beaten egg whites, folding together thoroughly. Pour into *ungreased* 2-quart casserole. For top hat make circle around top—see picture, next page. Bake in slow oven (300°) about 50 to 60 minutes or till mixture doesn't adhere to knife. Makes 5 servings.

Stand-up Cheese Souffle

A sturdy cheese souffle that's easy because the white sauce cooks itself!—

- 1½ cups shredded natural Cheddar cheese
- 3 tablespoons butter or margarine
- ¾ cup boiling water
- ¾ cup sifted enriched flour
- ⅔ cup instant nonfat dry milk
- 1 teaspoon salt
- Dash cayenne
- 4 eggs (at room temperature)
- ½ teaspoon cream of tartar
- 1 recipe Mushroom-Cheese Sauce

Place cheese and butter in bowl; stir in *boiling* water. Stir occasionally to help melt cheese. Measure flour, dry milk, salt, and cayenne into sifter. When cheese is melted (there may still be a few cheese flecks), sift dry ingredients on top. *Do not stir.*

Separate eggs; place yolks on top of dry ingredients; place whites in a large bowl. Beat egg whites with cream of tartar till stiff, but not dry, peaks form. Beat cheese mixture till *smooth.*

Into beaten whites, gently but thoroughly fold cheese mixture, by thirds. Pour into ungreased 2-quart souffle dish or casserole. Set in shallow pan; fill pan to 1 inch with *boiling* water. Bake in slow oven (325°) 50 to 60 minutes or till done. Pass Mushroom-Cheese Sauce. Makes 6 servings.

Mushroom-Cheese Sauce: Combine 1 can condensed cream of mushroom soup and ⅓ cup milk; heat through. Add ½ cup shredded Cheddar cheese; stir till melted.

Easy Asparagus Souffle

- 1 can condensed cream of asparagus soup
- ¾ cup shredded sharp process American cheese
- 4 egg yolks
- 4 stiff-beaten egg whites

Heat and stir soup over low heat; add cheese and stir till melted. Remove from heat. Beat egg yolks till thick and lemon-colored. Slowly add cheese mixture to beaten egg yolks, stirring constantly. Pour mixture slowly onto beaten egg whites, folding thoroughly. Pour into ungreased 2-quart casserole and bake in slow oven (300°) 1 hour and 15 minutes, or till mixture doesn't adhere to knife. Serve immediately. Makes 5 servings.

Tuna 'n Rice Souffle

Hearty with tuna and rice . . . simple to make with a can of mushroom soup—

- 1 can condensed cream of mushroom soup
- 1 6½- or 7-ounce can (1 cup) tuna, drained
- 1 cup cooked rice
- ¼ cup chopped pimiento
- 2 tablespoons chopped parsley

. . .

- 4 egg whites
- 4 egg yolks

Heat and stir the soup over low heat. Add tuna, rice, pimiento, and parsley; heat through. Remove from heat. Beat egg whites till stiff. Beat egg yolks till thick and lemon-colored; gradually stir in tuna mixture. Pour mixture slowly onto beaten egg whites, folding together thoroughly.

Pour into ungreased 2-quart casserole. Bake in moderate oven (350°) 30 to 35 minutes or till mixture is set in center.

Serve at once. Pass lemon wedges, if desired. Makes 6 servings.

tips *Here's how to give the souffle a high crown*

For a top hat (it puffs in the oven), use tip of spoon to trace circle in mixture 1 inch from edge and about 1 inch deep. To help the souffle "climb," use ungreased casserole.

Delicious French omelets

Traditional French omelets take the same ingredients as scrambled eggs, but get different in-the-skillet technique. After you take pan from heat, spoon sauteed mushrooms or chicken livers down center. Fold edges over and slip omelet onto plate.

1 The best French omelets are little ones. Use 2 or 3 eggs for each. With fork, beat 3 eggs, 1 tablespoon milk or water, ¼ teaspoon salt, and dash pepper till omelet mixture is blended but not frothy. Heat 8-inch skillet.

2 To skillet add 1 teaspoon butter; brown *lightly*. Tilt pan to grease sides. Add 1 teaspoon fines herbes. Pour in egg—leave heat moderately high. Rapidly stir through top of uncooked egg. Keep omelet at an even depth.

3 As you stir the uncooked egg back and forth, out to edges, cooked bits will come to center. Shake pan all the while to keep omelet sliding. Omelet cooks in 2 or 3 minutes. When egg is set but still shiny, take pan from heat.

Cheese French Omelet

4 well-beaten eggs
3 tablespoons milk
¼ teaspoon salt
Dash pepper
Dash garlic salt
⅛ teaspoon curry powder

• • •

2 tablespoons butter or margarine
½ cup diced sharp process American cheese

Combine eggs, milk, salt, pepper, garlic salt, and curry powder. Melt butter in 8-inch skillet; when hot, add the egg mixture.

Cook over medium heat, running spatula around the edge and lifting to allow the uncooked egg to flow underneath. When the bottom is set and lightly brown, top with diced cheese.

Remove from heat and cover the pan 3 minutes. Fold in half; slip onto warm plate. Trim with parsley fluff. Makes 2 or 3 servings.

Hashed-brown Omelet

4 slices bacon
2 cups shredded cooked potatoes*
¼ cup chopped onion
¼ cup chopped green pepper
• • •
4 eggs
¼ cup milk
½ teaspoon salt
Dash pepper
1 cup shredded sharp process
American cheese

In 10- or 12-inch skillet, cook bacon till crisp. Leave drippings in skillet; remove bacon and crumble.

Mix potatoes, onion, and green pepper; pat into the skillet. Cook over low heat till the underside is crisp and brown.

Blend eggs, milk, salt, and pepper; pour over potatoes. Top with cheese and bacon. Cover; cook over low heat. When egg is done, loosen omelet. Fold in half. Makes 4 servings.

*Or, if you like, use packaged hash-brown potatoes, cooked.

Country Blintze

It's an omelet filled with cottage cheese and onions. Beautiful for a spring brunch—

6 eggs
⅓ cup milk
½ teaspoon salt
Dash pepper
• • •
2 tablespoons butter
or margarine
1 cup large-curd cream-style
cottage cheese
1 to 2 tablespoons chopped green onions
• • •
Crisp-cooked bacon slices
Tomato slices
Parsley

Beat eggs slightly; beat in milk and seasonings. Heat butter in 10-inch skillet; pour in omelet mixture and cook slowly. Run spatula around edge, lifting to allow uncooked portion to flow underneath. When egg is just cooked but still shiny on top, loosen edge. Place cheese in center of omelet; sprinkle with onion; roll edges over.

Slip onto a warm platter. Garnish with bacon, tomato slices, and parsley fluffs. Makes 3 or 4 servings.

Golden Noodle Omelet

1 cup fine noodles
2 tablespoons chopped onion
3 tablespoons shortening
3 eggs
2 tablespoons milk
½ teaspoon salt
Dash pepper
• • •
Parmesan cheese
Speedy Cheese Sauce
1 10-ounce package frozen asparagus
spears, cooked and drained

Cook noodles in boiling salted water; drain. In 10-inch skillet, cook onion in hot fat till tender but not brown. Stir in noodles. Beat eggs, milk, salt, and pepper with a fork until blended but not frothy.

Pour egg mixture over noodles. Cook over medium heat. Shake skillet while cooking so omelet won't stick. When egg is cooked, slide spatula underneath to loosen omelet. Sprinkle top with Parmesan cheese. Fold in half; slip onto warm serving plate. Top with Cheese Sauce and surround with hot asparagus. Serve at once. Makes 4 servings.

Speedy Cheese Sauce: Melt 2 cups shredded sharp process cheese over hot water. Slowly stir in ⅓ cup milk. Makes 1 cup.

Supper Omelet

6 eggs
⅓ cup milk
¼ teaspoon salt
Dash pepper
1 tablespoon butter or margarine
1 recipe Chicken Sauce

Beat eggs slightly; beat in milk and seasonings. Heat butter in 10-inch skillet; pour in omelet mixture and cook slowly. Run the spatula around edge, lifting to allow uncooked portion to flow underneath. When egg is set but still shiny, loosen edge; roll or fold one half over. Serve on warm platter with Chicken Sauce. Makes 3 or 4 servings.

Chicken Sauce

Combine one can condensed cream of chicken soup, one 3-ounce can (⅔ cup) broiled sliced mushrooms with liquid, 2 tablespoons each of chopped green pepper, chopped pimiento, and chopped ripe olives, 2 teaspoons chopped chives, and ½ teaspoon monosodium glutamate. Heat thoroughly.

Red Caviar Omelet for gourmets Talk about flavor! The exotic, salty tang of red caviar and the tartness of sour cream contrast with the delicate goodness of a French Omelet. At Publick House, Sturbridge, Massachusetts, this luncheon may start off with melon appetizer.

Red Caviar Omelet with Sour Cream

(*Luncheon specialty from the Publick House*)

This famous omelet might be accompanied by iced melon, topped with lime sherbet. Bread is old-time johnnycake, oven-hot.

For omelet, use ingredients given in the step-by-step recipe for French Omelet, page 94; increase butter to 1 tablespoon and omit the fines herbes. Cook as directed.

While the omelet is still soft and creamy, let stand for a few seconds, then tilt pan at right angles toward a hot plate, and with fork, fold omelet over and turn out.

Garnish top of folded omelet with band of red caviar—as much as you can afford! Beside it, spoon on a band of snowy sour cream. Trim with parsley sprigs.

Olympia Oyster Hangtown Fry

(*Served at Tarantino's in San Francisco*)

⅓ cup (8) fresh medium oysters
2 slightly beaten eggs
1 tablespoon water
⅓ to ½ cup dry bread crumbs

• • •

2 slices bacon
Salt and pepper

Dip oysters in mixture of egg and water; roll in dry bread crumbs. Fry bacon in 6-inch skillet till crisp; remove bacon and all but about 1 tablespoon of fat. Add oysters and brown quickly, turning often.

Add bacon; pour in remaining egg mixture; season with salt and pepper. Cook till slightly brown and just set. Turn and brown. Serve on hot plate. Makes 1 or 2 servings.

Sunday-supper treat—scrambled eggs

Extra-special Scrambled Eggs

And we mean just that! The superb seasonings make these delicious—

6 eggs
½ teaspoon salt
¼ teaspoon monosodium glutamate
Dash pepper
1 teaspoon prepared mustard
⅓ cup light cream
2 tablespoons minced parsley
• • •
2 tablespoons minced onion
2 tablespoons fat

Beat eggs with salt, monosodium glutamate, pepper, and mustard; stir in light cream and minced parsley.

Cook onion in hot fat until tender but not brown; add egg mixture. Cook slowly, stirring frequently, until eggs are just set. Makes 3 or 4 servings.

Herbed Scrambled Eggs

Simple, but scrumptious! Parsley, chives, and thyme do the trick—

4 eggs
¼ cup light cream
½ teaspoon salt
Dash pepper
• • •
2 tablespoons butter or margarine
• • •
1 tablespoon chopped parsley
1 tablespoon chopped chives
Dash thyme, crushed

Beat eggs, cream, salt, and pepper with fork. (Mix slightly if you like eggs to have streaks of yellow and white; mix well if you prefer a uniform yellow.)

Melt butter in skillet; when hot, pour in egg mixture; sprinkle parsley, chives, and thyme on top. When mixture starts to set at bottom and sides, lift cooked portions with wide spatula so uncooked mixture goes to the bottom of skillet. Continue cooking till the eggs are cooked throughout, but still are glossy and moist.

Serve immediately on warm plate with little pork sausages or Canadian bacon. Garnish with parsley. Makes 2 to 3 servings.

Sausage-Egg Scramble

Light and fluffy, polka-dotted with color. A natural for your electric skillet—

3 tablespoons butter or margarine
2 4-ounce cans Vienna sausages
8 eggs
½ cup milk
1 teaspoon salt
Dash pepper
¼ cup chopped pimiento
¼ cup chopped green pepper
¼ cup chopped green onions

Preheat electric skillet (about 350°). Brown Vienna sausages in hot butter; reduce heat (to about 320°). Beat the eggs, milk, salt, and pepper with fork. (Mix slightly for streaks of yellow and white in eggs; mix well if you prefer eggs of a uniform yellow.) Pour in egg mixture; sprinkle chopped pimiento, green pepper, and onion on top. When mixture starts to set at bottom and sides, lift cooked portions with wide spatula so uncooked mixture goes to bottom of skillet.

Continue cooking till the eggs are cooked throughout, but still glossy and moist. Serve immediately. Makes 4 to 5 servings.

Mexican Scramble

1 cup chopped onion
1 cup chopped green pepper
2 tablespoons butter
  or margarine
1 cup canned solid-pack tomatoes
¾ teaspoon salt
½ teaspoon paprika
Dash pepper
¼ pound American process cheese,
  diced (1 cup)
3 beaten eggs
• • •
4 slices buttered toast

Cook onion and green pepper in butter till tender but not brown. Add tomatoes and simmer 5 minutes. Add seasonings and cheese; stir to melt cheese. Stir small amount of hot mixture into eggs; return to hot mixture.

Cook till thick (like scrambled eggs), but moist, stirring frequently. Serve over hot buttered toast. Makes 4 servings.

Light as air–fluffy omelets

1 For Fluffy Omelet, beat 4 egg yolks till *very thick*. Beat 4 whites frothy; add ¼ cup water and ¼ teaspoon salt; beat stiff but not dry. With rubber spatula, fold yolks into the whites.

2 Melt 1 tablespoon butter in 10-inch skillet. When hot, pour in omelet mixture; spread evenly. Reduce heat; cook slowly about 8 minutes. Brown top in oven at 325° 10 minutes.

3 Loosen sides. Make shallow cut across center of omelet at right angles to handle. Slip spatula under the half near handle; tilt pan. Fold omelet. Hold pan on platter; tip omelet out.

Follow the steps at left for a perfect fluffy omelet every time! You beat yolks and whites separately, then mix; puff the omelet top-of-range and bake to a golden brown. Spoon cheese sauce over the top; garnish platter. This Fluffy Omelet serves 3 or 4. Don't cut it—tear gently apart with two forks.

Puffy Cottage Cheese Omelet

3 eggs, separated
Dash pepper
1 cup cream-style small-curd cottage cheese, drained
¼ teaspoon salt
1 tablespoon butter or margarine
1 recipe Quick Mushroom Sauce
1 10-ounce package frozen asparagus, cooked and drained

Beat egg yolks till *very thick*; add pepper and the cheese; continue beating until well blended. Beat whites till frothy; add salt; beat till stiff but not dry. Fold yolks into whites. Melt butter in 10-inch skillet. When hot, pour in omelet mixture; spread evenly with spatula. Reduce heat, cook slowly 10 to 12 minutes or till puffy and golden on bottom.

Brown top in slow oven (325°) 12 to 15 minutes. Flip out of pan onto warm platter, following picture directions for Fluffy Omelet, left. Spoon Quick Mushroom Sauce over. Serve with hot cooked asparagus. Makes 4 to 6 servings.

Quick Mushroom Sauce

Stir 1 cup dairy sour cream into 1 can condensed cream of mushroom soup; heat through. Makes 4 to 6 servings.

Cheese-filled Omelet

Billowy omelet layers, with instant cheese sauce between—

8 egg yolks
¼ cup enriched flour
Dash pepper
• • •
8 egg whites
¼ cup water
1 teaspoon salt
1 8-ounce jar triple-use cheese spread
Currant jelly

Combine egg yolks, flour, and pepper; beat till *very thick*. Beat whites till frothy; add water and salt; beat till stiff but not dry. Fold yolk mixture into whites, gently but thoroughly. Pile into 2 *well-greased*, *hot* 8-inch shallow round baking dishes. Bake in moderate oven (350°) 15 minutes, or till done. Melt cheese over very low heat.

Put omelets together, layer-cake style, with cheese between. Dot top with jelly. Serve at once, cutting into pie-shaped wedges with two forks. Makes 6 servings.

Sour Cream-Ham Omelet

Serve with Glazed Apples—makes a tempting main dish for brunch or lunch—

5 egg yolks
1 cup dairy sour cream
¼ teaspoon salt
• • •
5 stiff-beaten egg whites
1 cup finely diced cooked ham
2 tablespoons butter, margarine, or fat

Beat egg yolks till thick and lemon-colored; beat in *half* of the sour cream and the salt. Fold in egg whites and ham. Heat butter in 10-inch skillet; pour in omelet mixture, leveling gently. Cook over low heat until lightly browned on bottom, about 5 minutes. Finish cooking in slow oven (325°) till top is golden brown, about 12 minutes. Loosen omelet; slide onto warm plate. Cut in wedges with two forks. Garnish with remaining sour cream and Glazed Apples. Makes 4 servings.

Glazed Apples

Sweet partner for omelets. Nice with sausage or roast pork, too—

3 tablespoons butter or margarine
⅓ cup brown sugar
¾ teaspoon cinnamon
Dash salt
3 unpared tart apples, thinly sliced

Melt butter in skillet; stir in brown sugar, cinnamon, and salt. Add the apples. Cook 10 to 15 minutes, stirring occasionally, till the apples are tender and glazed.

Macaroni Omelet

½ cup elbow macaroni
½ cup finely diced sharp process cheese
• • •
4 egg yolks
¼ teaspoon salt
4 stiff-beaten egg whites
2 tablespoons butter, margarine, or fat
1 recipe Creole Sauce

Cook macaroni in boiling salted water till tender; drain. Combine with cheese. Beat egg yolks with salt till thick and lemon-colored; add to macaroni mixture. Fold in egg whites. Melt butter in 10-inch skillet; when hot, pour in omelet mixture. Cook over low heat 8 to 10 minutes; finish cooking in slow oven (325°) 5 minutes or till lightly browned. Loosen with spatula. Make shallow cut across center of omelet; fold in half. Remove to hot platter; serve with Creole Sauce. Makes 4 to 6 servings.

Creole Sauce

3 tablespoons finely chopped onion
3 tablespoons finely chopped green pepper
2 tablespoons butter or margarine
• • •
1 8-ounce can (1 cup) seasoned tomato sauce
1 3-ounce can (⅔ cup) broiled sliced mushrooms, drained
¼ teaspoon salt
Dash pepper

Cook onion and green pepper in butter till tender but not brown. Add remaining ingredients. Simmer 10 minutes. Makes 1⅓ cups sauce. Serve with Macaroni Omelet.

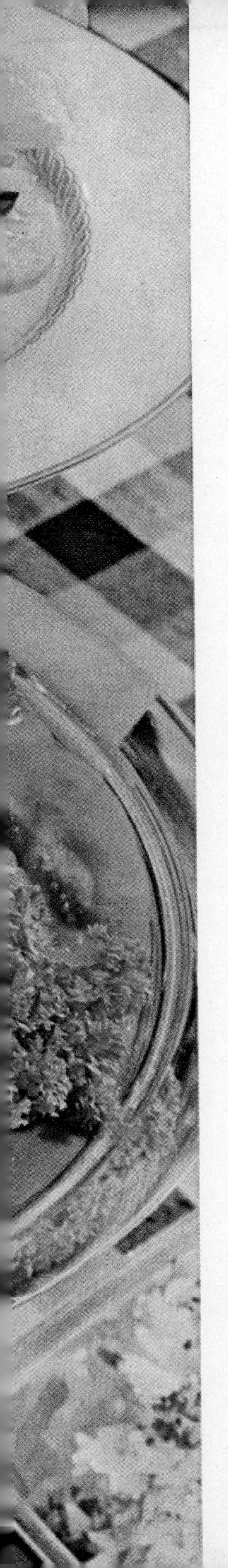

Chafing-dish classics

You couldn't ask for a more charming way to entertain than with a chafing-dish supper. The cooking flame adds its friendly glow to the candlelight. No chafing dish? Use an electric skillet. You serve casually in the living room, cook before guests with the fanfare of a magician. Choose from tangy Stroganoffs, sea-food Newburgs, a la Kings, rich cheese fondue or rabbits—fame is yours!

← ***Fit for a king—Beef Stroganoff***

It's a wonderful combination of tender beef strips, mushrooms, and lusciously rich sour-cream sauce. First served in the Gay '90s by a Russian count, Beef Stroganoff is so easy, impressive, and *good* that it's still a perfect choice for entertaining! See page 103.

Fanfare with meat, mushrooms

Here are glamour foods for your chafing dish—or electric skillet—that you can cook with a flourish, serve with pride. (Any of these tasty main dishes can be prepared in an on-the-range skillet, too, if you wish.)

First step toward cooking for an audience: Know your gear. Each chafing dish has a personality of its own which affects length of cooking time.

Chafing dishes come in many handsome styles, from tiny ones for single servings to jumbo sizes for more than 20. And they come with different kinds of heating devices.

For actual cooking at the table, most folks vote for heat you can adjust, whether alcohol, canned heat, or an electric unit.

Some chafing dishes are actually double boilers (*bain-marie*) with water pan and a cooking pan (blazer). The cooking pan is generally used directly over the flame. But when cooking sauces with several egg yolks, or cheese rabbits, you cook over hot water. When cooking in blazer pan, add water bath when cooking is done, to keep food warm.

Other chafing dishes are the deep skillet type with just one pan—cook in these as you would in blazer pan of the *bain-marie.*

There are special chafing dishes for fondues. The Continental choice for cheese fondue is an earthenware casserole on a heating unit, but any chafing dish can double nicely. Meat fondue calls for a deep one-pan chafing dish to hold hot oil. (An electric saucepan will work, too.)

Food warmers keep cooked foods at serving temperature on the buffet. They might be pottery casseroles, or metal dishes with heat-proof glass liners. Candles, alcohol burners, or electric units furnish heat. A *bain-marie* can serve as warmer, too.

Choose speedy recipes. If the sauce takes more than a few minutes, you'll probably want to thicken it ahead of time. Heat in the chafing dish, add remaining ingredients at the table.

Have everything ready for the main dish before guests arrive. Plan the rest of the meal so it takes minimum pre-serving preparation. Assemble cooking tools and ingredients on a tray for use at table. Now you're ready to go. Happy hostessing!

Company Ham in Sour Cream

1 cup cooked ham in julienne strips
¼ cup chopped onion
2 tablespoons butter or margarine
2 teaspoons enriched flour
1 cup dairy sour cream
1 6-ounce can (1⅓ cups) broiled sliced mushrooms, drained

In blazer pan of chafing dish, or skillet, cook ham and onion in butter till onion is tender but not brown. Sprinkle with flour; gradually stir in sour cream. Add mushrooms. Cook and stir over low heat, just till mixture thickens. Keep warm over hot water. Serve with fluffy rice. Makes 3 or 4 servings.

Chafing Chuck

Cook one 10-ounce package frozen Limas according to package directions; drain.

Combine 1 pound ground beef, 1 clove garlic, minced, 2 tablespoons cornstarch, 1½ tablespoons sugar, 1 teaspoon monosodium glutamate, 2 tablespoons soy sauce, few drops Tabasco sauce, and ½ cup water.

In blazer pan of chafing dish, cook meat mixture in hot oil till browned. Add Limas and 1 teaspoon horseradish. Cook and stir till hot through. Makes 6 servings. Pass hot buttered French bread, green salad.

Speedy Stroganoff with Noodles

3 minute steaks, cut in strips
1 medium onion, sliced
1 clove garlic, crushed
1 can condensed cream of mushroom soup
1 cup dairy sour cream
1 3-ounce can broiled sliced mushrooms
2 tablespoons catsup
2 teaspoons Worcestershire sauce

In blazer pan of chafing dish, or skillet, brown meat strips in hot fat. Add onion and garlic; cook till onion is just tender. Blend remaining ingredients. Pour over meat; heat through. Keep warm over hot water.

Cook 6 ounces noodles, drain, toss with 1 tablespoon each butter and poppy seed. Serve Stroganoff sauce over. Serves 4.

Perfect for cook-at-the-table drama—Beef Stroganoff

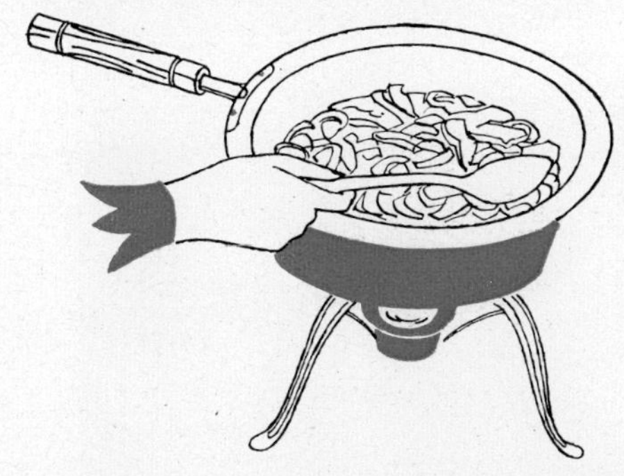

1 Use blazer pan of chafing dish over direct flame. Brown floured meat, then add mushrooms, onion, garlic; cook. Remove from pan.

2 Add more butter to drippings, thicken with flour, and add tomato paste. Slowly pour in the meat stock. Cook and stir till thick.

3 Return meat and mushrooms to pan. Stir in sour cream and sherry; heat. Place over hot-water bath. Serve over hot rice.

Classic Beef Stroganoff

How about caviar appetizers? And offer black-bread sandwiches, pickled-beet and cucumber salad, a fruit and cheese dessert—

1 tablespoon flour
½ teaspoon salt
1 pound beef sirloin, cut in
¼-inch strips
2 tablespoons butter
1 cup thinly sliced mushrooms
½ cup chopped onion
1 clove garlic, minced
2 tablespoons butter
3 tablespoons flour
1 tablespoon tomato paste
1¼ cups beef stock *or*
1 can condensed beef broth
1 cup dairy sour cream
2 tablespoons cooking sherry

Combine 1 tablespoon flour and the salt; dredge meat in mixture. Heat blazer pan of chafing dish, or skillet, then add 2 tablespoons butter. When melted, add the sirloin strips and brown quickly, flipping meat to turn all sides. Add mushroom slices, onion, and garlic; cook 3 or 4 minutes or till onion is barely tender. Remove meat and mushrooms from blazer pan to handy plate.

Add 2 tablespoons butter to pan drippings; when melted, blend in 3 tablespoons flour. Add tomato paste. Now slowly pour in cold meat stock. Cook and stir till thickened.

Return browned meat and mushrooms to blazer pan. Stir in sour cream and cooking sherry; heat briefly. Keep warm over hot water. Makes 4 or 5 servings.

Serve over parsleyed rice, hot buttered noodles, buckwheat groats, or pilaf.

Creamed Mushrooms

¼ cup butter or margarine
½ pound fresh mushrooms, sliced
2 tablespoons enriched flour
1¼ cups milk
1 to 2 teaspoons soy sauce
4 Toast Cups, page 113

Melt butter in blazer pan of chafing dish. Add sliced mushrooms; cook gently till tender and lightly browned. Push mushrooms to one side of pan; blend in flour. Slowly stir in milk. Cook and stir till thick. Add soy sauce and salt and pepper to taste.

Keep warm over hot water. Serve over crisp Toast Cups. Makes 4 servings.

Beef Fondue—terrific for a party; simple

It's a course by itself, or a whole snack. Each guest rates a bowl of cubed beef tenderloin. He spears a piece on long fondue fork, cooks it in chafing dish of hot oil. Then into a zesty sauce or butter—mighty good!

Beef Fondue

Salad oil
1½ pounds trimmed beef tenderloin, cut in ¾-inch cubes (3 cups)
Butters and sauces for dipping

Pour salad oil in beef fondue cooker or *deep* chafing dish* to depth of about 1½ inches. Place over direct heat on range and bring to 425° or just below smoking point. Then take to table and place over heating unit.

Have beef cubes at room temperature in serving bowl. Set out small bowls of several of the butters and sauces given at right. Each guest spears beef cube with fork, then holds it in hot oil until done as desired. He then dips it in a sauce on his plate.

Note: When salad oil cools so meat no longer cooks briskly, heat oil again on range. Treat hot oil with respect—be ever so careful in moving the pan.

*Or use an electric saucepan; oil can be heated at table, kept at proper temperature.

Garlic Butter

Whip ½ cup softened butter till fluffy. Stir in 1 clove garlic, minced. Makes ½ cup.

Anchovy Butter

Drain one 2-ounce can anchovies; place in mixer with ½ cup softened butter, 2 tablespoons olive oil, ½ teaspoon paprika, and ⅛ teaspoon pepper; beat smooth. Makes 1 cup.

Tomato Steak Sauce

Mix one 8-ounce can seasoned tomato sauce, ⅓ cup bottled steak sauce, 2 tablespoons brown sugar and 2 tablespoons salad oil. Bring to boil. Serve hot. Makes 1½ cups.

Creamy Horseradish Sauce

Combine 1 cup sour cream, 3 tablespoons drained prepared horseradish, ¼ teaspoon salt, dash paprika. Chill. Makes 1¼ cups.

Superb sea-food sauces

Shrimp Newburg

⅓ cup butter or margarine
2 tablespoons enriched flour
2 cups light cream
4 slightly beaten egg yolks
2 cups cleaned, cooked or canned shrimp (1½ pounds in shell)
½ teaspoon salt
¼ cup cooking sherry
2 teaspoons lemon juice

Melt butter in blazer pan of chafing dish, or in skillet; blend in flour; gradually stir in cream. Cook slowly, stirring constantly, till sauce thickens. Place hot water bath under blazer pan of chafing dish.

Stir small amount sauce into egg yolks; return to chafing dish and cook till blended, stirring constantly, about 1 minute. Add shrimp and salt; heat thoroughly.

Add cooking sherry and lemon juice. Sprinkle with paprika. Serve over pastry or toast shells, page 113. Makes 5 or 6 servings.

To round out the meal—jellied cranberry slices, buttered asparagus; a salad of orange and onion slices, curly endive and lettuce. For dessert, lemon chiffon pie, hot tea.

Speedy Shrimp Newburg

1 can frozen condensed cream of shrimp soup
½ cup milk
1 cup cooked cleaned shrimp (¾ pound shrimp in the shell or 7 or 8 ounces frozen shelled shrimp)
½ 10-ounce package (1 cup) frozen peas, cooked and drained
1 to 2 tablespoons triple-use cheese spread
1 to 2 tablespoons cooking sherry
4 Toast Rings, page 113

In blazer pan of chafing dish, or in saucepan, combine soup and milk; add shrimp and peas. Heat and stir just till simmering. Cook slowly about 5 minutes. Add cheese and cooking sherry. Keep warm over hot water. Serve over hot Toast Rings.

Garnish with additional cooked shrimp and water cress, if desired. Makes 4 servings.

Shrimp in Cheese Sauce

Nice for company—shrimp and green peas in well-seasoned cheese sauce. Serve in crisp pretty toast cups; pass fruit salad—

2 tablespoons butter or margarine
2 tablespoons enriched flour
1 cup milk

• • •

¼ teaspoon salt
Dash pepper
1 teaspoon Worcestershire sauce
½ cup shredded, sharp process American cheese

• • •

2 cups cooked cleaned shrimp (1½ pounds shrimp in shell)
½ 10-ounce package (1 cup) frozen peas, cooked and drained
1 teaspoon lemon juice

• • •

6 Toast Cups, page 113

Melt butter in blazer pan of chafing dish, or in skillet. Blend in flour. Add milk gradually and cook till thick, stirring constantly. Add salt, pepper, and Worcestershire sauce. Add cheese; stir till melted.

Add shrimp, peas, and lemon juice. Heat thoroughly. Serve in Toast Cups or other shells. Makes 6 servings.

Easy Shrimp Saute

Nothing could be quicker, and it's a real treat for shrimp fans!—

⅓ cup butter or margarine
1 clove garlic, minced
1½ pounds cleaned raw shrimp (2 pounds shrimp in shell)
⅓ cup cooking sherry
2 tablespoons snipped parsley
Hot yellow rice

Melt butter in blazer pan of chafing dish, or in skillet; add garlic and cook slightly. Add shrimp and cook till shrimp are tender and turn pink, about 5 minutes, stirring frequently. Stir in cooking sherry. Sprinkle with parsley. Serve with rice. Serves 4.

Lobster Newburg

⅓ cup butter or margarine
2 tablespoons enriched flour
1½ cups light cream
• • •
3 beaten egg yolks
• • •
1 5-ounce can (1 cup) lobster, cubed
3 to 4 tablespoons cooking sherry
2 teaspoons lemon juice
Salt
Paprika
• • •
4 Patty Shells, page 114, *or* 4 Toast Rings, page 113

Melt butter in blazer pan of chafing dish, or in skillet; blend in flour. Gradually stir in cream. Cook slowly, stirring constantly, till sauce thickens. Place hot water bath under blazer pan, if using chafing dish.

Stir small amount of hot mixture into egg yolks, return to hot mixture; cook, stirring constantly, till thick. Add lobster; heat. Add cooking sherry and lemon juice. Salt to taste. Sprinkle with paprika.

Serve on Patty Shells or on Toast Rings. Makes 4 servings.

Lobster Supreme

1 10-ounce package frozen artichoke hearts
1 bay leaf
• • •
1 can condensed cream of mushroom soup
½ cup light cream
2 tablespoons cooking sherry
• • •
½ cup shredded sharp process American cheese
1 tablespoon chopped onion
Dash garlic salt
1 5-ounce can (1 cup) lobster, drained and cut in bite-size pieces
4 Pastry Petal Cups, page 113

Cook artichoke hearts as directed on package, adding bay leaf. Drain; remove bay leaf.

Combine soup, cream, and sherry in blazer pan of chafing dish, or in skillet, stirring till smooth. Add cheese, onion, and garlic salt. Cook and stir till cheese is melted.

Add artichoke hearts and lobster; heat through. Keep warm over hot water or in skillet. Serve in Pastry Petal Cups, or over wild or fluffy rice. Makes 4 servings.

Real elegance in a chafing dish—creamy Lobster Newburg

This glamorous creation hails from the carefree Gay '90s, is as richly delicious now as it was then.

Prepare Newburg with a flourish, serve over flaky Patty Shells. Pass buttered green beans with mushrooms, broiled tomato halves, and crisp coleslaw with sour-cream dressing. Pick a Gibson Girl dessert favorite, too—Peaches Melba, with hot tea.

To make Peaches Melba: Thoroughly combine one 10-ounce package frozen raspberries, thawed and crushed, with 1½ teaspoons cornstarch; add ½ cup currant jelly. Bring to boil. Cook and stir till clear and slightly thick. Strain; cool. Serve over peach halves (two No. 2½ cans) put together with cream cheese and chopped nut mixture. Makes 6 to 8 servings.

Crab-meat Newburg

A gourmet dish for your fanciest party—

1½ tablespoons butter or margarine
1½ tablespoons enriched flour
1½ cups light cream
3 slightly beaten egg yolks
1 6½- or 7½-ounce can (about 1 cup) crab meat, flaked
2 tablespoons cooking sherry
1½ teaspoons lemon juice
¼ teaspoon salt
6 Popovers, page 113

Melt butter in blazer pan of chafing dish, or in skillet; blend in flour; add cream. Cook and stir till sauce thickens. Place hot water bath under blazer pan, if using chafing dish.

Stir small amount hot mixture into egg yolks; return to remaining hot mixture. Cook and stir till thick. Add crab meat, cooking sherry, lemon juice, and salt; heat.

Sprinkle with paprika. Serve in Popovers or pastry shells. Makes 6 servings.

Pass fresh-fruit cups, crisp crackers for guests to sample while they watch. Serve up the Newburg; let folks choose from colorful platter of chilled fresh and marinated vegetables. Last, an elegant torte and demitasse.

Tuna a la King with Cornsticks

1 box corn-muffin or corn-bread mix
¼ cup chopped green pepper
1 teaspoon minced onion
2 tablespoons butter or margarine
¼ cup enriched flour
1½ cups milk
1 6½- or 7-ounce can (1 cup) tuna
1 3-ounce can (⅔ cup) broiled sliced mushrooms, drained
¼ cup chopped pimiento
¼ teaspoon salt
¼ teaspoon paprika

Make corn-bread sticks or muffins, according to package directions. Bake; then keep warm till serving time.

In blazer pan of chafing dish or in skillet, cook green pepper and onion in butter till just tender, stirring frequently. Blend in flour; gradually stir in milk; cook and stir till thick.

Leave tuna in large pieces; add with mushrooms, pimiento, and seasonings. Heat through. Keep warm over hot water. Serve over crisp hot cornsticks or split muffins. Makes 6 servings.

Creamed Oysters on Toast

1 pint oysters
1 tablespoon butter
1 tablespoon enriched flour
1 cup canned beef broth or bouillon
1 cup light cream
4 egg yolks, beaten
2 teaspoons lemon juice
2 tablespoons minced parsley
6 Toast Rings, page 113

Simmer oysters in their own liquor over very low heat 8 to 10 minutes, or till edges curl and oysters are plump. Drain.

Melt butter in blazer pan of chafing dish, or in skillet. Blend in flour. Stir in broth. Cook and stir till thickened. Stir in cream; heat through.

Place hot water bath under blazer pan, if using chafing dish. Add a little hot sauce to egg yolks; return to hot mixture. Stir constantly till thickened.

Add oysters. Heat through. Stir in lemon juice. Sprinkle with parsley. Serve on Toast Rings. Makes 6 servings.

New England Creamed Codfish

1 pound salt codfish
2 tablespoons butter or margarine
2 tablespoons enriched flour
2 cups milk
2 egg yolks, beaten
2 tablespoons grated onion
2 teaspoons lemon juice

*To freshen codfish:** Wash codfish under running water 15 minutes. Cover with cold water; bring to boiling. Simmer uncovered 5 minutes. Drain, again cover with cold water and repeat simmering. Drain and flake, removing any skin and all bones.

In a skillet, melt butter; blend in flour and dash pepper. Slowly stir in milk, then cook and stir till thickened.

Now transfer mixture to blazer pan of chafing dish. Add small amount of hot sauce to egg yolks; return to remaining hot mixture. Add fish, onion, and lemon juice. Heat through.

Keep warm over hot water. Serve over boiled new potatoes or toast. Serves 6.

*You can also freshen salt codfish overnight: Wash fish 5 minutes. Soak in cold water overnight. Drain. Rinse in cold water and drain. Cover with cold water; bring to boiling and simmer 10 minutes. Drain and flake, removing any skin and all bones.

Elegant chafing-dish chicken

The Original Chicken a la King

¼ cup chopped green pepper
1 cup mushrooms, thinly sliced
2 tablespoons enriched flour
¾ teaspoon salt
2 cups light cream
3 cups cooked chicken cut in pieces
3 egg yolks
½ teaspoon paprika
¼ cup soft butter
1 teaspoon onion juice
1 tablespoon lemon juice
2 tablespoons cooking sherry
¼ cup diced pimiento

In blazer pan of chafing dish or in saucepan, cook green pepper and mushrooms in 2 tablespoons butter until tender but not brown. Push vegetables to one side and blend flour and salt into the butter. Gradually stir in cream; cook and stir until sauce thickens. Add chicken, and heat thoroughly, stirring occasionally.

Meanwhile, in small bowl, blend egg yolks, paprika, and soft butter; set aside.

To chicken mixture, add onion juice, lemon juice, and sherry. Be sure chicken is bubbling; place blazer pan over water bath. Add yolk mixture all at once, stirring till blended. (If using saucepan, remove from heat immediately.) Add pimiento.

Garnish with parsley, toast chickens (cut from bread with cooky cutter). Serve at once in Cheese Toast Cups. Serves 8.

Quick Chicken a la King

1 6-ounce can broiled sliced mushrooms
½ cup chopped green pepper
½ cup chopped celery
2 tablespoons butter or margarine
2 cans condensed cream of chicken soup
2 cups diced cooked chicken or turkey
¼ cup chopped pimiento
¼ teaspoon monosodium glutamate

Drain mushrooms, reserving ¼ cup liquid. In blazer pan, cook pepper and celery in butter till tender. Stir in soup and mushroom liquid. Add mushrooms, remaining ingredients. Season to taste. Heat. Serve in Cheese Toast Cups. Makes 7 servings.

Cheese Toast Cups

1 1-pound 4-ounce unsliced sandwich loaf
⅓ cup butter, melted

• • •

Cheese-custard Lining:
1 beaten egg
½ cup light cream
2 cups (½ pound) shredded sharp process American cheese

Freeze bread for easy handling. Trim crusts from unsliced loaf; cut in 6 jumbo slices, each 1¾ inches wide. Continue as below.

For triangular toast cups: Cut each big slice diagonally in half. On the long side of each triangle, cut a slit ¼ inch from the bottom, extending to within ¼ inch of the corners and other sides—careful, don't cut through. Leaving ¼ inch around all sides, cut a triangle straight down from the top all the way to the slit. Lift out inner triangle. Add Cheese-custard Lining. Bake in moderate oven (350°) 15 to 20 minutes or till golden brown and custard is set. Fill with Chicken a la King.

For Cheese-custard Lining: Place bread cups on ungreased baking sheet; brush with butter, inside and out. Combine egg, cream, and cheese; fill cups ½ full.

Cut slits in toast boxes as shown. *For square toast cups:* Prepare same as triangular cups, but make *one* cup from each slice of bread, cutting bottom and sides ½ inch thick.

No dish has enjoyed greater popularity than Chicken a la King!

Swiss fondue, saucy rabbits

Nothing could be simpler to serve than Cheese Fondue. It's simple, solos as the whole meal (just pass beverage afterward).

The key to perfect fondue is in constant stirring and in keeping mixture barely bubbling. To follow ancient custom, always stir in same direction with a wooden fork.

Guests take a turn with the cooking *while they eat*. Here's how: Spear a chunk of bread so tines go through soft part first, then through the sturdy crust. Now dip it in the melted cheese and keep the fondue in motion till your neighbor is ready to continue the chain stirring. Twirl your fork as you withdraw your morsel of cheese-coated bread.

When nearly all the fondue has been eaten, the remainder will brown. Gourmets consider this crust a special treat.

About gear: You'll want a wood fork for silent stirring, long-handled forks for guests to use. Page 102 tells about fondue cooker. See recipes for fondue, rabbits, next page.

Famous Swiss Cheese Fondue

This subtly flavored delicacy is the national favorite and no wonder! It's delicious *and* fun to eat—everyone dips from the cooking pot!

The Swiss say to skip salad and no cold drink, please. At the very last, offer freshly brewed coffee or tea, or steaming mugs of apple juice.

Cheese Fondue

¾ pound natural Swiss cheese, cut in julienne strips (about 3 cups)
1 tablespoon enriched flour
1 clove garlic, halved
1¼ cups cooking sauterne
Dash freshly ground pepper
Dash nutmeg
3 tablespoons cooking sherry
French bread, cut in bite-size pieces, each with at least one side of crust

Toss cheese with flour to coat. Rub inside of fondue cooker or chafing dish (use with water bath) vigorously with cut surface of garlic. Pour in sauterne; warm just till air bubbles start to rise (don't cover, don't boil).

Stir all the time from now on: Add a handful of cheese. Wait till cheese has melted (keep stirring!) before tossing in another handful. After all the cheese has been blended in, and mixture is bubbling *gently*, stir in seasonings and sherry. (Omit salt; cooking wines contain it.) Now invite guests to dunk. Each spears a cube of bread on a long-handled fork and dips into melted cheese. (If fondue becomes too thick, pour in a little *warmed* sauterne.) Makes 5 or 6 servings.

Give velvet-glove treatment to natural cheese—

To keep natural cheese smooth in cooking, place sauce over hot water before adding the cheese. (Use water bath with chafing dish, or a double boiler.) Crumble or shred cheese, or cut julienne style; stir into hot mixture.

Welsh Rabbit Sandwiches

½ pound shredded sharp process cheese
½ cup milk
1 teaspoon dry mustard
1 teaspoon Worcestershire sauce
2 dashes cayenne
1 egg, well beaten
4 slices hot buttered toast
4 tomato slices

Heat cheese and milk in blazer pan of chafing dish (use over water bath), or in skillet over *very low heat*, stirring constantly till cheese melts and sauce is smooth.

Add seasonings. Stir some hot mixture into egg; return to hot mixture; stir till mixture thickens and is creamy. Serve immediately over hot toast topped with tomato slices. Makes 4 servings.

Midnight-snack Rabbit

Combine 1 can condensed cream of mushroom soup and 2 cups shredded sharp process cheese in blazer pan of chafing dish or top of double boiler (use either one over hot water). Heat till cheese melts and mixture is hot, stirring occasionally.

Add ¼ cup sliced ripe olives and ¼ cup diced green pepper. Heat. Serve over hot toast points or slices of rye bread. Makes 4 or 5 servings. Pass chilled tomato juice, crisp celery sticks, mugs of hot coffee.

Swiss Rabbit Stack-ups

¼ cup finely chopped onion
3 tablespoons butter or margarine
3 tablespoons enriched flour
1 chicken bouillon cube
¾ cup hot water
1 cup milk
½ cup shredded process Swiss cheese
½ cup grated Parmesan cheese
4 or 5 open-face sandwiches of sliced boiled ham and hot asparagus on toast

In blazer pan of chafing dish, or in skillet, cook onion in butter till just tender. Blend in flour. Dissolve bouillon cube in hot water; gradually add bouillon and milk to flour mixture; cook and stir till thick.

Place blazer pan over water bath, if using chafing dish. Add cheeses, stirring till Swiss cheese melts and mixture is blended.

Spoon over open-face sandwiches. Makes 4 or 5 servings. Make it a luncheon with lemon meringue pie, freshly brewed tea.

For party sauces, pretty shells

Make ever-so-simple shells from pastry, bread; or bake Popovers

Pastry Petal Cups—Make Plain Pastry. (Recipe that calls for 1½ cups flour makes 4 to 6 Cups.) Roll to ⅛ inch on lightly floured surface. Cut with 1¾-inch round cutter.

Place one round in bottom of each muffin cup; overlap four rounds on sides; press together. Prick. Bake at 450° about 10 minutes.

Popovers

These golden puffs are crisp, feather-light—

2 eggs
1 cup milk
1 cup sifted enriched flour
½ teaspoon salt

• • •

1 tablespoon salad oil or
melted shortening

Place eggs in mixing bowl; add milk, flour, and salt. Beat 1½ minutes with rotary or electric beater. Add salad oil; beat ½ minute. (Do not overbeat.)

Fill 6 to 8 *well-greased* custard cups ½ full. Bake at 475° 15 minutes. Reduce heat to 350°; continue baking about 25 to 30 minutes, till popovers are browned and firm.

A few minutes before removing from oven, prick each popover with a fork to allow steam to escape. If you like your popovers dry inside, turn off oven and then leave in 30 minutes with door ajar. Makes 6 to 8 Popovers. Split and fill with creamed ham, chicken, or sea food.

Toast Rings—You'll need 3 sizes of cooky cutters. Slice bread in ¾-inch slices. Cut one slice with largest cutter. Cut second with medium one and remove center with smallest.

Brush big round with melted butter or margarine; top with "doughnut"; brush with melted butter or margarine. Toast in moderate oven (375°) for 10 to 12 minutes.

Toast Cups—Trim crusts from thin slices of day-old white bread. *Carefully* press down into ungreased medium muffin cups.

Brush bread thoroughly with melted butter or margarine—this makes the Cups more tasty and helps to brown them.

Toast in moderate oven (375°) about 12 minutes. Remove from muffin pan.

Puff Pastry

1 cup chilled butter or margarine
1¾ cups sifted enriched flour
½ cup ice water

Reserve 2 tablespoons butter; chill. Work remaining chilled butter with back of wooden spoon or in electric mixer just until as pliable as putty. Pat or roll between sheets of waxed paper in 8x6-inch rectangle, ¼ inch thick. Chill thoroughly (1 hour in refrigerator or 20 minutes in freezer.)

Measure flour into mixing bowl; cut in reserved 2 tablespoons of butter with pastry-blender or blending fork till mixture is like coarse meal. Gradually add ice water, tossing with fork to make a stiff dough. Shape in ball.

Turn onto lightly floured surface and knead till smooth and elastic, about 5 minutes (step 1, opposite page). Cover dough and let rest 10 minutes.

On *lightly* floured surface, roll dough in 15x9-inch rectangle, ¼ inch thick. Peel top sheet of waxed paper from chilled rectangle of butter; invert on half the dough; peel off other sheet of waxed paper. Fold over other half of dough over to cover butter (step 2, opposite page).

Seal edges of dough by pressing down with side or heel of hand (step 3). Wrap in waxed paper; chill thoroughly (1 hour in refrigerator or 20 minutes in freezer).

Unwrap. On lightly floured surface, roll dough in 15x9-inch rectangle, ¼ inch thick. (Roll dough from center, *just to* the edges. Don't flatten edges by allowing rolling pin to go over them.) Brush any excess flour from pastry; fold in thirds, turn dough around, fold in thirds again (steps 4 and 5).

Seal edges. Wrap in waxed paper; chill thoroughly. Repeat rolling, folding, and thorough chilling 2 or 3 times more. Now you are ready to make Patty Shells.

Patty Shells

Roll 1 recipe of Puff Pastry in 15x9-inch rectangle, ¼ inch thick. Cut out rounds with 3-inch cooky cutter. Remove centers from half the rounds with smaller 2-inch cutter to make rims. Slightly moisten edges of big rounds with cold water. Place rims atop, pressing edges together slightly (keep rim inside plain round).

Place on baking sheets covered with 3 to 4 thicknesses of paper towels. Chill thoroughly. (Small rounds may be baked separately for casserole toppers.)

Brush with mixture of 1 slightly beaten egg white and 1 tablespoon ice water. Bake in very hot oven (450°) 6 minutes, then in slow oven (300°) 25 to 30 minutes, or till lightly browned and crisp. Remove from pan; cool on rack. If baked ahead, reheat before serving—see directions, opposite page. Makes six 3-inch patty shells.

For a gourmet buffet— a la king in these featherweight shells!

Patty Shells made of puff pastry are really fabulous—so light and tender they melt in your mouth. What nicer frames for elegant a la kings and Newburgers?

You can bake the shells ahead and store them: Wrap in foil or saran; place in a box for protection, and store in the freezer.

Or store *unbaked* puff pastry: It will keep several weeks in the freezer or several days in the refrigerator. Wrap well.

Puff pastry takes time and attention. It must be chilled, rolled, and folded several times. But results are spectacular—there's nothing else like it!

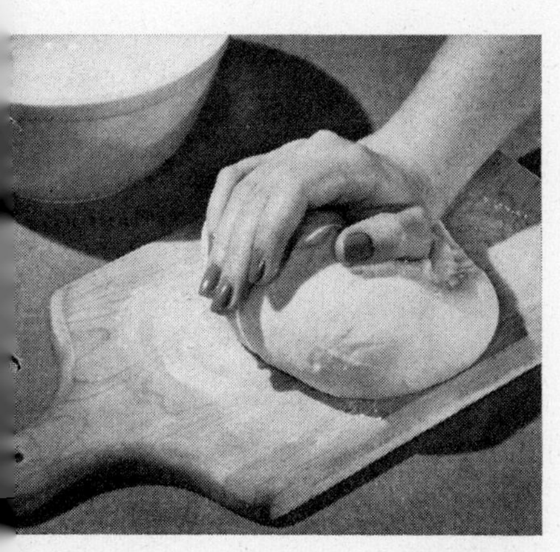

1 Prepare rectangle of butter according to recipe; chill in refrigerator as directed. Prepare dough, then knead it thoroughly on a lightly floured surface until a smooth elastic ball of dough is formed. This will usually take about 5 minutes.

After kneading, cover and allow dough to rest for 10 minutes—this makes the dough easier to roll.

2 Roll dough to a 15x9-inch rectangle, ¼ inch thick. Peel top sheet of waxed paper from chilled rectangle of butter (recipe tells how to prepare); invert on half the dough; peel off other sheet of waxed paper.

Fold over other half of the dough, envelope style, to cover butter.

Pointer: Butter must be firm at all times, never soft enough to melt, yet not so hard that it breaks through dough.

3 Seal edges of the dough together by pressing down with the side or heel of the hand. This helps keep butter enclosed when rolling and folding the dough.

Wrap pastry in waxed paper; chill thoroughly at least 1 hour in refrigerator or 20 minutes in the freezer. (Chill utensils and pastry cloth before each use also.)

4 On lightly floured surface, roll chilled pastry ¼ inch thick, shaping into 15x9-inch rectangle. (Roll from center *just to* edges, to avoid flattening them.) Always brush excess flour from the dough after rolling and before folding.

Fold dough in thirds, sealing edges together with side or heel of hand. Dough is now in 3 layers.

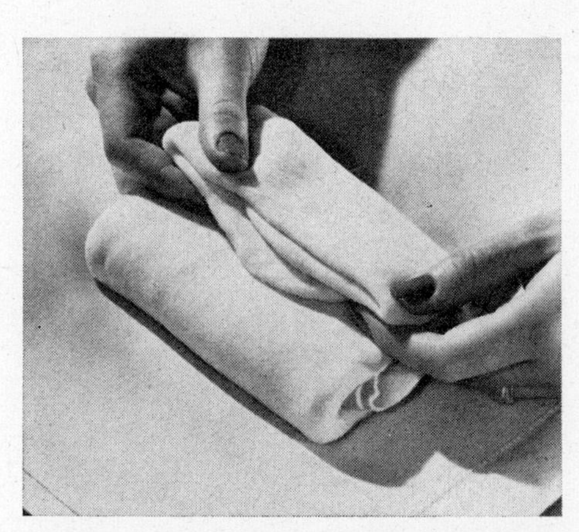

5 Turn folded dough around and fold again in thirds, as shown; seal edges. Wrap in waxed paper; chill thoroughly. Dough is now in 9 layers.

Repeat rolling, folding, and thorough chilling (steps 4 and 5) two or three times more.

Puff Pastry is ready to shape and bake.

Pointer: If dough seems to be getting soft at any time during rolling or folding, place in refrigerator or freezer till firm again.

6 To shape Patty Shells: Cut pastry rounds; remove centers from half of them. Lightly moisten edges of the big rounds, press the "rims" on top. Place on baking sheets covered with paper towels, chill. Brush with mixture of egg white and ice water; bake.

To reheat: Crisp in slow oven (300°) 10 to 15 minutes.

Chowders, soups, and stews

Whiff that wonderful aroma! Soup for supper bubbles lazily on the range. The rest of the meal is simple—just add crisp relishes and a fruit salad. Dessert might be your favorite cake. When you thumb the pages of this chapter, you'll find old-fashioned soups and stews that Grandma made her reputation on. There are new soup-can combinations that go together in nothing flat, yet taste as though you slaved all day. So, noontime or nighttime, cook up a big kettle of soup or stew. With these grand recipes, you'll turn out a masterpiece!

All-time greats! Chicken Pie with Puff-pastry Top, Split-pea Soup

Whole meal in a bowl–it's soup!

Split-pea Soup

1 pound (about 2¼ cups) green split peas
2 quarts cold water
1 meaty ham bone (about 1½ pounds)
1½ cups sliced onion
1 teaspoon salt
½ teaspoon pepper
¼ teaspoon marjoram
1 cup diced celery
1 cup diced carrots

Cover peas with the water and soak overnight. (*Or*, simmer gently 2 minutes, then soak 1 hour.) Don't drain. Add ham bone, onion, and seasonings. Bring to boiling; cover, reduce heat, and simmer (*don't boil*) 1½ hours. Stir occasionally.

Remove bone; cut off meat and dice. Return meat to soup; add vegetables. Cook slowly, uncovered, 30 to 40 minutes. Salt to taste. Makes 6 to 8 servings.

Pea Soup Royale

Blend 1 can condensed green-pea soup, 1 can condensed consomme, and ½ soup can milk; heat to boiling. Top with Skillet Croutons. Makes 4 servings.

Skillet Croutons: Cut slightly dry bread in ½-inch cubes. Melt a little butter in a skillet; add bread cubes; toss lightly. Heat and stir till croutons are golden brown.

tips *When soup is it, add these go-withs and garnishes!*

Trims for soups: For clear soups, add lemon slices, chopped parsley. Salted whipped cream, toasted almonds, minced chives are nice for cream soups. Try frankfurter slices in pea or bean soup; lemon slices with fish chowder.

Soup accompaniments: Use round wafers, cheese straws, toast strips spread with cheese, or Melba toast with clear soups. With cream soups, serve salted crackers, pretzels, croutons, sweet and dill pickles, or celery. With meat soups or chowders: Sour pickles, bread sticks, toasted hard rolls spread with garlic butter.

Cheese Chowder

The ultimate in cheese soups—

½ cup coarsely shredded carrots
½ cup chopped celery
¾ cup boiling water
¼ cup chopped onion
3 tablespoons butter or margarine
¼ cup enriched flour
2 cups milk
1 13½-ounce can (1¾ cups) chicken broth*
1½ cups shredded sharp process American cheese

Cook carrots and celery in boiling water until tender; do not drain. Cook onion in butter till tender but not brown; stir in flour. Gradually add milk and cook, stirring constantly, till thick. Add broth, cheese, and vegetables (with cooking liquid). Stir over low heat until cheese melts. Garnish with chopped parsley. Makes 6 servings.

*Or use 2 chicken bouillon cubes dissolved in 1¾ cups hot water.

Hearty Bean Soup

Thoroughly wash 1 pound dried navy beans. Add 2 quarts cold water. Soak overnight, *or* boil gently 2 minutes, then cover, soak 1 hour. Add 1 meaty ham bone, ½ teaspoon salt, 4 to 6 peppercorns, and 1 bay leaf. Cover; boil gently about 3 to 3½ hours, adding 1 medium onion, sliced, last half hour.

Mash beans slightly. Remove ham bone; cut off meat, dice, and return meat to soup. Season to taste. Makes 6 generous servings.

Chicken-Corn Soup

1 12-ounce or 1-pound can whole kernel corn, drained
2 tablespoons butter or margarine
1 can condensed chicken vegetable soup
1 can condensed chicken noodle soup
1½ cups water or corn liquid

Heat corn in butter in saucepan, about 5 minutes, stirring occasionally. Add soups and water; heat thoroughly. Float pretzels for trim. Makes 4 or 5 servings.

Vegetable Soup with Tiny Meat Balls

5 to 6 cups beef broth or stock*
1 can canned tomatoes
3 stalks celery and leaves, chopped
1 carrot, finely chopped
1 teaspoon crushed oregano
⅓ to ½ cup fine *pasta*
1 recipe Tiny Meat Balls
Grated Parmesan cheese

Heat beef broth to boiling. Add vegetables and the oregano. Cover; simmer 12 minutes. Add *pasta* to bubbling soup; cook till *pasta* is almost done (*don't overcook*). Drop Tiny Meat Balls into soup; simmer 2 minutes. Season to taste with salt and pepper. Pass grated Parmesan cheese. Makes 8 servings.

*Speedy with 3 cans condensed beef broth and 2 cans water. *Or make Beef Stock:* Have 6 pounds beef soup bones cut in several pieces. Dice meat coarsely. Put meat and bones in soup kettle; add 2½ quarts water. Simmer uncovered (*don't boil*) 3 hours. Add 1 cup sliced onion, ½ cup chopped celery with leaves, 1 bay leaf, 8 whole black peppers, and 2 teaspoons salt. Cook uncovered 2 hours longer. Strain; skim off excess fat. Refrigerate if stored. (Fix soup meat as hash.) Makes about 6 cups stock.

Tiny Meat Balls: Soak 2 slices dry bread or toast in water; squeeze out moisture. Lightly mix bread with 1 pound ground beef, 1 slightly beaten egg, 1 clove garlic, minced, and 1 teaspoon salt. Form in ¾-inch balls, using 1 teaspoon mixture for each. Brown in butter. Makes 5 dozen.

Soup-kettle Supper

Three soups make a grand new soup! Serve with crackers and crisp celery sticks—

1 can condensed cream of vegetable soup
1 can condensed cream of chicken soup
1 can condensed onion soup
1½ cups milk
1 12-ounce can (1½ cups) whole kernel corn
• • •
1 4-ounce can Vienna sausage

Mix soups together; stir in milk and corn. Slice sausage links in coins; add. Cover and heat slowly, stirring occasionally, till soup comes just to boiling. Ladle into bowls. Makes 6 to 8 servings.

Vegetable Soup with Tiny Meat Balls—or call it *Zuppa Vegetale con Polpettini.* You can get a head start with canned beef broth or make a real soup-bone soup—we give both ways. As with most Italian soups, the *pasta* is important, and traditionally ever so tiny. Here it's *rosa marina.* Could be any of the others clustered around the tureen.

Supper Corn Chowder

5 slices bacon
1 medium onion, thinly sliced and separated in rings
• • •
2 cups cooked or canned whole kernel corn
1 cup diced cooked potatoes (optional)
1 can condensed cream of mushroom soup
2½ cups milk
1 teaspoon salt
Dash pepper
Butter or margarine

In large saucepan, cook bacon till crisp. Remove bacon; pour off bacon drippings, returning 3 tablespoons to saucepan. Add onion and cook till lightly browned.

Add remaining ingredients except butter. Heat to boiling, reduce heat and simmer a minute or two. Crumble bacon; sprinkle over chowder. Top each serving with pat of butter. Makes 6 servings.

Tomato Chili Stew is delicious!
A snap to do with soup from a can

A meal at the drop of a hat! Pick a pair of soups—bean with bacon soup and tomato soup; add a spare—a can of chili con carne; heat. Pass corn chips for folks to sprinkle on top.

Tomato Chili Stew

1 can condensed bean with bacon soup
1 can condensed tomato soup
1 10½-ounce can chili con carne
 without beans
1 soup can water
Corn chips

Combine soups and chili con carne; stir in water. Heat to boiling. Ladle into bowls; top with corn chips. Makes 4 or 5 servings.

Ham-Potato Soup

Combine 1 can frozen condensed cream of potato soup, 1 can condensed cream of mushroom soup, 2 soup cans milk. Stir in one 2¼-ounce can deviled ham. Heat just to boiling. Makes 4 or 5 servings.

Beef Potage

Rich in flavor, full of vegetables and tender noodles. Satisfying and good—

½ cup sliced mushrooms,
 fresh or canned
½ cup thin green-pepper strips
1 tablespoon butter or
 margarine

. . .

1 can condensed beef-noodle
 soup
1 can condensed beef soup
1½ soup cans water

Heat mushrooms and green-pepper strips in butter, but do not brown. Add soups and water; heat to boiling. Ladle into bowls. Makes 4 or 5 servings.

Hearty sea-food chowders

Fish Chowder

The real New England kind! A favorite at Hartwell Farm, Lincoln, Massachusetts—

Put 1 cup diced potato and 3/4 cup diced onion through food chopper, using coarse blade. Fry 1 ounce (1/4 cup) cubed salt pork until lightly browned.

Cut 1 1/4 pounds boned haddock in 1/4-inch cubes; place alternate layers of potato mixture and fish in a deep kettle. Add salt pork and 2 cups water. Cover and bake in hot oven (400°) 15 minutes, then in moderate oven (350°) 45 minutes; *or* cover and simmer over low heat 1 hour.

Add 2 to 3 cups light cream; salt and pepper to taste. Heat. Makes 6 to 8 servings.

Manhattan Clam Chowder

3 slices bacon, finely diced
1 cup finely diced celery
1 cup chopped onion
2 7- or 7 1/2-ounce cans (about 2 cups) minced clams
1 1-pound can (2 cups) tomatoes
2 cups diced potatoes
1 cup finely diced carrots
1 1/2 teaspoons salt
1/4 teaspoon thyme
Dash pepper

Partially cook bacon. Add onion and celery and cook till tender but not brown. Drain clams, reserving liquor. Add water to the liquor to make 4 cups; add to bacon mixture. Add tomatoes, potatoes, carrots, and seasonings. Cover; simmer about 35 minutes.

Blend 2 tablespoons flour with 2 tablespoons cold water to make *smooth* paste. Stir into chowder; cook and stir till mixture comes to a boil. Add clams; heat through. Makes 6 to 8 servings.

Or use fresh clams in shells: Thoroughly wash 2 to 3 dozen clams. Cover with salt water (1/3 cup salt to 1 gallon cold water); let stand 15 minutes; rinse. Repeat two more times. Place clams in large kettle; add 1 cup water. Cover and steam just until shells open, 5 to 10 minutes. Remove clams, reserving liquid. Remove clams from shells and dice finely. Strain liquid.

Oyster Stew

2 tablespoons enriched flour
1 1/2 teaspoons salt
1 teaspoon Worcestershire sauce
Dash Tabasco sauce
2 tablespoons water
1 pint oysters
1 quart milk, scalded*

Combine flour, seasonings, and water; blend to smooth paste. Stir into oysters and their liquor. Simmer over very low heat 10 minutes or just till edges curl, stirring gently. Then pour into hot milk. Remove pan from heat. Cover; let stand 15 minutes.

Place 1/4 cup butter in tureen. Reheat stew to serving temperature. Pour into tureen; dash with paprika. Makes 4 servings.

*Or use 3 cups milk and 1 cup light cream.

Pacific Chowder

4 slices bacon
1/4 cup chopped onion
2 tablespoons chopped green pepper
1 can frozen condensed cream of potato soup
2 cups milk
1 6 1/2-, 7-, or 9 1/4-ounce can tuna, drained and broken in chunks

Cook bacon till crisp. Drain, reserving 2 tablespoons drippings. In reserved drippings, cook onion and green pepper just till tender. Add soup and milk; heat just to boiling. Add tuna; crumble bacon; add. Heat. Dash with paprika. Makes 4 servings.

Crab Meat Bisque

1 can condensed cream of mushroom soup
1 can condensed cream of asparagus soup
1 1/2 soup cans milk
1 cup light cream
1 6 1/2-ounce can (about 1 cup) crab meat, drained and flaked
1/4 cup cooking sherry

Blend soups, milk and cream. Heat just to boiling. Add crab meat, heat. Add sherry. Float butter atop. Serves 6 to 8.

Savory STEW

Chuck-wagon stew—rib-sticking fare! Long, slow cooking is the secret for its delicious flavor

Simmer browned beef and vegetables at a slow jog—the flavors blend, the meat goes fork-tender.

Here, chef ladles his stew into little iron kettles to pass around. 'S wonderful!

Chuck-wagon Stew

2 pounds beef chuck, cut in 1½-inch cubes
4 cups water*
1 medium onion, sliced
1 clove garlic, sliced
1 tablespoon salt
1 teaspoon sugar
½ teaspoon pepper
1 teaspoon Worcestershire
1 tablespoon lemon juice

• • •

½ cup cut celery
6 carrots, quartered
½ pound small white onions or 1 1-pound can, drained
3 potatoes, quartered
2 or 3 tomatoes, cut in wedges, or 1 1-pound can*

Trim excess fat from beef; heat fat in Dutch oven. Brown meat slowly on all sides in hot fat. Add water, sliced onion, and seasonings. Cover; simmer (*don't boil*) 2 hours, stirring now and then to keep from sticking. Add vegetables except tomatoes; cook covered 20 minutes. Add tomatoes and cook 15 minutes longer or till meat and vegetables are done. Skim fat from stew.

To thicken liquid: Put 4 tablespoons flour in small bowl; slowly stir in ½ cup cold water—mixture must be *smooth*. Stir into stew; cook and *stir* till thickened. Cook 5 minutes more. Makes 6 to 8 servings.

*If you use canned tomatoes, drain; use juice as part of the liquid.

Speedy Vegetable-Beef Stew

2 pounds beef chuck, cut in 1-inch cubes
2 tablespoons fat
2 teaspoons salt
¾ teaspoon paprika
¼ teaspoon basil leaves
Dash pepper
1 cup onion slices
1 cup celery slices
6 whole medium carrots
6 whole medium potatoes
1 12-ounce can (1½ cups) vegetable-juice cocktail

Brown meat slowly in hot fat in pressure pan (about 15 minutes). Add seasonings, vegetables, and juice. Cook at 10 or 15 pounds pressure 10 to 12 minutes. Cool pan normally 5 minutes; then reduce pressure under cold running water. Thicken stew, if desired. Makes 4 to 6 servings.

Chili Con Carne

1½ cups dry red or kidney beans*

• • •

1 large onion, sliced
1 green pepper, chopped
1 pound ground beef
1 tablespoon fat
1 1-pound can (2 cups) tomatoes
1 8-ounce can (1 cup) seasoned tomato sauce
1 to 1½ tablespoons chili powder
1½ teaspoons salt
Dash paprika
Dash cayenne pepper
1 bay leaf

Rinse the beans; then add to 1½ quarts cold water and let stand overnight. Add 1 teaspoon salt to beans and soaking water; cover, and simmer until *tender*, about 1 hour. Drain, reserving the bean liquid.

Brown onion, green pepper, and meat in hot fat. Add beans, tomatoes, tomato sauce, and seasonings. Cover; simmer 1½ hours, adding reserved bean liquid or water, if needed. Makes 6 servings.

*Or use two 1-pound cans (4 cups) red or kidney beans. Drain beans, add to meat mixture with tomatoes.

Brunswick Stew

1 4- to 5-pound ready-to-cook stewing chicken,* disjointed
4 cups water
1 tablespoon salt
½ teaspoon pepper
1 bay leaf
Dash thyme
1 cup diced onion
1 1-pound can (2 cups) tomatoes
1 1-pound can (2 cups) cream-style corn
1½ cups green Limas, fresh, frozen or canned (drained)
1 cup sliced okra, fresh, frozen, or canned (drained)

Place chicken in Dutch oven or deep kettle. Add water, seasonings, and onion. Cover and simmer (*don't boil*) till tender, 3 to 4 hours. (If desired, remove chicken from broth, take meat from bones and cut in bites; return to stew for last hour of cooking.) Skim fat from stew; add vegetables and simmer uncovered 1 hour. Salt and pepper to taste. Makes 8 servings.

*Or use 2 "bro-hens" (older broiler-fryers), about 2½ to 3 pounds each, and cook 2½ to 3 hours or till tender.

Hungry for Old-time Beef Stew? Here's how to make it

1 Cut 2 pounds beef chuck in 1½-inch cubes (or have the meatman cut it for you). In Dutch oven or deep heavy kettle, brown meat cubes slowly in 2 tablespoons hot fat. Don't hurry this step—it takes about 20 minutes to develop color and flavor. If kettle is too crowded, brown only part of the beef cubes at one time. Turn cubes often for even browning.

For the fat for browning, you can use the trimmings from the meat; or use a piece of suet—ask your meatman for a small chunk.

2 When meat's well browned, measure and pour in 4 cups boiling water. Lower heat; shift meat with fork to make sure cubes aren't sticking to pan. Add 1 tablespoon lemon juice—makes meat more tender, adds a slight tang.

Meal planning is no problem when you're having stew—it's a meal in a bowl! Just pass crisp fresh relishes, or fix a fruit salad. For dessert? Oven-warm gingerbread. Remember to give each person a soupspoon—no one will want to waste a drop of that good gravy!

3 In go seasonings: 1 teaspoon Worcestershire sauce, 1 clove garlic, 1 medium onion, sliced, 1 to 2 bay leaves. Sprinkle on 1 tablespoon salt, 1 teaspoon sugar, ½ teaspoon pepper, ½ teaspoon paprika, and dash allspice or cloves. Cover; simmer till tender—2 hours. *Don't boil.* Stir occasionally so meat doesn't stick. Remove bay leaves and garlic.

Prepare vegetables: 6 carrots and 1 pound (18 to 24) small white onions. Leave small carrots whole; if large, halve or quarter.

4 Now add carrots and onions. (Cubed potatoes may be added, too.) Cover; simmer 30 minutes or till vegetables are done. Remove meat and vegetables. Thicken liquid for gravy.

To make gravy: Skim most of fat from stew liquid. For 3 cups liquid, blend ½ cup cold water with ¼ cup enriched flour. Mixture must be *smooth.* Add flour mixture slowly to meat stock, stirring constantly till gravy thickens. Cook 5 minutes longer, stirring. Pour over meat and vegetables. Makes 6 to 8 servings.

Chicken Pie with Puff-pastry Top

½ cup chopped onion
⅓ cup butter or chicken fat
⅓ cup enriched flour
1½ teaspoons salt
3 cups chicken broth*
4 cups cooked chicken cut in pieces
1 cup drained cooked or canned peas
1 6-ounce can (1⅓ cups) broiled sliced mushrooms, drained
¼ cup chopped pimiento

Cook onion in butter till tender, but not brown; blend in flour and salt. Gradually stir in broth. Cook and stir until thick. Add chicken and vegetables; heat to bubbling. Pour into *heated* shallow 2-quart casserole. Add *hot* Puff-pastry Top and serve immediately. Makes 10 to 12 servings.

*You can use canned broth or dissolve 4 chicken bouillon cubes in 3 cups hot water.

Puff-pastry Top: Make Puff Pastry, page 114. Chill, roll, and fold as directed.

Now shape top for Chicken Pie: Cut a paper pattern to fit top of casserole. Again roll dough into 15x9-inch rectangle, ¼ inch thick. Place pattern on top; cut out with pastry wheel or knife.

Place pastry on baking sheet covered with 3 or 4 thicknesses of paper towels. Chill thoroughly at least 1 hour in refrigerator or 20 minutes in freezer. Cut design in top with sharp knife. Brush with mixture of 1 slightly beaten egg white and 1 tablespoon ice water. Bake in very hot oven (450°) 6 minutes, then in slow oven (300°) 25 to 30 minutes or till lightly browned and crisp. Place on hot filling just before serving.

If baked ahead, place on baking sheet on 3 or 4 thicknesses of paper towels. Heat in slow oven (300°) about 10 minutes.

Favorite Lamb Stew

Flour 1½ pounds lean boneless lamb shoulder, cut in 1-inch cubes. Brown in a little hot fat. Add 3 cups water, 1 clove garlic, minced, 2 teaspoons salt, and ¼ teaspoon pepper. Cover; simmer (don't boil) 1½ hours or till meat is almost tender.

Add 4 carrots, cut in 2-inch lengths, 6 tiny onions, and 3 small potatoes, halved. Cook till almost done, about 20 minutes.

Add 2 tablespoons minced parsley and one 10-ounce package frozen peas. Cook 5 minutes or till done. Season. Serves 5.

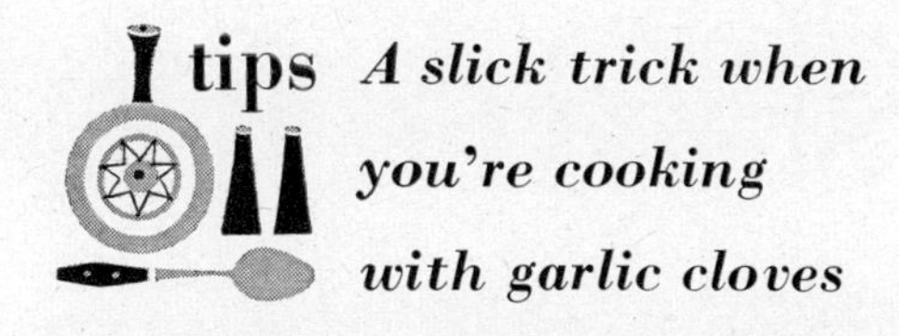

A slick trick when you're cooking with garlic cloves

Before adding garlic to cooking liquid, slash cloves several times. Spear each clove with a toothpick to hold it together. Come serving time, it's a snap to find and remove garlic.

Old-time Oxtail Stew

2 pounds oxtail, cut in 1½-inch lengths
1 medium onion, sliced
2 cups hot water
1 1-pound can (2 cups) tomatoes
1 can condensed beef broth
1½ teaspoons salt
¼ teaspoon pepper

• • •

8 small whole onions
4 potatoes, halved
4 carrots, halved

Flour meat; brown in small amount hot fat in Dutch oven. Add next 6 ingredients. Cover; simmer 2½ hours or till meat is just tender. Add vegetables; cover and simmer 30 to 45 minutes or till done. Skim off excess fat.

Pressure saucepan: Flour meat; brown. Add sliced onion, tomatoes, broth, seasonings (omit water). Cook at 15 pounds pressure 30 minutes. Cool pan normally 5 minutes; then reduce pressure under cold running water. Add vegetables; return to 15 pounds pressure 10 minutes. Reduce pressure immediately under cold running water. Skim off excess fat. Makes 4 to 6 servings.

Stew toppers—package start

Beef Pie with Lattice Squares

Cook beef-and-vegetable mixture as for Old-time Potpie below. Turn into shallow baker or serving dish (at least 11x7 inches). Top with 6 rafts of hot Lattice Squares.

Lattice Squares: For 6 little lattice rafts, prepare 2 sticks pastry mix according to package directions. Divide dough in half; form each in ball and roll to 1/8 inch on lightly floured surface.

Cut in strips 3/4 inch wide, making 24 strips 3 inches long, and 18 strips 4 inches long. Weave in 6 lattice sections: For each, line up three 4-inch strips side by side, 1/4 inch apart. Weave four 3-inch strips crosswise. Bake on ungreased baking sheet in very hot oven (450°) 8 to 10 minutes.

Old-time Potpie with Thimble Rolls

2 pounds beef stew meat, cut in 1½-inch cubes
3 cups boiling water
1 teaspoon Worcestershire sauce
1 clove garlic
1 medium onion, sliced
1 bay leaf
1 tablespoon salt
1 teaspoon sugar
¼ teaspoon pepper
½ teaspoon paprika
6 small carrots, halved
6 small potatoes, pared and halved
6 small onions

Brown meat on all sides in small amount hot fat; add next 9 ingredients. Cover; simmer 2 hours, stirring occasionally. Remove bay leaf and garlic. Add vegetables. Cover and cook 30 minutes longer or till meat and vegetables are done. Remove stew from heat. Transfer meat and vegetables to a 2-quart round casserole. Skim fat from stew liquid.

To thicken liquid: Put 4 tablespoons flour in small bowl; slowly stir in 1/2 cup cold water—mixture must be *smooth;* stir into stew liquid. Cook and *stir* till thickened; cook 5 minutes more, stirring. Pour gravy over meat and vegetables. Top with hot Thimble Rolls. Makes 6 to 8 servings.

Thimble Rolls

1 package active dry yeast *or* 1 cake compressed yeast
¾ cup water
2½ cups packaged biscuit mix

Soften active dry yeast in *warm* water or compressed yeast in *lukewarm* water. Stir in biscuit mix; beat vigorously, about 3 minutes. Turn out on surface well dusted with biscuit mix. Knead till smooth, about 20 strokes. Roll to slightly less than 1/2 inch. Cut with floured 1-inch cutter.

In greased 8x1 1/2-inch round pan, arrange 2 rows of rolls close together around edge. Brush tops with butter; cover with damp cloth; let rise in warm place till double, 30 to 45 minutes. Bake in hot oven (400°) 12 to 15 minutes or till done. (Bake remaining rolls in another pan.) Brush again with butter. Immediately place ring of rolls on top of Old-time Potpie and serve.

Lamb Pie with Pastry Tricorns

For meat and seasonings, follow recipe for Favorite Lamb Stew, page 125, except decrease the water to 1 1/2 cups.

When meat is almost tender, add 6 small onions; cover and continue cooking till almost done, about 15 minutes.

Add 3 small potatoes, pared and quartered, one 10-ounce package frozen green Limas, and 2 tablespoons minced parsley; cook 15 to 18 minutes longer or till done. Top with Pastry Tricorns. Makes 6 servings.

Pastry Tricorns

Prepare 1 stick packaged pastry mix according to package directions. Roll on lightly floured surface to an 8-inch circle, a little less than 1/4 inch thick.

With pastry wheel or sharp knife, cut in 6 pie-shaped wedges. Roll back center point of each; crumple small pieces of foil and place one under each point (these will support points). Bake on ungreased baking sheet in very hot oven (450°) 12 to 15 minutes. Immediately arrange on hot lamb stew.

Top stew with Lattice Squares, Thimble Rolls, Pastry Tricorns

Light-as-a-cloud Fluffy Dumplings

1 Fluffy Dumplings go atop Old-time Beef Stew. Make stew as directed, page 124. For Dumplings, sift 1½ cups sifted enriched flour with 3½ teaspoons baking powder and ½ teaspoon salt. Add ¾ cup milk all at once. Stir just until flour is dampened.

2 When stew is done, drop dumplings atop from a teaspoon. Let meat and vegetables be landing base. The dumplings will slide off the spoon easily if each time you dip spoon in stew first.

3 Cover dumplings with a tight lid and *leave it on* the full time. No fair peeking (unless lid is glass), or dumplings will fall. Cook about 12 minutes or till dumplings are done. Remove dumplings, stew to serving platter. Thicken liquid for gravy.

Short-rib Stew with Parsley Dumplings

2 pounds short ribs
¼ cup enriched flour
1 tablespoon salt
¼ teaspoon pepper
2 tablespoons fat
2 1-pound cans (4 cups) tomatoes
2 cloves garlic, minced
1 tablespoon Worcestershire sauce
4 to 5 carrots, sliced
2 medium onions, sliced
1 medium potato, diced
• • •
1 recipe Parsley Dumplings

Cut short ribs in serving pieces. Combine flour, salt, and pepper; dredge ribs in mixture. Brown in hot fat. Combine tomatoes, garlic, and Worcestershire sauce; pour over ribs. Cover; simmer 1½ hours.

Add carrots, onions, and potato. Simmer 45 minutes longer, or till meat and vegetables are tender. Skim off fat. Season stew to taste. Drop Parsley Dumpling mixture from tablespoon atop bubbling stew. Cover tightly; bring to boiling. Reduce heat (don't lift cover) and simmer 15 minutes longer. Makes 4 or 5 servings.

Parsley Dumplings

Sift together 1 cup enriched flour, 2 teaspoons baking powder, and ½ teaspoon salt. Add ¼ cup chopped parsley. Combine ½ cup milk and 2 tablespoons salad oil or melted shortening; add to dry ingredients, stirring just till flour is dampened.

Easy Dumplings

¾ cup milk
2 cups packaged biscuit mix

Add milk to biscuit mix all at once; stir just until mix is dampened. Drop by rounded tablespoons atop hot, bubbling stew. Cook uncovered over low heat 10 minutes; cover, continue cooking 10 minutes more.

Biscuit Dumplings

1 package refrigerated biscuits
1 tablespoon snipped parsley

Place biscuits on hot, bubbling stew; sprinkle with parsley. Cover tightly and steam 15 minutes or till "dumplings" are done.

Veal Stew with Corn-meal Dumplings

1½ pounds veal stew meat, cut in 1-inch cubes
4 cups tomato juice
2 teaspoons salt
1½ teaspoons monosodium glutamate
4 to 6 dashes Tabasco sauce
Dash pepper

• • •

1 cup diced pared potatoes
½ cup sliced celery
½ cup chopped onion
1 recipe Corn-meal Dumplings

Flour meat. Brown slowly in small amount hot fat in Dutch oven; add tomato juice and seasonings. Cover and simmer (don't boil) 1 hour. Add vegetables; cover and continue cooking 30 minutes or till vegetables are almost done. Drop rounded tablespoons of Corn-meal Dumplings onto hot stew. Cover tightly and steam (don't lift cover) 10 minutes or till dumplings are done. Serves 6.

Corn-meal Dumplings

2 tablespoons minced parsley
1 10-ounce package corn-bread mix

Add parsley to corn-bread mix. *Using only ⅓ cup milk,* prepare batter according to package directions. Drop rounded tablespoons onto hot bubbling stew.

Raisin Polka-dot Dumplings

Wonderful with stewed chicken—

Sift together 1 cup sifted enriched flour, 3 teaspoons baking powder, and 1 teaspoon salt. Cut in 1 tablespoon shortening.

Add ½ cup seedless raisins and ¾ cup dry bread crumbs. Combine 1 beaten egg, ¾ cup milk, and 2 teaspoons grated onion. Add to raisin mixture; mix just to moisten.

Drop by teaspoons atop hot stewed chicken pieces. Cover tightly; steam 20 minutes. Remove chicken and dumplings; thicken broth.

Flavorful Veal Stew with Corn-meal Dumplings— The meat is superbly seasoned with tomato and Tabasco; the from-a-mix dumplings are airy and flecked with parsley. Folks will appreciate the old-fashioned goodness of a dish like this. You'll appreciate the speedy dumpling topper! Corn-bread mix gives you a head start—make them in minutes!

Speedy suppers

Suppertime again! And you're at your wit's end to find a just-right main dish—one that takes only a jiffy to make . . . that doesn't tax the budget . . . one that will make a big hit.

Well, stop here for suppers that beat the clock! Helpers from can and package, and a handy pressure pan, put you minutes ahead—fancy fare with no fuss!

Keep this chapter of fast recipes at your finger tips. Pull them out at the end of a busy day when an easy meal is just the ticket!

Baked Corned-beef Burgers—easy on the cook!

← Open a can of corned beef for the patties . . . make the scrumptious sauce with cheese and a can of soup. Pass generous slices of French bread; another time serve burgers atop toasted English muffin halves. A tossed green salad rounds out the meal.

Fast meat fix-ups

Speedy Chop Suey

1 pound pork, veal or beef, cut in ½-inch cubes or thin slices
2 tablespoons fat
1 cup sliced celery
1 cup onion slices
1 cup water
½ teaspoon salt
1 6-ounce can (1⅓ cups) broiled, sliced mushrooms
¼ cup soy sauce
3 tablespoons cornstarch
1 No. 2 can (2½ cups) bean sprouts
4 cups hot cooked rice

Brown meat slowly in hot fat in pressure saucepan. Add celery, onions, water, salt, and dash pepper. Cook at 10 pounds pressure 5 minutes. Cool pan normally 5 minutes; then reduce pressure under cold running water. Remove cover. Add mushrooms (and liquid). Mix soy sauce and cornstarch; tip pressure pan slightly; slowly stir cornstarch mixture into hot liquid. Cook stirring constantly till thick. Add drained bean sprouts. Serve over rice. Makes 6 servings.

Chipped-beef Chow Mein

4 ounces dried beef, coarsely torn
2 tablespoons butter or margarine
1 can condensed cream of mushroom soup
1 can condensed chicken-rice soup
1 10-ounce package frozen asparagus, cooked and drained
2 cups chow-mein noodles, heated

Cook dried beef in butter till slightly crisp. Stir in soups; simmer 5 minutes. Add asparagus, heat through. Serve over crisp chow-mein noodles. Makes 4 to 6 servings.

10-minute Spaghetti Sauce

2 tablespoons salad oil
1 pound ground beef
2 large onions, sliced
3 cloves garlic, minced or crushed
2 8-ounce cans (2 cups) seasoned tomato sauce
1 6-ounce can (⅔ cup) tomato paste
2 to 3 teaspoons chili powder
1 teaspoon salt
1 teaspoon sugar
Dash red pepper

Combine all ingredients in pressure saucepan. Cook at 15 pounds pressure 10 minutes. Reduce pressure quickly under cold running water. Serve over cooked spaghetti (one 8-ounce package long spaghetti). Top with grated Parmesan cheese. Makes 6 servings.

Bologna-Rice Barbecue

1 4⅝-ounce package precooked rice (1⅓ cups)
½ pound big Bologna cut in ½-inch cubes (about 1⅔ cups)
½ cup extra-hot catsup
⅔ cup hot water
1 3-ounce can (⅔ cup) broiled sliced mushrooms, undrained
¼ cup finely chopped onion
2 tablespoons chopped green pepper
½ teaspoon salt
2 tablespoons butter or margarine

Combine all ingredients in skillet. Cook over medium heat, stirring often, till hot. Cover tightly, reduce heat and let stand about 5 minutes or till done. Fluff rice with a fork; serve. Makes 4 servings.

Bologna Bake

¾ pound big Bologna, diced (2 cups)
1 cup celery slices
¼ cup sliced stuffed olives
4 hard-cooked eggs, diced
¼ cup chopped onion
1 tablespoon prepared mustard
Dash pepper
¾ cup mayonnaise
1 cup crushed potato chips

Combine all ingredients except potato chips. Place in 8x2-inch round baking dish; sprinkle with chips. Bake in hot oven (400°) 20 to 25 minutes. Makes 4 or 5 servings.

Speedy Chop Suey—it's ready to serve in less than a half hour!

Sausage-top Casserole

6 ounces medium noodles
1 can condensed cream of celery soup
1 cup drained cooked or canned peas
1 cup grated pimiento cheese
1 10-ounce can sausage links
½ cup buttered dry bread crumbs

Cook noodles in boiling salted water till tender; drain. Combine noodles, soup, peas, and cheese in greased 1½-quart casserole. Top with sausage. Sprinkle crumbs around edge of casserole. Bake in hot oven (400°) 25 minutes. Makes 4 servings

Sausage-Noodle Skillet

1 package brown-and-serve sausage links
1 8-ounce package chicken-noodle dinner
1 8-ounce can (1 cup) tomatoes
2 tablespoons instant minced onion
2 teaspoons parsley flakes

Halve sausage links and brown according to label directions. Add sauce mix and cook following directions for packaged dinner.

Meanwhile cook noodles as directed; drain. Add to skillet along with remaining ingredients. Heat thoroughly. Serves 5.

Wiener Towers

Place 8 onion slices in greased skillet; top each with ½-inch slice peeled tomato. Sprinkle with salt and pepper.

Cut 1 small green pepper in strips. Place 2 or 3 strips on each tomato. Top with thin bias-cut celery slices (½ cup in all).

Halve 8 frankfurters lengthwise, then crosswise; place 2 pieces, cut side up, on each tower; top with 2 more.

Cover and heat slowly 10 to 15 minutes. Sprinkle with 1 cup shredded sharp process American cheese and paprika. Serve with hot French bread. Makes 4 servings.

Jiffy Cheesefurters

Split 1 pound (8 to 10) frankfurters lengthwise, cutting only about ¾ the way through. Place in a shallow baking dish or jelly-roll pan. Spread cut surfaces with one 6-ounce roll process cheese food—pepper, garlic, smoky, or bacon flavor.

Sprinkle cheese generously with one 3-ounce package corn chips, coarsely crushed. Bake at 350° till heated through, about 15 minutes. Makes 4 or 5 servings.

Hot Dog Bar-B-Q

Count on these to make a hit! The sauce is terrific—it's not too sweet or too tangy—

½ cup chopped onion
1 tablespoon fat
1 14-ounce bottle (1¼ cups) extra-hot catsup
2 tablespoons pickle relish
1 tablespoon sugar
1 tablespoon vinegar
¼ teaspoon salt
Dash pepper
1 pound (8 to 10) frankfurters
8 to 10 coney buns, split and toasted

Cook onion in hot fat till tender but not brown. Stir in catsup, pickle relish, sugar, vinegar, and seasonings. Score franks; add to sauce. Simmer until frankfurters are thoroughly heated, about 10 minutes. Serve in hot toasted buns. Makes 8 to 10 servings.

Wiener Bean Pot

Pork-and-bean fans will rejoice over the extra-special seasoning—

2 1-pound cans (4 cups) pork and beans
1 envelope onion-soup mix
⅓ cup catsup
¼ cup water
2 tablespoons brown sugar
1 tablespoon prepared mustard
1 pound (8 to 10) frankfurters, sliced

Combine all ingredients in 2-quart casserole or bean pot. Bake uncovered in moderate oven (350°) 1 hour. Makes 6 to 8 servings.

Deviled-ham Bean Bake

½ cup sliced onion, separated in rings
1 tablespoon fat
1 4½-ounce can deviled ham
1 tablespoon molasses
1 teaspoon prepared mustard
Dash salt
1 1-pound can (2 cups) Boston style pork and beans
1 medium tomato, peeled and sliced, or 1 cup well-drained canned tomatoes

Cook onion in hot fat till tender but not brown. Combine deviled ham, molasses, mustard, salt, and beans. In 1-quart casserole, alternate layers of bean mixture with onion and tomato. Bake in moderate oven (350°) 30 minutes. Makes 6 to 8 servings.

Chili con Wiene

- 1 pound ground beef
- ½ cup chopped onion
- 1 tablespoon fat

• • •

- 1 1-pound can (2 cups) chili with beans
- 8 frankfurters, cut diagonally in ¼- to ½-inch slices
- 1 can condensed tomato soup
- ½ cup chili sauce
- ½ teaspoon salt

• • •

- ¼ cup diced green pepper

• • •

- 8 hamburger buns, split and toasted

In large skillet, lightly brown meat and onion in hot fat. Add chili, frankfurters, soup, chili sauce, and salt. Heat thoroughly. Add green pepper. Garnish with some of the frankfurter slices and ripe-olives. Serve over bun halves. Makes 8 servings.

Western Rabbit

- 1 package corn-bread mix

• • •

- 1 can condensed cheese soup
- 2 tablespoons milk
- Few drops Tabasco sauce
- ¼ cup ripe-olive slices

Bake corn bread according to package directions. Combine soup, milk, and Tabasco. Heat slowly, stirring frequently, until hot. Add olives; heat just to boiling. Cut hot corn bread in squares; split in half and spoon rabbit over. Pass extra corn-bread squares and plenty of butter. Makes 3 servings.

Tomato Rabbit: Combine and heat 1 can condensed cheese soup, one 8-ounce can seasoned tomato sauce (1 cup), and few drops Tabasco. Add ½ cup ripe-olive slices; heat just to boiling. Serve over hot corn-bread squares, as above. Makes 4 servings.

Chili con Wiene—easy does it!

Here, bias-cut wiener slices heat in a delicious mixture of browned ground beef and onion, canned chili with beans, condensed tomato soup. Just before serving, top with a ring-around of wiener cuts and a few ripe-olive slices. Spoon over toasty bun halves.

Hurry Supper Bake

Golden cheese-capped potatoes atop beef and brown gravy from a can—

1 1-pound can brown gravy and sliced beef*
¼ cup chopped onion

• • •

Packaged instant mashed potato
½ cup shredded process American cheese

Spread meat and gravy in small baking dish (we used an 8-inch shallow round baking dish). Sprinkle with chopped onion. Bake in hot oven (425°) 10 minutes or till hot.

Meanwhile, prepare instant potato (enough for 4 servings) according to package directions, but add last of liquid slowly, so you can omit a little if necessary, to make potatoes stiff enough to hold their shape. Drop hot potatoes by spoonfuls over meat, making 4 mounds; sprinkle potato with shredded cheese. Return to oven and bake about 3 minutes longer. Makes 4 servings.

*Or use one 12-ounce can roast beef, and thicken meat broth for gravy.

Supper Stew Bake

Flaky onion pastry is the lid for this easy meat pie. Pass catsup and pickles—

Mix 1 stick pastry mix and 1 tablespoon instant minced onion; prepare dough according to package directions. Roll in 8½-inch circle; cut in 6 wedges. Heat one 1-pound 8-ounce can beef stew till bubbling hot; turn into 9-inch pie plate; top with pastry wedges. Bake in very hot oven (450°) 20 minutes or till pastry topper is done. Makes 4 servings.

Deviled-ham Hot Lunch

1 tablespoon butter or margarine
1 1-pound can tiny whole potatoes, drained

• • •

¼ cup chopped celery
¼ cup chopped onion
1 4½-ounce can deviled ham

Melt butter in skillet; add potatoes, turning to coat. Sprinkle celery and onion over. Drop deviled ham by teaspoon in between potatoes; heat 10 minutes or till hot. Snip parsley over top. Makes 2 or 3 servings.

Ham Sandwich, Spring Style

8 thick slices enriched bread, toasted
Prepared mustard
2 4½-ounce cans deviled ham
8 thin slices (about 3½ inches square) sharp process American cheese

• • •

2 10-ounce packages frozen asparagus spears, cooked and drained

• • •

1 recipe Jiffy Mustard Sauce

Trim off crusts, then spread toast lightly with prepared mustard; spread generously with deviled ham. Top each slice with cheese. Cut toast in half, diagonally. Place on baking sheet and heat in hot oven (400°) 3 to 5 minutes, or till cheese starts to melt. Arrange on platter with hot buttered asparagus; serve with warm Jiffy Mustard Sauce. Makes 8 servings. See picture at right.

Jiffy Mustard Sauce

Combine ½ cup mayonnaise and 1½ teaspoons prepared mustard in small saucepan. Heat over *very low* heat, stirring constantly.

Meat-ball Pie

Caraway seed on the biscuit topper is flavor complement for the meat balls in this one-dish meal—

½ cup chopped onion
1 tablespoon butter or margarine

• • •

1 1-pound can meat balls and gravy
1 1-pound can (2 cups) cut green beans, drained
½ cup milk
1 teaspoon Worcestershire sauce

• • •

¾ cup rice flakes, crushed
1 tablespoon caraway seed
½ teaspoon salt
1 package refrigerated biscuits

Cook onion in butter till tender but not brown. Add meat balls and gravy, beans, milk, and Worcestershire. Heat till bubbling. Pour into 10x6x1½-inch baking dish.

Mix cereal, seed, and salt. Brush tops of 6 biscuits with milk; then dip in cereal mixture. Arrange biscuits atop *hot* meat. Bake in hot oven (425°) 10 to 12 minutes or till biscuits are done. (Bake remaining biscuits on cooky sheet.) Makes 6 servings.

Fancy Ham Sandwich, Spring Style

A good meal is no farther away than your can opener! Keep a can of deviled ham on hand for this luncheon special. For a gay look, arrange the platter of asparagus as shown; tuck in "sails" of deviled-ham-and-cheese toast. Spoon Jiffy Mustard Sauce down center of the platter.

Baked Corned-beef Burgers

Delicious! See picture on page 130—

1 12-ounce can corned beef, finely chopped
½ cup finely chopped green pepper
½ cup finely chopped onion
½ cup mayonnaise or salad dressing
1 egg, beaten
1 tablespoon water
¾ cup fine dry bread crumbs
¼ cup fat
3 slices sharp process American cheese
1 can condensed cream of vegetable soup
⅓ cup milk
3 large English muffins, halved, toasted

Mix corned beef, green pepper, onion, mayonnaise, and dash pepper. Shape in 6 patties. Blend egg and water; dip patties into egg, then into crumbs. Brown lightly in hot fat. Arrange patties in 11½x7½x1½-inch baking dish. Quarter cheese slices diagonally; overlap 2 triangles atop each patty.

Combine soup and milk; heat; pour around patties. Bake at 350° for 12 to 15 minutes or till heated through. Serve on hot muffin halves. Makes 6 servings. Quick salad—lettuce wedges, bottled dressing.

Pizza Hash

Corned-beef hash with an Italian flair; it takes only a few minutes to put the ingredients together—

1 1-pound can corned-beef hash*

• • •

¼ pound sharp process American cheese, shredded (1 cup)

• • •

1 8-ounce can (1 cup) seasoned tomato sauce
1 3-ounce can (⅔ cup) broiled chopped mushrooms, drained
½ teaspoon garlic salt
½ teaspoon crushed oregano

• • •

2 tablespoons grated Parmesan cheese

Cut hash in 6 slices;* arrange in ungreased 11½x7½x1½-inch baking dish. Sprinkle American cheese over hash.

Combine tomato sauce, mushrooms, garlic salt, and oregano; spoon over hash. Sprinkle with Parmesan cheese.

Bake uncovered in moderate oven (375°) about 20 minutes or till hot. Makes 3 servings (double the recipe to serve 6).

*Chill hash in can for easier slicing.

Easy Ham and Potatoes au Gratin

Cut one 12-ounce can chopped ham in 8 slices; place in 10x6x1½-inch baking dish.

Top with potato slices from 1 package au gratin potatoes. Add one 3-ounce can broiled sliced mushrooms, drained, and cheese-sauce mix. Continue as directed on package, but add 1 teaspoon Worcestershire sauce to butter and boiling water called for. Cover; bake in moderate oven (375°) 30 to 35 minutes. Makes 4 servings.

Big-meal Combo

1 can condensed cream of chicken soup
1 cup shredded sharp process American cheese
¼ teaspoon salt
2 1-pound cans (4 cups) tiny whole potatoes, drained
2 1-pound cans (4 cups) small whole onions, drained
1 3-ounce can (⅔ cup) broiled sliced mushrooms, drained
½ cup diced green pepper
1 12-ounce can corned beef, chilled
1 cup buttered soft bread crumbs or corn-flake crumbs

Combine soup, cheese, and salt; add vegetables. Pour into greased 8x8x2-inch baking dish. Top with corned beef, cut in 8 slices. Add crumbs. Bake in moderate oven (375°) about 25 minutes. Makes 8 servings.

DINNER'S IN THE OVEN!

Big-meal Combo
Sliced Tomatoes
Toasty Garlic Bread   Dill Pickles
Chocolate Pudding
Milk   Coffee

Toasty Garlic Bread: Melt ½ cup butter in 13x9x2-inch baking dish. Add 2 cloves of garlic, minced. Add eight 1-inch slices of French bread; turn quickly to butter both sides. Let stand 10 minutes. Heat at 375° with Big-meal Combo last 15 minutes.

15-minute Banquet

Cut one 12-ounce can luncheon meat in 8 slices; stud with whole cloves.

In skillet, brown meat on both sides in 1 tablespoon butter or margarine, then push to one side of pan. Add one 11-ounce can whole yams, drained; sprinkle with salt. Spoon ⅓ cup peach or pineapple preserves over meat and yams; heat uncovered over low heat, basting often, till hot and glazed, about 5 minutes. Makes 4 servings.

Dandy Dixie Bake

1 1-pound can (2 cups) applesauce
¼ teaspoon ginger
1 12-ounce can luncheon meat, cut in 8 slices
Whole cloves
1 1-pound 2-ounce can (3 cups) sweet potatoes

. . .

½ cup apricot jam
½ teaspoon dry mustard
¼ teaspoon salt
1 tablespoon water

Combine applesauce and ginger; spread in 10x6x1½-inch baking dish. Lightly score meat slices and stud with cloves. Arrange potatoes and meat on applesauce. Combine remaining ingredients; spread over meat and potatoes. Bake in hot oven (400°) 25 minutes or till heated. Makes 4 servings.

Garden Skillet Meal

1 12-ounce can luncheon meat, cut in strips
3 tablespoons butter or margarine

. . .

1½ to 2 cups cut fresh corn
3 to 4 onions, cut in thick slices
2 green peppers, cut in strips
2 to 3 firm-ripe tomatoes, quartered
Dash basil

Brown meat in butter in large skillet. Push to one side; add corn and onions.* Sprinkle vegetables with salt and pepper. Cover and cook till vegetables are almost tender, about 10 minutes. Place green-pepper strips in skillet; cover and cook about 3 minutes. Arrange tomato wedges; sprinkle with salt and the basil. Cover and cook 2 to 3 minutes longer. Trim with parsley. Makes 4 servings.

*If you like green pepper tender instead of crisp, add with corn and onions.

Quick Spanish Rice

Meat and rice—a complete meal. Fast, too—

½ cup chopped green pepper
½ cup chopped onion
1 4⅝-ounce package (1⅓ cups) precooked rice
¼ cup fat

• • •

1 beef bouillon cube
1¼ cups hot water

• • •

2 8-ounce cans (2 cups) seasoned tomato sauce
1 12-ounce can luncheon meat, cut in thin strips

Cook green pepper, onion, and rice in hot fat, stirring constantly, until lightly browned. Dissolve bouillon cube in hot water; add to rice along with the tomato sauce and meat; mix. Bring quickly to a boil; reduce heat and simmer uncovered 5 minutes or till rice is tender. Makes 5 servings.

Squaw Corn

Cube one 12-ounce can luncheon meat; brown the cubes in a little hot fat.

Combine 3 slightly beaten eggs, one 1-pound can (2 cups) golden cream-style corn, ¼ teaspoon salt, and dash of pepper. Add to meat. Cook over low heat, stirring occasionally, just till the eggs are set. Serve immediately. Makes 6 servings.

Busy-day Barbecue

¾ cup sliced onion
2 tablespoons fat
1 cup catsup
¼ cup sugar
¼ cup Worcestershire sauce
1 tablespoon vinegar
½ teaspoon salt
Dash pepper

• • •

1 12-ounce can luncheon meat, cut in thin strips
⅔ cup packaged precooked rice

Cook onion in hot fat till tender but not brown. Add catsup, sugar, Worcestershire sauce, vinegar, salt and pepper. Add meat; heat to boiling. Prepare rice according to package directions. Spoon rice around edge of large platter; arrange barbecued meat in center. Makes 3 or 4 servings.

Lazy-lady's Casserole

¼ cup chopped onion
1 tablespoon butter or margarine
2 1-pound cans (4 cups) pork and beans in tomato sauce or smoke-flavored beans
¼ cup catsup
1 tablespoon prepared mustard

• • •

1 12-ounce can luncheon meat
3 pineapple slices, cut in half
¼ cup brown sugar
1 tablespoon prepared mustard

• • •

1 package refrigerated biscuits

Cook onion in butter till tender but not brown. Add pork and beans, catsup, and prepared mustard; bring to boiling. Pour into 11½x7½x1½-inch baking dish.

Cut luncheon meat in 12 strips; arrange over beans to match picture below. Center with row of pineapple half-slices. Mix 1 tablespoon pineapple syrup or other fruit juice with the brown sugar and mustard. Spread over meat and pineapple.

Place 3 biscuits at each end of casserole. Bake in moderate oven (375°) 15 to 20 minutes or till biscuits are done. (Bake extra biscuits on baking sheet.) Makes 6 servings.

Note: Or, make biscuits with 2 cups packaged biscuit mix by package directions.

Lazy-lady's Casserole is a meal-in-one! Glazed luncheon meat and pineapple go atop baked beans. Hot biscuits, too! More good news: You give the high-sign for supper in no time!

Sleight-of-hand main dishes! These

Put ready-mades through their paces—turn out glamorous Chicken 'n Biscuit Pie

Call on canned, frozen, or packaged foods—exciting dishes fairly jump off the shelf! For instance, Chicken 'n Biscuit Pie is a delicious combination of chicken and vegetables plus a topper of refrigerated biscuits. Trim with pimiento bits. Offer slices of jellied cranberry sauce.

Below is our 15-minute Banquet—canned luncheon meat and sweets glazed with peach preserves. Recipe is on page 138.

star chicken, sea food

Chicken 'n Biscuit Pie

1 1-pound can chicken in gravy
1 can condensed cream of chicken soup
1 tablespoon instant minced onion
½ teaspoon rosemary, crushed
1 8-ounce can (1 cup) peas, drained
1 3-ounce can (⅔ cup) mushrooms
1 5-ounce can (⅔ cup) boned chicken
1 package refrigerated biscuits

Mix chicken in gravy, soup, seasonings; add peas and mushrooms. Dice chicken; add. Heat slowly, stirring now and then, until bubbling hot; turn into a 1½-quart casserole. Snip biscuits in thirds; arrange, point up, in 2 rows around edge of casserole. Bake in very hot oven (450°) 15 minutes or till biscuits are done. Makes 5 servings.

Chicken Pot Pie

Old-fashioned cooking can be this quick!—

2 1-pound cans (4 cups) chicken in gravy

• • •

⅓ cup milk
1 cup packaged biscuit mix
Paprika

Place chicken in gravy in wide 3-quart saucepan (to make room for dumplings). Heat till bubbling. Add milk to biscuit mix, and prepare and cook dumplings according to package directions. Before serving, sprinkle with paprika. Makes 6 servings.

Speedy Chicken Divan

1 10-ounce package frozen broccoli
2 5-ounce cans boned chicken
1 tablespoon light cream
½ 8-ounce jar (½ cup) triple-use cheese spread

Cook broccoli in unsalted water according to package directions; drain thoroughly. Heat chicken in liquid from the can. Add cream to cheese spread and heat.

To serve, place a layer of broccoli on each plate, then a layer of chicken; top with cheese sauce. Makes 4 servings.

Cheese-Noodle Ring with Chicken

Delicious, simple to fix. No one will suspect that protein-padding is afoot—

6 ounces noodles
1½ cups milk
¾ cup grated sharp process American cheese
3 slightly beaten eggs
½ teaspoon salt
½ teaspoon Worcestershire sauce

• • •

2 10½-ounce cans chicken a la king

Cook noodles in boiling, salted water; drain. Arrange in *well-greased* 5-cup ring mold. Combine milk, cheese, eggs, salt, and Worcestershire sauce; pour over noodles.

Place mold in shallow pan, filling pan to 1 inch with hot water. Bake in moderate oven (350°) about 45 minutes, or until firm.

Heat chicken a la king. Unmold ring and fill center with the hot chicken. Trim with pimiento, if desired. Makes 8 servings.

Herbed Chicken and Rice

Aluminum foil

• • •

4 onion slices, ¼ inch thick
½ cup packaged precooked rice
1 2½- to 3-pound ready-to-cook broiler-fryer chicken, cut up
Kitchen bouquet

• • •

1 can condensed cream of mushroom soup
3 tablespoons chopped parsley
2 teaspoons marjoram
1 teaspoon salt
Dash pepper

Cut four 12-inch squares of foil. On each, place a slice of onion; sprinkle with 2 tablespoons rice. Top with a serving of chicken, skin side up. Brush chicken lightly with kitchen bouquet.

Mix remaining ingredients; spoon over chicken. Fold foil over and seal securely. Place packages on baking sheet. Bake in very hot oven (450°) 40 minutes or till done. Trim with parsley. Makes 4 servings.

Fillet Company Dinner

The orange juice makes it tangy . . . your broiler makes it fast—

1 pound fresh or frozen fish fillets
¼ cup orange juice
2 tablespoons melted butter or margarine

• • •

½ teaspoon salt
Dash paprika
1 tablespoon grated orange peel

• • •

Cooked or canned asparagus, drained
Melted butter or margarine
4 strips pimiento

Thaw frozen fish just long enough to separate. Place fillets on greased broiler pan. Combine orange juice and butter; pour half over fish. Sprinkle fish with salt, paprika, orange peel. Broil 3 inches from heat for 5 minutes.

Pour remaining sauce over fish; place asparagus in 4 stacks on broiler pan; brush with butter and top with strips of pimiento. Broil 3 to 6 minutes longer until fish flakes easily and is golden. Transfer to platter. Pass lemon wedges. Makes 4 servings.

Quick Tuna Bake

A natural for Friday-night suppers!—

1 7½-ounce package macaroni-and-cheese dinner
3 tablespoons soft butter or margarine
1 7½-ounce can (1 cup) tomatoes
½ cup milk
2 tablespoons instant minced onion
1 slightly beaten egg
1 6½-, 7-, or 9¼-ounce can tuna, drained
2 tablespoons snipped parsley
¼ teaspoon salt
Dash pepper

• • •

2 tablespoons corn-flake crumbs

Cook macaroni according to package directions; drain. Add cheese (from packaged dinner) and butter. Toss to mix. Drain tomatoes, reserving liquid. Dice tomatoes; add with reserved liquid and remaining ingredients, except crumbs.

Pour mixture into greased 1-quart casserole. Sprinkle with crumbs. Bake uncovered in moderate oven (350°) 35 minutes or till thoroughly heated. Makes 5 servings.

Chopstick Tuna

1 can condensed cream of mushroom soup
1 3-ounce can chow-mein noodles
1 6½-, 7-, or 9¼-ounce can tuna
1 cup sliced celery
½ cup salted toasted cashews
¼ cup chopped onion
Dash pepper

Mix soup with ¼ cup water. Add *1 cup* chow-mein noodles and remaining ingredients; toss lightly. Place in ungreased 10x6x1½-inch baking dish. Sprinkle remaining noodles over top.

Bake in moderate oven (375°) 15 minutes or till heated. Trim with canned mandarin-orange slices. Makes 4 or 5 servings.

15-minute Tuna Curry

⅓ cup chopped onion
¼ cup chopped green pepper
1 clove garlic, minced
2 tablespoons butter or margarine
1 cup dairy sour cream
1 teaspoon curry powder
¼ teaspoon salt
Dash pepper
1 6½-, 7-, or 9¼-ounce can tuna

Cook onion, green pepper, and garlic in butter till tender but not brown. Stir in sour cream and seasonings. Break tuna in bite-size pieces; add. Heat slowly, stirring often, just till hot, Serve over hot rice dotted with raisins. Makes 4 servings.

Jiffy Shrimp Skillet

1 can frozen condensed cream of shrimp soup
¾ cup boiling water
⅔ cup packaged precooked rice
1 8-ounce package frozen cleaned shrimp
½ cup diced celery
½ cup diced green pepper
1 to 1½ teaspoons curry
½ teaspoon salt
½ cup sliced pitted ripe olives
¼ cup toasted slivered blanched almonds

Place shrimp soup in skillet; pour boiling water over. Cover; bring to boiling. Stir in rice, shrimp, celery, green pepper, curry, salt, and dash pepper. Cover; bring to boiling and cook 10 minutes or till rice and shrimp are done, stirring occasionally. Add olives; top with almonds. Makes 4 servings.

Encore-luscious leftovers

Do you look longingly at a big juicy roast, knowing full well your family can "never eat all that"? Look again—there's more than one delicious meal in that roast! The same goes for a ham, a turkey, a plump stewing hen. With good recipes at hand, you can turn that meat-counter buy into good meals for several days. Here are ways to use up every last smidgen of beef, pork, chicken, and turkey. So *plan* to have some leftovers for a delicious return!

Leftover chicken goes company best

← Chicken 'n Chips Bake is really a hot chicken salad. Celery and almonds add crunch, lemon juice and cheese give wonderful flavor. Border casserole with potato chips; add a fluff of parsley.

Twice good—beef and pork

Best Oven Hash

1½ cups coarsely ground cooked beef
1 cup coarsely ground cooked potatoes
½ cup coarsely ground onion
¼ cup chopped parsley
1 teaspoon salt
Dash pepper
2 teaspoons Worcestershire sauce
1 6-ounce can (⅔ cup) evaporated milk
⅓ cup slightly crushed corn flakes
1 tablespoon butter, melted

Lightly mix first eight ingredients. Turn into greased 1-quart casserole. Mix corn flakes and butter; sprinkle over top. Bake in moderate oven (350°) 30 minutes or till heated through. Makes 4 servings.

Skillet Hash

2 tablespoons butter
2 cups cooked beef roast, cut in ½-inch cubes
2 cups raw potato cut in ½-inch cubes
⅓ cup finely diced onion
½ cup beef broth
½ teaspoon salt

Melt butter in skillet; add remaining ingredients. Mix well. Cover; cook over low heat, stirring often, till potatoes are tender, about 15 minutes. Uncover and cook 5 minutes more. Makes 4 servings.

Ham Puffs

1½ cups ground cooked ham
½ pound sharp process American cheese, ground
1 small green pepper, ground
1 small onion, ground

. . .

1¼ cups milk
2 beaten egg yolks
½ cup cracker crumbs
2 stiff-beaten egg whites

. . .

1 recipe Mushroom Sauce

Combine first 4 ingredients. Stir in milk, egg yolks, and crumbs. Fold in egg whites. Fill six greased 6-ounce custard cups. Bake in moderate oven (350°) 40 to 50 minutes or till set. Turn out on plates; top with Mushroom Sauce. Makes 6 servings.

Mushroom Sauce

Melt 2 tablespoons butter or margarine; blend in 2 tablespoons enriched flour. Gradually stir in 1 cup milk and one 3-ounce can broiled sliced mushrooms (with liquid).

Cook, stirring constantly, till mixture thickens. Add 1 tablespoon grated onion and 1 tablespoon chopped parsley. Season to taste with salt and pepper. Spoon over Ham Puffs just before serving.

Turn leftover beef into Best Oven Hash

Roast beef and potatoes return second day as Best Oven Hash. It's expertly seasoned with Worcestershire sauce and onion, has evaporated milk for richness. The crisp topper is buttered corn flakes.

Your family will vote for this hash treat crowned with poached eggs. Have eggs ready when hash comes from the oven. Garnish with sprigs of parsley. Pass catsup and mustard.

Sandwiches Stroganoff

Canned gravy with sour cream—grand finale for Sunday's roast. Try on burgers, too—

1 tablespoon chopped onion
1 tablespoon butter or margarine
1 can (1¼ cups) beef gravy
¼ cup dairy sour cream
1 tablespoon cooking sherry
¼ teaspoon monosodium glutamate
Dash basil
6 slices leftover roast beef
6 slices toast

Cook onion in butter till tender but not brown; stir in gravy, sour cream, sherry, and seasonings. Add beef slices; heat 8 to 10 minutes, stirring occasionally. Serve over hot toast. Makes 6 servings.

Yankee Red-flannel Hash

1½ cups finely chopped cooked corned beef
3 cups finely chopped cooked potatoes
1½ cups finely chopped cooked or canned beets
⅓ cup finely chopped onion
⅓ cup milk
1 teaspoon salt
Few drops Tabasco sauce

• • •

3 to 4 tablespoons fat

Lightly toss together all ingredients except fat; season to taste. Melt fat in skillet; spread hash evenly over bottom. Cook over medium heat till underneath side is brown and crusty. Makes 4 servings.

Ham Patties with Sour Cream

2 cups ground cooked ham
½ cup soft bread crumbs
¼ cup chopped green onion
⅓ cup milk
1 slightly beaten egg
Dash pepper

• • •

1 cup dairy sour cream

Combine ham with remaining ingredients except sour cream. Shape mixture in 6 small or 4 large patties. Brown slowly on both sides in a small amount of hot fat.

Heat sour cream just until hot; serve with patties. Trim with chopped green onion tops or chives. Makes 3 or 4 servings.

LUNCHEON DELIGHT

Savory Ham-Tomato Casserole
Buttered Peas
Pineapple Salad Mold
Dill Pickles — Cloverleaf Rolls
Double-chocolate Pudding
Milk — Coffee

Double-chocolate Pudding: Cook 1 package chocolate pudding following label directions, but *adding ¼ cup more milk*. While hot, add ½ cup semisweet chocolate pieces; stir till melted. Cool. Add 1 teaspoon vanilla; beat till fluffy; fold in 1 cup heavy cream, whipped. Spoon into 6 to 8 sherbets. Chill. Trim with chocolate pieces.

Savory Ham-Tomato Casserole

Use the last of the ham for this flavorful meal-in-one. To round out lunch, see plan above. Salad and dessert wait in refrigerator—

6 ounces 7-minute macaroni

• • •

1 No. 2 can (2½ cups) tomatoes
1 cup chopped celery
½ cup chopped onion
½ cup chopped green pepper
2½ teaspoons salt
¼ teaspoon pepper

• • •

1½ cups cooked ham, cut in matchstick strips
2 tablespoons chopped parsley
1 cup shredded sharp process American cheese

• • •

Parsley sprigs

Cook the macaroni according to the package directions; drain. Combine tomatoes, celery, onion, green pepper, and seasonings; cook gently 30 minutes.

Combine macaroni, vegetables, meat, parsley, and ¾ cup of the cheese; turn into greased 2-quart casserole.

Bake in slow oven (325°) 1 hour. Top with ¼ cup of the cheese during last 5 minutes of baking. Garnish casserole with sprigs of parsley. Makes 8 servings.

Barbecued Pork Sandwiches give leftover roast a flavor bonus—the sauce has plenty of spunk! In fact, this fix-up is so good—you'll *plan* to have some roast pork left from dinner.

Monday Meat Pie

Inside: Savory meat and vegetables. On top: Fluffy, delicious spoon bread—

2½ cups cooked beef, in ½-inch cubes
1½ cups cubed, cooked potatoes
1 cup sliced, cooked carrots
½ cup chopped onion
1 cup shredded sharp process cheese
1 tablespoon chopped pimiento
¾ cup leftover beef gravy
⅔ cup salad dressing
Spoon-bread Topper

Combine ingredients except topper. Heat to bubbling. Turn into greased 2-quart casserole; pour Spoon-bread Topper over hot meat mixture. Bake in hot oven (400°) about 40 minutes. Makes 6 to 8 servings.

Spoon-bread Topper

1 cup corn meal
½ teaspoon salt
1 cup boiling water
½ cup cold milk
2 eggs
1 tablespoon butter, melted
2 teaspoons baking powder

Combine corn meal and salt; add water and mix well. Add milk; beat thoroughly. Beat in eggs; add melted butter and baking powder; mix well. Spoon over *hot* meat mixture.

Barbecued Pork Sandwiches

¼ cup chopped onion
1 tablespoon salad oil

• • •

1 8-ounce can (1 cup) seasoned tomato sauce
¼ to ⅓ cup bottled steak sauce
2 tablespoons brown sugar
Dash salt
1½ to 2 cups thinly sliced roast pork

• • •

6 to 8 hamburger buns, split and toasted

Cook onion in hot oil till tender but not brown. Stir in tomato sauce, steak sauce, sugar, and salt; bring to boiling. Add meat. Reduce heat, cover and cook gently 10 minutes. Serve in toasted hamburger buns. Makes 6 to 8 servings.

Creamed Ham

Delicious over toasted corn bread! Sauce boasts good ham flavor accented with green olives, parsley, spunky Worcestershire—

3 tablespoons butter or margarine
3 tablespoons enriched flour
1½ cups milk

• • •

2 cups diced cooked ham
¼ cup chopped stuffed green olives
1 tablespoon chopped parsley
1 teaspoon Worcestershire sauce

Melt butter; blend in flour. Gradually add milk. Cook and stir till mixture thickens. Add remaining ingredients. Heat thoroughly, about 5 minutes. Serve in patty shells or over toast points. Garnish with snipped parsley. Makes 6 servings.

Hurry-up Luncheon Waffles

Pair off ham and green beans in a quick cheese sauce. Next time serve over rice—

1 8-ounce jar (1 cup) triple-use cheese spread
1 cup diced cooked ham
1 10-ounce package frozen cut green beans, cooked and drained

• • •

4 frozen waffles

Heat cheese spread in top of double boiler or over very low heat. Stir in ham and green beans; heat thoroughly. Heat waffles according to directions on package. To serve, spoon sauce over waffles. Makes 4 servings.

Tag-ends of chicken and turkey

Turkey Tetrazzini

8 ounces spaghetti
¼ cup butter or margarine
½ cup enriched flour
2½ cups chicken broth
1 cup light cream
¼ cup cooking sherry
1¼ teaspoons salt
½ teaspoon monosodium glutamate
Dash pepper
1 6-ounce can mushrooms, drained
¼ cup chopped green pepper
2 cups diced cooked turkey
½ cup shredded Parmesan cheese

Cook spaghetti in boiling salted water till just tender (*don't overcook*); drain.

Melt butter; blend in flour. Gradually stir broth into flour mixture. Add cream. Cook and stir till mixture thickens. Add cooking sherry and seasonings. Divide sauce in half. To one half of sauce, add drained spaghetti, mushrooms, and green pepper. Place in an 11½x7½x1½-inch baking dish.

Add turkey to remaining sauce. Make well in center of spaghetti and pour in turkey mixture. Sprinkle Parmesan cheese over all.

Bake in moderate oven (350°) about 25 minutes or till hot. Makes 5 or 6 servings.

Turkey Curry with Crisp Noodles

Melt 3 tablespoons butter or margarine in skillet. Add 1½ cups finely chopped pared tart apples and ⅓ cup chopped onion. Cook till tender but not brown.

Stir in 2 tablespoons enriched flour and 2 to 2½ teaspoons curry powder. Slowly stir in 2 cups milk. Cook, stirring constantly, till mixture thickens.

Add 1 teaspoon salt and 2 to 3 cups coarsely diced cooked turkey. Heat through. Serve over heated chow-mein noodles. Offer curry condiments. Makes 6 or 7 servings.

Turkey Chop Suey

1 1-pound can (2 cups) bean sprouts
½ cup onion slices
2 tablespoons butter or margarine
1½ to 2 cups diced cooked turkey
1 cup celery slices
1 5- or 6-ounce can (about ⅔ cup) water chestnuts, drained and sliced
½ cup turkey broth*

• • •

2 tablespoons cornstarch
¼ teaspoon salt
¼ teaspoon monosodium glutamate
¼ cup water
2 tablespoons soy sauce

• • •

4 cups hot cooked rice
½ cup slivered blanched almonds, toasted

Drain bean sprouts, reserving liquid. Cook onion in butter till tender but not brown; add the turkey, celery, water chestnuts, broth, and bean-sprout liquid; heat to boiling. Combine cornstarch, seasonings, water, and soy sauce; stir into turkey mixture. Cook, stirring constantly, till thick. Add bean sprouts and just heat through. Serve with hot rice and almonds. Pass bottle of soy sauce. Makes 4 to 6 servings.

*Or use 1 chicken bouillon cube dissolved in ½ cup water in place of turkey broth.

Turkey Chop Suey—a good idea for those last two cups of turkey! Bean sprouts and water chestnuts give an Oriental flair. Serve over fluffy rice; pass slivered almonds.

Chicken 'n Chips Bake

2 cups cubed cooked chicken
2 cups sliced celery
½ cup slivered blanched almonds, toasted (optional)
½ teaspoon salt
½ teaspoon monosodium glutamate
2 teaspoons grated onion
2 tablespoons lemon juice
1 cup mayonnaise or salad dressing

• • •

½ cup shredded sharp process cheese
1½ cups crushed or whole potato chips

Combine all ingredients except cheese and potato chips. Pile lightly in greased 8-inch shallow round baking dish or shallow 1½-quart casserole. Sprinkle with shredded cheese. Border casserole with potato chips. Bake in hot oven (425°) 15 minutes or till heated through. Makes 5 or 6 servings. See picture of this casserole, page 144.

Leftover turkey inspires a luscious meal! Here golden corn bread, crusty and brown, becomes part of the main course. Fill center of Hot Corn Ring with Creamed Turkey, or an a la king.

Hot Corn Ring

Prepare batter from corn-muffin mix or corn-bread mix according to package directions. Fill greased ring mold ⅔ full and bake in hot oven (400°). (Bake any extra batter as muffins.) Allow 18 to 20 minutes for a 5½-cup (8-inch) ring mold. Allow 25 to 30 minutes for larger ring molds.

Unmold; while hot, fill center with Creamed Turkey or a ham or chicken a la king. Trim with pimiento bits and parsley.

Creamed Turkey

¼ cup butter or margarine
¼ cup enriched flour
2 cups milk
½ teaspoon salt
Dash pepper
1 teaspoon Worcestershire sauce
2 cups cubed cooked turkey or chicken

Melt butter; blend in flour. Gradually stir in milk. Cook, stirring constantly till thick. Add seasonings and turkey. If you like a thinner sauce, add a little more milk. Heat thoroughly. Serve in Hot Corn Ring or on toast. Makes 6 servings.

Turkey-salad Souffle

6 slices white bread
2 cups diced cooked turkey
½ cup chopped onion
½ cup chopped green pepper
½ cup finely chopped celery
½ cup mayonnaise
¾ teaspoon salt
Dash pepper

• • •

2 beaten eggs
1½ cups milk

• • •

1 can condensed cream of mushroom soup
½ cup shredded sharp process cheese

Cube *2 slices* of the bread; place in bottom of 8x8x2-inch baking dish. Combine turkey, vegetables, mayonnaise, and seasonings. Spoon over bread cubes.

Trim crusts from remaining bread; arrange slices atop turkey mixture. Combine eggs and milk; pour over all. Cover and chill 1 hour or overnight. Spoon soup over top. Bake in slow oven (325°) about 1 hour or till set. Sprinkle cheese over top last few minutes of baking. Makes 6 servings.

Easy Chicken a la King

There's nothing to it! Use canned mushroom soup for the sauce—

1 can condensed cream of mushroom soup
¼ cup light cream
1½ cups diced cooked chicken
¼ cup diced green pepper
2 tablespoons diced pimiento
1 teaspoon Worcestershire sauce

Slowly heat soup and cream, stirring constantly. Add remaining ingredients; heat thoroughly, stirring occasionally. Serve over toast points. Makes 4 to 6 servings.

Chicken Balls with Mushrooms

2 tablespoons butter or margarine
3 tablespoons enriched flour
1 cup milk or chicken broth
2 cups diced cooked chicken
1 tablespoon snipped parsley
¾ teaspoon salt
Dash pepper
6 to 8 slices white bread
1 beaten egg
1 recipe Mushroom Sauce

Melt butter; blend in flour. Gradually stir in milk. Cook, stirring constantly, till mixture thickens; cool. Add chicken and parsley. Season to taste with salt and pepper. Cover and chill 2 or 3 hours.

Cut crusts from bread. Tear slices into ½-inch pieces. Shape chicken mixture into 8 balls about 2½ inches in diameter (use about ¼ cup mixture for each ball). Dip into beaten egg, then roll in bread pieces, coating well. Place on greased jelly roll pan and chill 2 to 3 hours.

Brush balls with melted butter. Bake in moderate oven (350°) about 20 minutes or till heated through and crumbs are toasted.

To serve, spoon Mushroom Sauce on plate; place chicken balls atop. Makes 4 servings.

Mushroom Sauce
(*for Chicken Balls*)

2 tablespoons melted butter or margarine
1 cup coarsely chopped fresh mushrooms
1 can condensed cream of chicken soup
⅓ cup chicken broth

Melt butter in skillet; add mushrooms and cook 1 to 2 minutes. Add soup and broth; heat just until bubbling hot, stirring often.

Toll House Pancakes

A long-time luncheon favorite at this hospitable inn in Whitman, Massachusetts—

1¼ cups buttermilk
½ teaspoon soda
2 beaten egg yolks

• • •

1 cup sifted enriched flour
2 teaspoons sugar
¾ teaspoon baking powder
¼ teaspoon salt
2 tablespoons soft butter
2 stiff-beaten egg whites

• • •

1 recipe Chicken Filling and Mushroom Sauce
2 tablespoons grated Parmesan cheese

Beat buttermilk and soda into egg yolks with rotary beater, or use your electric mixer at low speed. Sift together flour, sugar, baking powder, and salt; add to egg yolk mixture along with butter; beat till just smooth. Fold in egg whites.

Heat griddle or heavy frying pan. Grease with piece of fat salt pork. (Rub salt pork over pan between each batch.)

Drop batter from ⅓ cup measure onto griddle to make 5-inch pancakes. When cakes are full of bubbles, and edges are cooked well, turn cakes and cook on other side. (To keep first pancakes warm, place on towel-covered baking sheet in very slow oven.) Put a tablespoon of Chicken Filling on each pancake; roll. Place cakes, edges down, in 11½x7½x1½-inch baking dish. Top with Mushroom Sauce; sprinkle with Parmesan cheese. Broil till golden. Makes 4 servings.

Chicken Filling and Mushroom Sauce

3 tablespoons butter
3 tablespoons enriched flour
½ teaspoon salt
1⅓ cups chicken broth
1 cup ½-inch cubes cooked chicken

• • •

⅓ cup sliced mushrooms
3 tablespoons light cream

Chicken Filling: Melt butter; blend in flour and salt. Gradually stir in broth; cook till thick, stirring constantly. Reserve *half* of this sauce for Mushroom Sauce. To other half, add chicken; heat through.

Mushroom Sauce: Stir mushrooms and cream into reserved sauce; heat.

Indoor picnic on a raft—Broiler Bean-er Wiener

One sandwich serves the whole family! Makings are all old favorites—zipped-up baked beans, cheese, and franks broil till bubbly hot. Mustard and pickles top it off! Pass potato chips, relishes, cold milk. Then—big chocolate sundaes.

Vienna Egg-salad Sandwich—hot 'n cold combo

Sizzling-hot Vienna sausages and cool dill-pickle chips make a parade of peppy flavor the full length of this sunny salad sandwich. Whack into eighths and serve everybody two slices, with steaming bowls of onion soup, chilled tomato rounds. →

Seven-league Pizzaburger—good Italian flavor

You split a French loaf, make a yard-long sandwich to divide among 4 or 5 pizza fans. The ground-beef filling is fragrant with oregano and Parmesan, the broiled-on tomato-cheese topper melty and good. Serve chilled green salad, hot coffee.

Whole-meal sandwiches

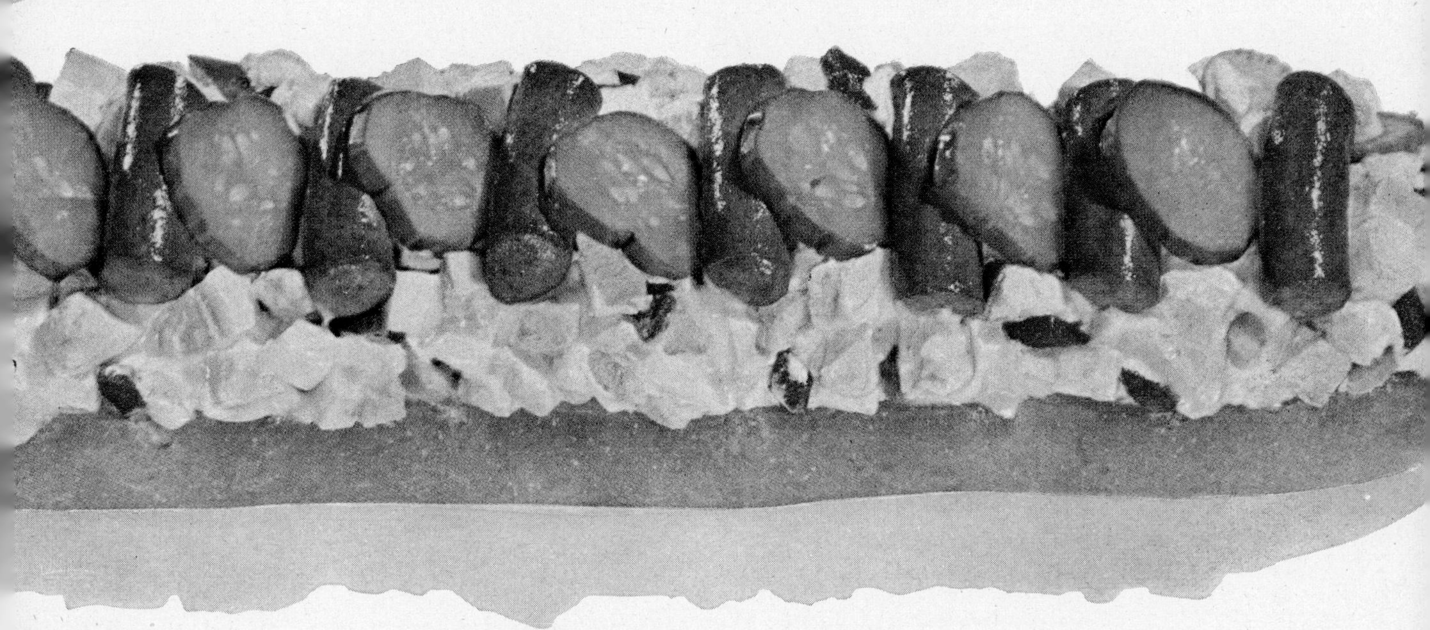

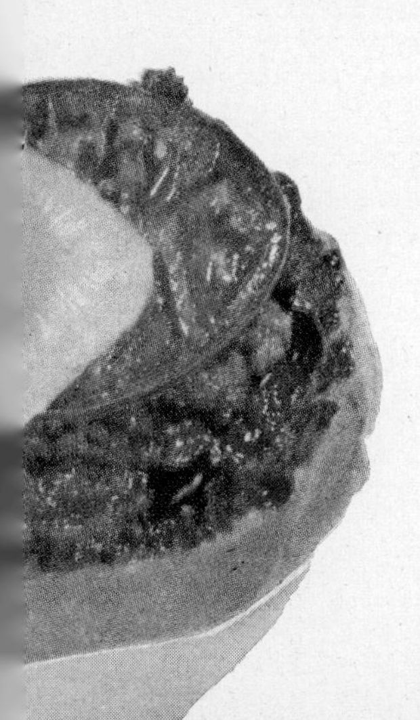

You can build luncheon or supper, even a party, around these sandwiches! Pick a whopper like one of these half-a-loafers—it makes a main dish that's fast and fun, serves 4 to 6. Or hollow out a roll and stuff—easy and impressive. For a teen-age party, serve Submarines, or California Bacon Burgers—filled full, flavor-packed!

Offer hearties by the yard

Vienna Egg-salad Sandwich

2 4-ounce cans Vienna sausage
¼ cup chopped green pepper
¼ cup chopped celery
2 tablespoons chopped green onions
3 hard-cooked eggs, chopped
¼ cup salad dressing or mayonnaise
Dash salt
1 loaf French bread,
  about 18 inches long
Soft butter or margarine
Dill-pickle slices

Reserve 8 sausages for trim; chop remaining sausages and combine with green pepper, celery, onions, eggs, salad dressing, and salt.

Cut bread lengthwise in half; butter one half* and spread with egg mixture. Brown the reserved sausages in small amount hot fat; drain. Place the browned sausages crosswise on half loaf. Tuck pickle slices in between sausages. To serve, slash in 8 sandwiches. Offer knives and forks for neat eating.

*Other half of loaf can be used for garlic bread. Or double filling and use both halves.

Seven-league Pizzaburger

1 loaf French bread,
  about 18 inches long
1 pound ground beef
⅓ cup grated Parmesan cheese
¼ cup finely chopped onion
¼ cup chopped ripe olives
1 teaspoon salt
½ to 1 teaspoon oregano
Dash pepper
1 6-ounce can (⅔ cup) tomato paste
3 tomatoes, peeled and thinly sliced
5 slices sharp process cheese,
  halved diagonally

Cut loaf lengthwise in half. Combine meat, Parmesan cheese, onion, olives, seasonings, and tomato paste. Spread evenly on each half loaf. Broil about 5 inches from heat 12 minutes or till meat is done.

Alternate tomato and cheese slices down top. Broil 1 to 2 minutes more or just till cheese starts to melt. Cut each half loaf in 4 or 5 slices. Allow 1 or 2 slices each.

Broiler Bean-er Wiener Loaf

1 loaf French bread, 18 inches long
1 tablespoon prepared mustard
2 tablespoons soft butter or margarine
1 1-pound can (2 cups) baked beans or
  pork and beans, drained
¼ cup chopped onion
2 tablespoons brown sugar
½ cup shredded sharp process cheese
5 frankfurters
5 small sweet pickles, cut in fans

Cut bread lengthwise in half; blend mustard and butter, spread on half* of loaf. Mix beans, onion, and brown sugar; spoon on the buttered bread. Sprinkle with cheese.

Broil about 7 inches from heat 5 minutes. Split franks lengthwise, without cutting clear through along one side; place split side up on beans, crosswise of loaf; broil 5 minutes longer. Add pickle fans; drizzle mustard down center of franks. Cut loaf in 5 slices so each serving has frank and pickle.

*Use other half for garlic bread, croutons.

Shrimp Boat

1 loaf French bread, 18 inches long
Leaf lettuce
1 8-ounce package cream cheese,
  softened
1 tablespoon lemon juice
½ teaspoon salt
½ teaspoon dill seed
½ cup coarsely chopped cucumber
2 cups cleaned cooked or canned shrimp,
  chilled (1½ pounds in shell)
¾ cup stuffed green olives

Cut bread lengthwise in half; butter both halves; cover with layer of lettuce. Gently press on lettuce so butter holds it in place.

Blend cream cheese, lemon juice, and salt; stir in dill seed and cucumber. Reserve *half* the shrimp and several olives for trim; coarsely chop remaining shrimp and olives. Stir chopped shrimp and olives into cream-cheese mixture and spread evenly over lettuce leaving a green ruffle all around.

Trim with whole shrimp and sliced olives. Cut each half loaf in 4 or 5 slices.

Hot Cheese-Salami Sandwiches

2 cups shredded process cheese *or*
  2 5-ounce jars spreading cheese
¼ cup mayonnaise or salad dressing
1 teaspoon prepared mustard
1 teaspoon grated onion
⅔ cup chopped ripe olives
1 unsliced sandwich loaf,
  about 11 inches long
18 to 20 thin slices large salami
2 tablespoons butter, melted

Blend first 4 ingredients; stir in olives. Cut crusts from top and sides of loaf. Make ½-inch slices, cutting to, *but not through*, bottom crust. Spread facing sides of first cut with cheese filling. Repeat with *every other* cut. Insert 2 salami slices in each "cheese sandwich." Carefully spread remaining cheese mixture over top of loaf.

Tie loaf together with string. Brush sides with butter. Toast on baking sheet in moderate oven (350°) 25 to 30 minutes or till hot.

To serve, snip string and cut through bottom crust in sections without filling.

Makes 9 or 10 sandwiches.

Take-two Sub Sandwich

Each takes one meat, one cheese sandwich—

1 loaf French bread, 18 inches long
Soft butter or margarine
Leaf lettuce
5 thin slices boiled ham
5 thin slices large salami
Large dill pickles, sliced thin
  lengthwise
5 slices Swiss cheese
5 thin slices tomato

Cut French loaf in ¾-inch slices, *almost to, but not through*, bottom crust, making 19 cuts in all. Butter facing sides of first cut and line with lettuce. Repeat with *every other* cut—this will leave unfilled cuts in between, where sandwiches can be broken off.

In first lettuce-lined cut, insert a folded slice *each* of ham and salami with a slice of pickle in the middle. In second lettuce-lined cut, insert a cheese slice folded in half around a tomato slice. Alternate these fillings in remaining lettuce-lined cuts.

Makes 5 double-sandwich servings.

Hot Cheese-Salami Sandwiches—good! This dandy loaf serves 10, goes in the oven in minutes. Filling is salami and melty cheese spiked with mustard, onion, olives. You brush loaf with butter so it toasts a delicious golden brown! Cut apart; serve hot with iced fruit punch or mugs of steaming soup.

Stuffed rolls, stack sandwiches

All-in-a-Roll Burgers

¾ pound ground beef
¼ cup chopped onion
2 large brown-and-serve French rolls, each about 8 inches long*
1 egg, beaten
3 tablespoons snipped parsley
1 to 2 tablespoons prepared mustard
2 tablespoons water
¾ teaspoon salt
¼ teaspoon oregano
Dash pepper
2 tablespoons butter or margarine, melted
1 clove garlic, minced

Brown ground beef. Add onion; cook till tender but not brown. Drain off excess fat.

Cut off one end of each roll; reserve. With a fork, hollow out roll centers and pull apart enough bread to make 1 cup crumbs. Mix crumbs with meat and next 7 ingredients.

Fill rolls, replacing ends; tack with toothpicks. Mix butter and garlic; brush over rolls. Heat on baking sheet in moderate oven (375°) 20 minutes or till hot. Cut each roll in 2 or 3 servings.

*Or 6 coney buns. Fill, wrap in foil; heat.

Henny Penny Rolls

2 cups coarsely diced cooked chicken
½ cup diced celery
⅓ cup chopped sweet pickles
1 tablespoon diced pimiento
½ cup mayonnaise
Salt and pepper

• • •

4 large hard rolls, each about 8 inches long
Soft butter or margarine

Combine chicken, celery, pickle, and pimiento. Moisten with mayonnaise. Season with salt and pepper to taste.

Cut slice off top of each roll; scoop out some of center. Butter the hollows and lids. Fill with chicken salad; replace tops.

Wrap each roll in foil and heat in hot oven (400°) 15 to 20 minutes or till heated through. Makes 4 servings.

Here's hamburger done up in style! The well-seasoned meat filling is corraled in hollowed-out French rolls. More zip—brush crusts of All-in-a-Roll Burgers with garlic butter.

Tuna Toastwiches

15 thin slices bread
1 6½- or 7-ounce can tuna, flaked
1 2-ounce can (½ cup) mushroom stems and pieces, drained
4 hard-cooked eggs, chopped
½ cup chopped ripe olives
¼ cup chopped green onions
¼ cup mayonnaise
1 can condensed cream of chicken soup
1 cup dairy sour cream

Trim bread; butter on both sides. Combine tuna, mushrooms, eggs, olives, onions, and mayonnaise; spread on 10 bread slices.

Put together 5 triple-decker sandwiches, with remaining buttered slices on top. Fasten corners with toothpicks. Toast on baking sheet in moderate oven (350°) 20 minutes or till crisp and lightly browned.*

Mix soup and sour cream; heat and stir just till hot. Serve over hot sandwiches.

*Sandwiches may be wrapped and chilled in refrigerator; heat 5 minutes longer.

Submarines

Brown giant brown-and-serve French rolls (about 8 inches long) according to package directions. Split rolls in half, but don't cut quite through. (If you like, scoop out centers to make extra room for filling.)

Spread generously with mustard, garlic butter, and/or mayonnaise with curry powder. (Or sprinkle bread with clear French or Italian dressing and dash with oregano or basil or other favorite herb.)

Line bottom halves with leaf lettuce. Pile on slices of corned beef, ham, Bologna, salami, pickled tongue, chicken, tuna, herring —several or all. Add sliced American and Swiss cheese, onion, olives, dill pickles—you name it. More lettuce, too. Anchor with cocktail picks; top with cherry tomatoes. Each roll makes one *big* sandwich.

Grilled Corned-beef Sandwiches

12 slices pumpernickel
½ cup Thousand Island dressing
6 slices Swiss cheese
6 tablespoons drained sauerkraut
¼ pound cooked or canned corned beef, sliced
Butter or margarine, softened

Spread 6 slices of bread with dressing. Top each with cheese, 1 tablespoon sauerkraut, corned beef, and bread slice. Butter top and bottom of sandwiches. Grill on both sides on griddle till cheese melts. Makes 6 sandwiches.

California Bacon Burger

1 pound ground beef
¼ cup catsup or barbecue sauce
¾ teaspoon salt
4 slices Canadian-style bacon
4 hamburger buns, split and buttered
2 slices sharp process American cheese, cut in half diagonally
Leaf lettuce
4 slices tomato
8 slices avocado

Combine beef, catsup, salt, and dash pepper; shape in 4 patties. Broil 3 to 4 inches from heat 6 minutes; turn. Place bacon on broiler rack with patties. Broil 6 minutes, turning bacon once. Toast buns last 2 to 3 minutes.

On bottom half of each bun stack bacon slice, beef patty, cheese triangle; on top half place lettuce, tomato slice, 2 avocado slices. Serve open face; offer Thousand Island Dressing, catsup, mustard. Makes 4.

Thousand Island Dressing

½ cup mayonnaise or salad dressing
¼ cup chili sauce
1 hard-cooked egg, finely chopped
2 tablespoons finely chopped green pepper
2 tablespoons finely chopped celery
1 teaspoon paprika
¼ teaspoon salt

Combine all ingredients. Makes 1 cup.

Submarines—high-hat sandwiches that have some of everything!

Invite guests with hearty appetites for these filling-on-filling sandwiches! Serve with tomato consomme, maybe dessert. That's all!

Index

A

Apples, Glazed, 99
Artichokes With Crab Stuffing, 41
Asparagus dishes, 16, 66, 93

B

Bacon Curls, 45
Beef dishes, *see Meat and Hamburger*
Biscuits
Biscuit Rolls, 16
Cheese Pretzels, 46
Cheese Swirls, 46
Onion Biscuits, 46
Pimiento Drop Biscuits, 21
Pinwheel Biscuits, 46
Yam Biscuits, 17
Blintze, Country, 95
Blue-cheese Dressing, 66
Bouquet garni, 62, 72
Bread
French Bread Parmesan, 42
Toasty Garlic Bread, 138

C

Casseroles, 6-53
Artichokes With Crab Stuffing, 41
Asparagus-Ham Bake, 16
Baked beans, 37, 38, 134
Beef dishes
Baked Corned-beef Burgers, 137
Beefsteak and Kidney Pie, 70
Best Oven Hash, 146
Big-meal Combo, 138
Chipped-beef Noodle Bake, 17
Chipped-beef Puff, 17
Monday Meat Pie, 148
Pizza Hash, 137
Round-steak Supper, 14
Steak Supper, Foil-wrapped, 13
Vegetable-Beef Bake, 14
Big-meal Combo (*meal plan*), 138
Bologna Bake, 133
Cheese dishes
Cheese-Noodle Ring with Chicken, 141
Hungarian Noodle Bake, 33
Jiffy Cheesefurters, 134
Macaroni and Cheese, 11, 31, 51
Pizza Supper Pie, 32
Quiche Lorraine, 72
Swiss Cheese-Onion Pie, 34
Swiss Onion Bake, 32
Swiss Pies, 34
Three-cheese Lasagne, 33
Chicken dishes
Bombay Chicken, 22
Casserole Chicken a la King, 20
Chicken-Biscuit Pie, 18
Chicken 'n Biscuit Pie, 141
Chicken and Biscuits, 21
Chicken 'n Chips Bake, 150
Chicken Dinner Bake, 20
Chicken with Noodles, 21
Chicken Pot Pie, 141
Chicken Strata, 18, 51
Chicken Upside-down Pie, 22
Classic Chicken Divan, 18
Club Chicken, 20
Creamy Chicken-Rice Casserole, 20
Curried Chicken Casserole, 19
Curried Chicken in Pepper Cups, 40
Easy Chicken Divan, 19
Herbed Chicken and Rice, 141
Party Chicken-Noodle Bake (*meal plan*), 22
Speedy Chicken Divan, 141
Corn Puff, 39
Crowd casseroles, 50-51
Dandy Dixie Bake, 138

Casseroles, *continued*
Egg dishes
Curried Eggs in Shrimp Sauce, 35
Deviled Egg-Ham Casserole, 34
Eggs in Spanish Sauce, 34
Ham 'n Egg Divan, 35
Ham and Eggs en Casserole, 16
Sunday-Supper Egg Cups, 35
Fillet Company Dinner, 142
Freezing casseroles, 47
Garnishes for casseroles, 44-45
Ham dishes
Asparagus-Ham Bake, 16
Deviled Egg-Ham Casserole, 34
Easy Ham and Potatoes au Gratin, 138
Ham-Chicken Bake, 17
Ham 'n Egg Divan, 35
Ham and Potato Scallop, 42
for 24, 50
Ham Puffs, 146
Savory Ham-Tomato Casserole (*meal plan*), 147
Veal-Ham Foldovers, 13
Hamburger dishes
Burger Chili and Chips, 10
Burger-Noodle Bake, 10
Hamburger-Biscuit Bake, 9
Hamburger-Corn Casserole, 10
Hamburger Pie, 8, 50
Hamburger Pielets, 9
Jumbo Cornburger, 39
Mexican Tamale Pie, 74
Old-time Stuffed Peppers, 40
Salmagundi Bake, 10
Stuffed Manicotti, 9
Vegetable-Meat Pie, 36
Hash-stuffed Onions, 41
Honey-baked Squash, 41
Hot Potato Salad with Franks (*meal plan*), 42
Hungarian Noodle Bake, 33
Hurry Supper Bake, 136
Indian Corn Casserole, 39
Jiffy Cheesefurters, 134
Jumbo Cornburger, 39
Lasagne, Baked, 82, 50
Lasagne, Short-cut Style, 83
Lasagne, Three-cheese, 33
Lazy-lady's Casserole, 139
Macaroni and Cheese, 11, 31, 51
Meat-ball Pie, 136
Monday Meat Pie, 148
Mushroom Casserole, Club, 43
Oven Spanish Rice, 33
Parsley Rice Squares with Chicken, 33
Pizza Hash, 137
Pizza Supper Pie, 32
Pork dishes
Pork-Apple Bake, 15
Pork-chop Oven Dinner (*meal plan*), 15
Spareribs with Caraway Kraut, 13
Tenderloin-Noodle Treat, 15
Salmagundi Bake, 10
Salmon dishes
Salmon Florentine, 28
Salmon Macaroni, 28
Seattle Salmon Pie, 28
Sausage dishes
Gourmet Sausage and Noodles, 11
Honey-baked Squash, 41
Sausage Macaroni and Cheese, 11
Sausage Pilaf, 12
Sausage Polenta, 11
Sausage-Stuffing Towers, 12
Sausage Strata (*meal plan*), 12
Sausage and Sweets, 43
Sausage-top Casserole, 134
Scalloped Potatoes With Sausage, 42
Squash-Sausage Bake, 41
Scalloped Eggplant Italian, 36

Casseroles, *continued*
Sea-food dishes
Artichokes With Crab Stuffing, 41
Brazilian Shrimp Pie, 75
Creole Stuffed Peppers, 40
Golden Shrimp Bake, 27
Lobster en Coquille, 23
Luncheon Crab Bake, 23
Rice and Shrimp Casserole, 27
Scalloped Oysters, 29
Sea Food Fancy, 23
Shrimp New Orleans, 27
Shrimp Pinwheel Casserole, 27
Spareribs with Caraway Kraut, 13
Squash-Sausage Bake, 41
Stuffed Manicotti, 9
Stuffed peppers, 40
Supper Stew Bake, 136
Swedish Cabbage Rolls, 70
Tamale Pie, Mexican, 74
Tenderloin-Noodle Treat, 15
Tips
Common casserole sizes, 8
How to grease casserole, 9
How to measure casseroles, 8
How to mix in casserole, 39
Trims for casseroles, 44-45
Toppers for casseroles
Biscuits, 16, 17, 21, 46
Potato Fluff Topper, 8
Spoon-bread Topper, 148
Tuna
Chopstick Tuna, 142
Cream-cheese Tuna Bake, 26
Quick Tuna Bake, 142
Tuna with Cheese Swirls, 26
Tuna Italian, 25
Tuna-Noodle Casserole, 25
Turkey-salad Souffle, 150
Turkey Tetrazzini, 149
Veal-Ham Foldovers, 13
Veal and Rice, Chopstick, 13
Vegetable-Beef Bake, 14
Vegetable-Meat Pie, 36
Wiener Bean Pot, 134
Zucchini Dolmas, Turkish, 70
Chafing-dish Classics, 100-115
Beef Fondue, 104
Beef Stroganoff, Classic, 103
Chafing Chuck, 102
Cheese Fondue, 110-112
Chicken a la King, 109
Crab-meat Newburg, 107
Creamed Codfish, New England, 107
Creamed Mushrooms, 103
Creamed Oysters on Toast, 107
General information, 102
Ham in Sour Cream, Company, 102
Lobster Newburg, 106
Lobster Supreme, 106
Midnight-snack Rabbit, 112
Rabbits, 112
Shells for creamed dishes, 109, 113-115
Shrimp in Cheese Sauce, 105
Shrimp Newburgs, 105
Shrimp Orleans, 143
Shrimp Saute, Easy, 105
Speedy Stroganoff with Noodles, 102
Swiss Rabbit Stack-ups, 112
Tuna a la King with Cornsticks, 107
Welsh Rabbit Sandwiches, 112
Cheese dishes
Cheese Chowder, 118
Cheese Fondue, 110-112
Cheese French Omelet, 94
Cheese souffles, 92, 93
Egg and Cheese Scallop, 67
Hot Cheese-Salami Sandwich, 155
Macaroni and Cheese casseroles, 11, 31, 51
Omelets, 94-96, 98-99
Quiche Lorraine, 72
Rabbits, 67, 112, 135, 143
Souffles, 92, 93
Swiss Cheese-Onion Pie, 34
Swiss Pies, 34
Chicken dishes
Bombay Chicken, 22
Brunswick Stew, 123
Cheese-Noodle Ring with Chicken, 141
Chicken a la King, 109, 151

Chicken dishes, *continued*
Chicken Almond, 86
Chicken Balls with Mushrooms, 151
Chicken 'n Chips Bake, 150
Chicken-Corn Soup, 118
Chicken Curry, 88
Chicken Dinner Bake, 20
Chicken Divan, 18, 19, 141
Chicken Livers Stroganoff, 63
Chicken with Noodles, 21
Chicken Strata, 18
for 24, 51
Club Chicken, 20
Company Chicken and Potatoes, 63
Creamed Chicken or Turkey, 64
Creamy Chicken-Rice Casserole, 20
Curried Chicken Casserole, 19
Curried Chicken in Pepper Cups, 40
Dumplings for stewed chicken, 129
Gourmet Chicken with Noodles, 63
Ham-Chicken Bake, 17
Herbed Chicken and Rice, 141
How much chicken to slice and dice; how to slice chicken, 18
Parsley Rice Squares with Chicken, 33
Party Chicken-Noodle Bake (*meal plan*), 22
Pies
Casserole Chicken a la King, 20
Chicken-Biscuit Pie, 18
Chicken 'n Biscuit Pie, 141
Chicken and Biscuits, 21
Chicken Pie with Puff-pastry Top, 125
Chicken Pot Pie, 141
Chicken Upside-down Pie, 22
Sandwiches
Chicken-Tomato Whirl, 71
Henny Penny Rolls, 156
Spanish-style Chicken Skillet (*meal plan*), 63
Toll House Pancakes, 151
Chili
Burger Chili and Chips, 10
Chili Con Carne, 123
for 24, 52
Jiffy Tamale Chili, 74
Chinese Fried Rice, 86
Chinese Hot Pot, 85
Chop Suey, 133, 149
Chow Mein, Chipped-beef, 133
Chowders, *see Soups, Chowders*
Chutney, Currant, 89
Cioppino (Italian Fish Stew), 82
Creamed dishes
Cheese-Noodle Ring with Chicken, 141
Chicken a la King, 109, 151
Chicken Curry, 88
Chipped-beef Chow Mein, 133
Crab-meat Newburg, 107
Creamed Chicken or Turkey, 64
Creamed Eggs a la Asparagus, 66
Creamed Ham, 148
Creamed Mushrooms, 103
Creamed Oysters on Toast, 107
Creamed Turkey, 150
Curried-egg Biscuit Topper, 66
Curried Shrimp, 88
Curry of Shrimp, Suzanne, 89
Eggs a la King, 66
Hurry-up Luncheon Waffles, 148
Lobster Newburg, 106
Lobster Supreme, 106
New England Creamed Codfish, 107
Quick Shrimp Curry, 143
Shrimp Newburg, 105
Shrimp Orleans, 143
Speedy Shrimp Newburg, 105
Tuna a la King with Cornsticks, 107
Tuna Curry, 15-minute, 142
Crowd main dishes, 48-53
Curry
Chicken, 88
Condiments, 89
Lamb, 88
Shrimp, 88, 89, 143
Tuna, 142
Turkey, 149

D-E

Desserts
Double-chocolate Pudding, 147
Peaches Melba, 106
Persian Peaches, 12
Speedy Apple Pie, 60
Dumplings, 128-129
Egg dishes
Chipped Beef-Egg Patties, 67
Country Blintze, 95
Creamed Eggs a la Asparagus, 66
Curried-egg Biscuit Topper, 66
Curried Eggs in Shrimp Sauce, 35
Deviled Egg-Ham Casserole, 34
Egg and Cheese Scallop, 67
Eggs a la King (*meal plan*), 66
Eggs in Spanish Sauce, 34
Ham 'n Egg Divan, 35
Ham and Eggs en Casserole, 16
Omelets, 94-96, 98-99
Scrambled, 97
Souffles, 92-93
Squaw Corn, 139
Sunday-Supper Egg Cups, 35
Vienna Egg-salad Sandwich, 154

F-G

Fish, *see also Sea Food*
Cioppino (Italian Fish Stew), 82
Fillet Company Dinner, 142
Fish Chowder, 121
New England Creamed Codfish, 107
Salmon casseroles, 28
Tuna dishes
Chopstick Tuna, 142
Church-supper Tuna Bake for 24, 51
Cream-cheese Tuna Bake, 26
15-minute Tuna Curry, 142
Pacific Chowder, 121
Quick Tuna Bake, 142
Sweet-Sour Tuna, 65
Tuna a la King with Cornsticks, 107
Tuna with Cheese Swirls, 26
Tuna Italian, 25
Tuna-Noodle Casserole, 25
Tuna 'n Rice Souffle, 93
Tuna Toastwiches, 156
Foil dinners
Foil-wrapped Steak Supper, 13
Herbed Chicken and Rice, 141
Foreign fare, 68-89
Brazilian Shrimp Pie, 75
Chinese
Chicken Almond, 86
Fried Rice, 86
Hot Pot, 84-86
Chop Suey, 133, 149
Danish Smorrebrod, 71
English Beefsteak and Kidney Pie, 70
French
Quiche Lorraine, 72
Veal Stew, 72
Hungarian
Gulyas, 72
Spaetzels, 72
Indian and Pakistani
Chicken Curry, 88
Condiments for curry, 89
Currant Chutney, 89
Curried Lamb, 88
Curried Shrimp, 88
Curry of Shrimp, Suzanne, 89
Orange Rice, 89
Saffron Rice, 88
Shrimp Curry In A Hurry, 88
Italian
Cioppino, 82
Fine Spaghetti with Green Sauce, 78
Green Noodles, 78
Lasagne, Baked, 82
for 24, 50
Lasagne, Short-cut Style, 83
Meat Balls, 77
Meat Sauce, 78
Mushroom Pasta Sauce, 78
Pizzas, 79-81
Polenta with Meat Sauce, 83
Spaghetti and Meat Balls, 77
Stuffed Manicotti, 9
Vegetable Soup with Tiny Meat Balls, 119
Foreign fare, *continued*
Japanese Sukiyaki, 87
Mexican
Eggplant Skillet, 74
Jiffy Tamale Chili, 74
Tamale Pie, 74
Russian Classic Beef Stroganoff, 103
Spanish Fried Rice, 75
Spanish Paella (*meal plan*), 75
Swedish Cabbage Rolls, 70
Swiss fondue, 110
Turkish Zucchini Dolmas, 70
Frankfurters
Broiler Bean-er Wiener Loaf, 154
Chili con Wiene, 135
Hot Dog Bar-B-Q, 134
Hot Potato Salad with Franks (*meal plan*), 42
Jiffy Cheesefurters, 134
Saucy Franks, 59
Wiener Bean Pot, 134
Wiener Towers, 134
Freezing main dishes, 47
Garnishes for casseroles, 44-45
Goulash, 62, 72

H-I-J-K

Ham dishes
Asparagus-Ham Bake, 16
Company Ham in Sour Cream, 102
Creamed Ham, 148
Ham-Chicken Bake, 17
Ham and Eggs en Casserole, 16
Ham and Potato Scallop, 42
for 24, 50
Ham and Potatoes au Gratin, 17
Easy, 138
Ham and Squash Skillet (*meal plan*), 60
Ham Patties with Sour Cream, 147
Ham-Potato Soup, 120
Ham Puffs, 146
Hawaiian Sweet-Sour Ham, 60
Hurry-up Luncheon Waffles, 148
Savory Ham-Tomato Casserole (*meal plan*), 147
Sour Cream-Ham Omelet, 99
Veal-Ham Foldovers, 13
Hamburger dishes
All-in-a-Roll Burgers, 156
Bow-tie Noodles with Meat Sauce, 58
Burger Chili and Chips, 10
Burger-Noodle Bake, 10
Burger-Q Buns, 58
California Bacon Burger, 157
Chafing Chuck, 102
Chili Con Carne, 52, 123
Chili con Wiene, 135
Ground Beef and Noodles in Sour-cream Sauce, 57
Hamburger-Biscuit Bake, 9
Hamburger-Corn Casserole, 10, 50
Hamburger Pie, 8, 50
Hamburger Pielets, 9
Italian Meat Balls, 77
Spaghetti sauces, 51, 78, 133
Jumbo Cornburger, 39
Meat-ball Garden Skillet, 57
Old-time Stuffed Peppers, 40
Salmagundi Bake, 10
Seven-league Pizzaburger, 154
Stroganoff Beefburgers, 57
Stuffed Manicotti, 9
Texas Straw Hats, 58
Vegetable-Meat Pie, 36
Vegetable Soup with Tiny Meat Balls, 119
Hash, 137, 146, 147
Herbed Chips, 28
Italian dishes, *see Foreign fare*
Jiffy dishes, *see Speedy Suppers*
Kabobs, Scallop, 143

L

Lasagne, 50, 82, 83
Leftovers, 144-151
Beef, 146, 148
Chicken 150, 151
Ham, 146-148
Pork, 148
Turkey, 149-150
Luncheon-meat dishes
Busy-day Barbecue, 139
Dandy Dixie Bake, 138
15-minute Banquet, 138
Garden Skillet Meal, 138
Lazy-lady's Casserole, 139
Quick Spanish Rice, 139
Squaw Corn, 139

M-N

Macaroni
Best-ever Macaroni and Cheese, 31
Cream-cheese Tuna Bake, 26
Hurry-up Macaroni and Cheese, 31
Macaroni-and-Cheese Puff, 31
Macaroni Omelet, 99
Olive Macaroni-Cheese Bake, 31
Quick Tuna Bake, 142
Salmon Macaroni, 28
Sausage Macaroni and Cheese, 11
Stuffed Manicotti, 9
Meal plans
Casserole Luncheon, 12
Chicken and Biscuits, 63
Chicken for Company, 22
Dinner's in the Oven, 138
Family Fare, 42
Homespun and Hearty, 15
Luncheon Delight, 147
Savory Sausage Dinner, 59
Sea-breeze Supper, 28
Southern Supper, 60
Spanish Feast, 75
Spring Special, 66
Meat, *see also Ham, Hamburger, and Sausage*
Beef dishes
Baked Corned-beef Burgers, 137
Beef Fondue, 104
Beef Goulash—Poppy-seed Noodles, 62
Beef Potage (soup), 120
Beef Stroganoff, 102, 103
Big-meal Combo (*meal plan*), 138
Chipped-beef Chow Mein, 133
Chipped Beef-Egg Patties, 67
Chipped-beef Noodle Bake, 17
Chipped-beef Puff, 17
Curried Beef Cubes, 61
English Beefsteak and Kidney Pie, 70
Foil-wrapped Steak Supper, 13
Grilled Corned-beef Sandwiches, 157
Meat-ball Pie, 136
Monday Meat Pie, 148
Round-steak Supper, 14
Savory Beef and Spaghetti, 62
Steak 'n Potato Dinner, 61
Stews, 123-124, 126, 128
Vegetable-Beef Bake, 14
Bologna Bake, 133
Bologna-Rice Barbecue, 133
Chop Suey, Speedy, 133
Deviled-ham Bean Bake, 134
Deviled-ham Hot Lunch, 136
Ham dishes, *see Ham*
Hamburger dishes, *see Hamburger*
Hash, 137, 146, 147
Hungarian Gulyas, 72
Lamb dishes
Curried Lamb, 88
Favorite Lamb Stew, 125
Lamb Pie with Pastry Tricorns, 126
Luncheon-meat dishes, 138-139
Pizza, 79-81
Pork dishes
Barbecued Pork Sandwiches, 148
Pork-Apple Bake, 15
Pork-chop Oven Dinner (*meal plan*), 15
Pork-chop Spanish Rice, 60
Tenderloin-Noodle Treat, 15
Sandwiches
Grilled Corned-beef Sandwiches, 157
Ham Sandwich, Spring Style, 136
Sandwiches Stroganoff, 147
Submarines, 157
Take-two Sub Sandwich, 155
Sausage, *see Sausage dishes*
Meat, *continued*
Stews, 122-129
Veal dishes
Chopstick Veal and Rice, 13
French Veal Stew, 72
Veal-chop Dinner, 62
Veal-Ham Foldovers, 13
Veal Parmesan, 62
Veal Stew with Corn-meal Dumplings, 129
Newburgs, 105, 106, 107
Noodles, Italian Green, 78

O-P-Q-R

Omelets, 94-96, 98-99
Paella, Spanish (*meal plan*), 75
Pizzas, 79-81
Polentas, 11, 83
Popovers, 113
Pressure-pan dishes
Old-time Oxtail Stew, 125
Speedy Chop Suey, 133
10-minute Spaghetti Sauce, 133
Pudding, Double-chocolate, 147
Puff Pastry, 114-115, 125
Quantity recipes, 48-53
Cabbage Slaw, 53
Chicken Strata, 51
Chili Con Carne, 52
Church-supper Tuna Bake, 51
Ham-and-Potato Scallop, 50
Hamburger-Corn Casserole, 50
Hamburger Pie, 50
Italian Spaghetti Sauce, 51
Lasagne, 50
Macaroni and Cheese, 51
Roaster Baked Beans, 52
Shopping for 24, 52-53
Tossed Green Salad for 50, 53
Quiche Lorraine, 72
Rabbits
Creole Rabbit, 67
Midnight-snack Rabbit, 112
1-2-3 Lobster Rabbit, 143
Swiss Rabbit Stack-ups, 112
Tomato Rabbit, 135
Welsh Rabbit Sandwiches, 112
Western Rabbit, 135
Rice dishes
Chinese Fried Rice, 86
Chopstick Veal and Rice, 13
Club Chicken, 20
Creamy Chicken-Rice Casserole, 20
Herbed Chicken and Rice, 141
Honolulu Shrimp and Rice, 65
How to mold rice, 65
Orange Rice, 89
Oven Spanish Rice, 33
Parsley Rice Squares with Chicken, 33
Pork-chop Spanish Rice, 60
Quick Spanish Rice, 139
Rice and Shrimp Casserole, 27
Rice rings, 64
Saffron Rice, 88
Salmagundi Bake, 10
Sausage Pilaf, 12
Spanish Fried Rice, 75
Spanish Tomato Rice, 60

S

Salads for a crowd, 53
Salmon casseroles, 28
Sandwiches, 152-157
All-in-a-Roll Burgers, 156
Barbecued Pork Sandwiches, 148
Broiler Bean-er Wiener Loaf, 154
Burger-Q Buns, 58
California Bacon Burger, 157
Danish Smorrebrod, 71
Grilled Corned-beef Sandwiches, 157
Ham Sandwich, Spring Style, 136
Henny Penny Rolls, 156
Hot Cheese-Salami Sandwiches, 155
Sandwiches Stroganoff, 147
Seven-league Pizzaburger, 154
Shrimp Boat, 154
Submarines, 157
Take-two Sub Sandwich, 155
Tuna Toastwiches, 156
Vienna Egg-salad Sandwich, 154
Welsh Rabbit Sandwiches, 112

Sausage dishes
Gourmet Sausage and Noodles, 11
Hawaiian Sausage Platter, 59
Honey-baked Squash, 41
Lasagne, 50, 82, 83
Polenta with Meat Sauce, 83
Sausage Creole, 59
Sausage-Egg Scramble, 97
Sausage Macaroni and Cheese, 11
Sausage-Noodle Skillet, 134
Sausage Pilaf, 12
Sausage Pizza, 81
Sausage Polenta, 11
Sausage Strata (*meal plan*), 12
Sausage-Stuffing Towers, 12
Sausage and Sweets, 43
Sausage-top Casserole, 134
Sausage with Parsley Noodles (*meal plan*), 59
Scalloped Potatoes With Sausage, 42
Squash-Sausage Bake, 41
Vienna Egg-salad Sandwich, 154
Sauces
Anchovy Butter, 104
Chicken Sauce, 95
Chinese Mustard, 86
Creamy Horseradish Sauce, 104
Creole Sauce, 99
Cucumber Sauce, 28
Currant Chutney, 89
Garlic Butter, 104
Ginger Soy, 86
Jiffy Mustard Sauce, 136
Mushroom-Cheese Sauce, 93
Mushroom Sauce, 146
Peanut Sauce, 86
Quick Mushroom Sauce, 99
Red Sauce, 86
Spaghetti Sauces, 77-78, 133
Speedy Cheese Sauce, 95
Tomato Steak Sauce, 104
Vegetable Sauce, 9
Scrambled Eggs, 97
Sea Food, *see also Fish*
Cioppino (*Italian Fish Stew*), 82
Clam Chowder, Manhattan, 121
Crab dishes
Artichokes With Crab Stuffing, 41
Crab Meat Bisque, 121
Crab-meat Newburg, 107
Luncheon Crab Bake, 23
Lobster dishes
Lobster en Coquille, 23
Lobster Newburg, 106
Lobster Rabbit, 1-2-3, 143
Lobster Supreme, 106
Oyster dishes
Creamed Oysters on Toast, 107
Olympia Oyster Hangtown Fry, 96
Oyster Stew, 121
Scalloped Oysters, 29
Pacific Chowder, 121
Scallop Kabobs, 143
Sea Food Fancy, 23
Shrimp dishes
Brazilian Shrimp Pie, 75
Creole Stuffed Peppers, 40
Curried Eggs in Shrimp Sauce, 35
Curried Shrimp, 88, 89, 143
Easy Shrimp Saute, 105
Golden Shrimp Bake, 27
Honolulu Shrimp and Rice, 65
How to measure shrimp, 27
Jiffy Shrimp Skillet, 142
Rice and Shrimp Casserole, 27
Shrimp Boat, 154
Shrimp Creole, 65
Shrimp in Cheese Sauce, 105
Speedy Shrimp Newburg, 105
Shrimp New Orleans, 27
Shrimp Newburg, 105
Shrimp Orleans, 143
Shrimp Pinwheel Casserole, 27
Spanish Paella (*meal plan*), 75
Shells, rings for creamed dishes
Cheese-Noodle Ring, 141
Cheese Toast Cups, 109
Confetti Rice Ring, 64
Corn Ring, Hot, 150
Parsley Rice Ring, 64
Pastry Petal Cups, 113
Patty Shells, 114-115
Popovers, 113
Toast Cups, 113
Toast Rings, 113
Shopping for 24 people, 52-53
Shrimp dishes, *see Sea Food*
Skillet meals, 54-67, *see also Chafing-dish classics*
Beef dishes
Beef Goulash—Poppy-seed Noodles, 62
Chipped-beef Chow Mein, 133
Chipped Beef-Egg Patties, 67
Curried Beef Cubes, 61
Savory Beef and Spaghetti, 62
Skillet Hash, 146
Steak 'n Potato Dinner, 61
Bologna-Rice Barbecue, 133
Chicken dishes
Chicken a la King, Easy, 151
Chicken Almond, 86
Chicken Curry, 88
Chicken Livers Stroganoff, 63
Company Chicken and Potatoes, 63
Creamed Chicken or Turkey, 64
Gourmet Chicken with Noodles, 63
Spanish-style Chicken Skillet (*meal plan*), 63
Speedy Chicken Divan, 141
Chili con Wiene, 135
Chinese Hot Pot, 85
Creamed Eggs a la Asparagus, 66
Curried-egg Biscuit Topper, 66
Eggs a la King (*meal plan*), 66
Egg and Cheese Scallop, 67
Eggplant Skillet, Mexican, 74
Frankfurter skillets, 59, 134
Ham dishes
Creamed Ham, 148
Deviled-ham Hot Lunch, 136
Ham Patties with Sour Cream, 147
Ham and Squash Skillet (*meal plan*), 60
Hawaiian Sausage Platter, 59
Hawaiian Sweet-Sour Ham, 60
Hurry-up Luncheon Waffles, 148
Hamburger dishes
Bow-tie Noodles with Meat Sauce, 58
Burger-Q Buns, 58
Ground Beef and Noodles in Sour-cream Sauce, 57
Meat-ball Garden Skillet, 57
Sandwiches Stroganoff, 147
Spaghetti and Meat Balls, 77
Stroganoff Beefburgers, 57
Texas Straw Hats, 58
Luncheon meat dishes, 138-139
Pork-chop Spanish Rice, 60
Sausage dishes
Polenta with Meat Sauce, 83
Sausage Creole, 59
Sausage-Noodle Skillet, 134
Sausage with Parsley Noodles (*meal plan*), 59
Shrimp dishes
Honolulu Shrimp and Rice, 65
Jiffy Shrimp Skillet, 142
Quick Shrimp Curry, 143
Shrimp Creole, 65
Shrimp Orleans, 143
Spanish Fried Rice, 75
Spanish Tomato Rice, 60
Sukiyaki, 87
Tamale Chili, Jiffy, 74
Tuna Curry, 15-minute, 142
Tuna, Sweet-sour, 65
Turkey Chop Suey, 149
Turkey, Creamed, 150
Turkey Curry with Crisp Noodles, 149
Veal-chop Dinner, 62
Veal Parmesan, 62
Yankee Red-flannel Hash, 147
Souffles, 92-93
Soups, Chowders, 118-121
Beef Potage, 120
Cheese Chowder, 118
Chicken-Corn Soup, 118
Chili Con Carne, 123
for 24, 52
Chilled Tomato-Cream Soup, 75
Crab Meat Bisque, 121
Fish Chowder, 121
Ham-Potato Soup, 120
Hearty Bean Soup, 118
Manhattan Clam Chowder, 121
Oyster Stew, 121
Pacific Chowder, 121
Soups, Chowders, *continued*
Pea Soup Royale, 118
Soup-kettle Supper, 119
Split-pea Soup, 118
Supper Corn Chowder, 119
Tomato Chili Stew, 120
Trims for soups; soup accompaniments, 118
Vegetable Soup with Tiny Meat Balls, 119
Spaghetti sauces, 51, 77, 78, 133
Spanish Rice
Pork-chop Spanish Rice, 60
Quick Spanish Rice, 139
Spanish Fried Rice, 75
Spanish Tomato Rice, 60
Spareribs with Caraway Kraut, 13
Speedy Suppers
Bologna Bake, 133
Bologna-Rice Barbecue, 133
Chicken, 109, 141
Chipped-beef Chow Mein, 133
Corned beef, 137-138
Deviled-ham dishes, 134, 136
Easy Ham and Potatoes au Gratin, 138
Frankfurter dishes, 134-135
Fillet Company Dinner, 142
Hurry Supper Bake, 136
Luncheon meat dishes, 138-139
Meat-ball Pie, 136
1-2-3 Lobster Rabbit, 143
Pizza On The Run, 81
Sausage-Noodle Skillet, 134
Sausage-top Casserole, 134
Scallop Kabobs, 143
Shrimp dishes
Jiffy Shrimp Skillet, 142
Quick Shrimp Curry, 143
Shrimp Curry In A Hurry, 88
Shrimp Orleans, 143
Speedy Shrimp Newburg, 105
Speedy Chop Suey, 133
Squaw Corn, 139
Supper Stew Bake, 136
10-minute Spaghetti Sauce, 133
Tomato Rabbit, 135
Tuna dishes, 142
Western Rabbit, 135
Stews, 122-129
Beef Pie with Lattice Squares, 126
Beef Stew, Old-time, 124
Brunswick Stew, 123
Chicken Pie with Puff-pastry Top, 125
Chuck-wagon Stew, 123
Cioppino, 82
French Veal Stew, 72
Hungarian Gulyas, 72
Lamb Stew, Favorite, 125
Lamb Pie with Pastry Tricorns, 126
Old-time Potpie with Thimble Rolls, 126
Oxtail Stew, Old-time, 125
Short-rib Stew with Parsley Dumplings, 128
Spanish Paella, 75
Speedy Vegetable-Beef Stew, 123
Supper Stew Bake, 136
Toppers for stew
Dumplings, 128, 129
Lattice Squares, 126
Pastry Tricorns, 126
Puff-pastry Top, 125
Thimble Rolls, 126
Veal Stew with Corn-meal Dumplings, 129
Sukiyaki, 87
Swedish Cabbage Rolls, 70

T

Tamale Pie, Mexican, 74
Tetrazzini, Turkey, 149
Thousand Island Dressing, 157
Tips
Artichokes, how to prepare and cook, 41
Casserole, how to grease, 9
Casserole saves a mixing bowl, 39
Casserole sizes, 8
Casserole toppers, biscuits, 46
Cheese, how to measure, 33
Cheese, how to melt, 33, 112
Chicken, how much to buy, 18
Chicken, how to slice, 18
Chopsticks, how to use, 86
Tips, *continued*
Garlic cloves, removing, 125
Rice, how to mold, 65
Seasonings from Italy, 82
Shrimp, how to measure, 27
Souffle tips, 92, 93
Soups, accompaniments for, 118
Soups, garnishes for, 118
Spaghetti tips, 76, 78
Toll House Pancakes, 151
Toppers for casseroles
Biscuits, 16, 17, 21, 46
Potato Fluff Topper, 8
Spoon-bread Topper, 148
Toast bonnets, 45
Toppers for stews
Dumplings, 128, 129
Lattice Squares, 126
Pastry Tricorns, 126
Puff-pastry Top, 125
Thimble Rolls, 126
Tuna dishes, *see Fish*
Turkey
Creamed Chicken or Turkey, 64
Creamed Turkey, 150
Turkey Chop Suey, 149
Turkey Curry with Crisp Noodles, 149
Turkey-salad Souffle, 150
Turkey Tetrazzini, 149

V-Y-Z

Veal dishes, *see Meat*
Vegetables
Artichokes With Crab Stuffing, 41
Asparagus
Creamed Eggs a la Asparagus, 66
Easy Asparagus Souffle, 93
-Ham Bake, 16
Beans
Bean-pot Limas, 38
Boston-style Beans, 38
Calico Bean Bake, 37
Deviled-ham Bean Bake, 134
Limas and Franks, 37
Roaster Baked Beans for 24, 52
Wiener Bean Pot, 134
Cabbage Rolls, Swedish, 70
Corn
Corn Puff, 39
Hamburger-Corn Casserole, 10
for 24, 50
Indian Corn Casserole, 39
Jumbo Cornburger, 39
Squaw Corn, 139
Eggplant Skillet, Mexican, 74
Eggplant Italian, Scalloped, 36
Meat-ball Garden Skillet, 57
Mexican Scramble, 97
Mushroom Casserole, Club, 43
Mushroom Pasta Sauce, 78
Mushrooms, Creamed, 103
Onions
Hash-stuffed Onions, 41
Swiss Cheese-Onion Pie, 34
Swiss Onion Bake, 32
Peppers, stuffed, 40
Potatoes
Company Chicken and Potatoes, 63
Easy Ham and Potatoes au Gratin, 138
Ham and Potato Scallop, 42, 50
Ham and Potatoes au Gratin, 17
Hashed-brown Omelet, 95
Hot Potato Salad with Franks (*meal plan*), 42
Sausage and Sweets, 43
Scalloped Potatoes With Sausage, 42
Savory Ham-Tomato Casserole (*meal plan*), 147
Squash
Ham and Squash Skillet (*meal plan*), 60
Honey-baked Squash, 41
-Sausage Bake, 41
Turkish Zucchini Dolmas, 70
Vegetable-Beef Bake, 14
Vegetable-Meat Pie, 36
Vegetable soups, 118-120
Yam Biscuits, 17
Zucchini Dolmas, Turkish, 70